THE CITROËN 2CV

A 425 cc engined 2CV AZ of 1954/5. The 2CV was aimed deliberately at women drivers, just as André Citroën's 5CV had been thirty years earlier.

THE CITROËN 2CV

John Reynolds

Third Edition

Haynes Publishing

© John Reynolds, 2005

All rights reserved. No part of this publication may be reproduced, stored in a retrieval system, or transmitted, in any form, or by any means, electronic, mechanical, photocopying, recording or otherwise, without prior permission in writing from the publisher.

First published in 1997 by Sutton Publishing Limited
Revised paperback edition first published in 2001
This revised and expanded third edition published in 2005

A catalogue record for this book is available from the British Library

Whilst the publisher has made every effort to trace the copyright ownership of photographs, this has not proved possible in every case. If a copyright owner has inadvertently been offended, then please do discuss the matter with the Editorial Director of the Books Division at Haynes Publishing

ISBN 1 84425 207 8

Library of Congress control no. 2005925520

Published by Haynes Publishing, Sparkford, Yeovil, Somerset BA22 7JJ, UK
Tel: 01963 442030 Fax: 01963 440001
Int. tel: +44 1963 442030 Int. fax: +44 1963 440001
E-mail: sales@haynes.co.uk
Website: www.haynes.co.uk

Haynes North America Inc.,
861 Lawrence Drive, Newbury Park, California 91320, USA

Printed and bound in Britain by J.H. Haynes & Co. Ltd, Sparkford

CONTENTS

Preface 7
Acknowledgements 9
Foreword 10
The CV of the Citroën 2CV 12
Introduction 16

Part One: Autobiography

Chapter One
Ancestry 21

Chapter Two
Conception & Birth 31

Colour section 65–72

Chapter Three
Life & Death 73

Part Two: Family Relations

Chapter Four
The Sahara, the Mehari & the Fourgonnette vans 101

Chapter Five
The Ami-6 & Ami-8 111

Chapter Six
The Dyane & Acadiane 125

Part Three: Parentage

Chapter Seven
The Four Fathers of the 2CV 133

Colour section 137–44

Part Four: Foreign Affairs

Chapter Eight
The 2CV in the UK 161

Chapter Nine
Exploration & Adventure 178

Chapter Ten
2CV Publicity & Advertising 185

Chapter Eleven
The 2CV's Competitors 191

Part Five: Conclusion

Chapter Twelve
The End of the Road? 207

Part Six: Appendices

Production Data 214
Bibliography 218
Picture Credits 219
Filmography 220
Index 221

Toute dynamique implique une continuité: à qui veut un aprés, il faut un avant.
On ne peut conduire bien sans rétroviseur ...

Jacques Wolgensinger

(All progress implies continuity: whoever wants a future must have a past. One cannot steer a forward course without an occasional glance in the rear view mirror.)

PREFACE

Seeing the 2CV's recent TV appearances in the title sequence of the BBC's *Antiques Roadshow*, viewers may well conclude that the little car has itself become an antique, a relic of motoring times gone by that no longer has any practical purpose or relevance in the modern automobile world, and which is unfit for regular daily use on today's congested arterial roads and motorways.

On the contrary, as its many faithful owners and enthusiasts will be glad to confirm, its virtues are timeless. As long as the location and occasion are right, the Citroën Deux Chevaux still represents a viable means of transport even today. Fifty-five years after its first appearance it remains much more than just a motoring museum-piece, suitable only for driving, slowly and carefully, to classic car rallies. Although the numbers in service both in France and the United Kingdom have certainly declined over the past decade, numerous examples can still be seen hard at work on the back roads and byways of the UK as well as in France, Germany, and the Netherlands. Clearly, far from being merely an object of curiosity and nostalgia, despite its age it still serves as a useful and reliable domestic machine as well as a desirable and fast-appreciating collector's item. Rather like the grandfather clock protruding from the roof of the example in the *Antiques Roadshow* titles, in fact.

To drive a 2CV *pied à plancher* (flat out) in the places and conditions for which it was created – the quiet, traffic-free *routes touristique* of rural France, where risk of a collision with a forty-ton truck is remote – is to rediscover the true joys of motoring, especially in summer, with the roof open to the sunshine and fresh air. It's an experience that few modern Eurobox cars can rival for agility, for comfort, for economy, and for fun. *Évidemment, la Deux Cheveaux est en plein vie toujours!*

The recent series of BBC TV's highly popular collectors' programme, the *Antiques Roadshow*, featured a 2CV in its title sequence, doubtless in recognition of the fast appreciating value of the car as a collectors' item. But was the idea inspired by this Citroën publicity shot first seen in a brochure produced by the Delpire agency in the 1960s, showing the 2CV transporting a grandfather clock and other bric-a-brac to demonstrate its carrying capacity?

Acknowledgements

Just like the 2CV itself, this book has a long history behind it, as the date of its conception can be traced back fifteen years, to 1990. Since its first appearance in 1997 (by which time it had been more than five years in gestation) it has been reprinted four times; but now it has been reborn, in this completely revised and updated edition, containing, for the very first time, a gallery of colour photographs.

There are many people who must be thanked for their outstanding efforts in providing material and assistance for the original edition.

In Holland: Wouter Jansen, Jan de Lange, Bart Vanderveen, and Erik Verhaest.

In France: Gilles Blanchet, Fabien Sabatès, Olivier de Serres, and Jacques Wolgensinger, plus Sylvie Bader and Gro Hoeg of SA Citroën and Anne Pezant of Renault SA.

In England: Graham Barnes, Malcolm Bobbitt, George Burton, Alan Cofflard, David Conway, Bob Date, John Dodson, the late Anthony Heal, Steve Hill, Dennis Lewis, Julian Leyton, Stephen Loft-Simson, Bob MacQueen, Tony Searle, Nick Thompson, and, of course, Ken Smith (former Chief Engineer of Citroën UK Ltd), whose contribution in supplying information and reading the manuscript was, as ever, well beyond the call of duty!

In addition my thanks go to Jean-Luc Bénard, Zoe Harrison, and Aart aan der Wiel for permission to reproduce their original photographs, and to Posy Simmonds for kindly allowing the reproduction of an example of her famous cartoons from the *Guardian*.

I'm also grateful to several individuals who played no part in the production of the first edition but have made important contributions to the second, in the form of new information and additional illustrations. These are: Neill Bruce, Giles Chapman, Antoine Demetz, Anne-Marie Michel, Annick Rouaud, Garry Whelan, and Olwen Gillespie of BBC TV's *Antiques Roadshow*.

John Reynolds, Lutterworth,
Leicestershire, Summer 2005

The 2CV was originally designed to serve the needs of the peasant farmers and winegrowers of France who were suspicious of cars and who had little experience of owning and operating machinery. It succeeded so well that it continued to serve these country folk for three generations.

FOREWORD to the First Edition

That was a long day, back in the 1970s, when I had to go from darkest Esher to some bleak turnabout in the north, and chose – inspired either by its everlasting improbability or by its enduring optimism – to do the journey in a 2CV. It was also a frustrating day: there were a lot of roundabouts on the A1 by which I returned, and a roundabout is no place for the driver of a 2CV.

However fast one may have been coming flat-out for a quarter of an hour along the preceding straight, there is always a paroxysm of annoyance that one cannot enter the roundabout fast enough to exploit the roadholding which is the most improbable of all 2CV attributes. One tries to accelerate into every roundabout, but it does not work: the 2CV is not a car which accelerates. Like some other classic Citroën models, it is a car which is content to gather speed.

Mine gathered what it could before reaching the last real roundabout of my journey, at Chiswick Flyover, somewhere around two in the morning. The place looked deserted, and as far as I could see there was nothing coming from any direction. Any promptings to precautionary braking were dismissed; throttle wide open, the blessed little 2CV hurtled (these things are relative) into the roundabout, heeled around it, and hotfooted it away towards and over Kew Bridge. But I had been wrong about the place being deserted: during my impassioned semicircle I found myself passing beneath the nose (more truly somewhere above the eyebrows, for the 2CV is not a low car) of a waiting police car. On Kew Green, he caught up with me.

Don't bother to explain that this car has fantastic roadholding, said the Metropolitan stalwart as I folded my window. *And don't waste your time telling me that what you did just now was perfectly safe in this car. I know all that – but there are some people who don't, and you will give them a heart attack. Don't do it!*

It was nice to have my opinions backed by an obvious authority. I had always admired the 2CV – liked it, indeed, but admiration is a prerequisite to liking a car – since the dear distant day when I first saw it at the Earls Court motor show. Prompted by curiosity to reach for the top rail and rock the car where it stood (can you imagine doing that to *any* other car at a motor show?) I noted with interest that it behaved in roll very like my blessed 1926 Citroën Cloverleaf, the 5CV, which was my regular transport until the late '50s. Subsequent practical assessment showed that it also behaved similarly in pitch, and in fuel consumption and speed and (for want of a better word) acceleration, and – given that my Cloverleaf was the balloon-tyred version – it had similarly defiant roadholding.

The main difference seemed to be that the modern car (a gross misdescription in many ways, for it was truly a timeless car) also had effective brakes; but, had anything gone wrong with it, I might also have discovered the ease with which one could remove a panel or two and walk into the engine bay to attend to the few but clever items of importance to be found there. I am, you see, not of the school which believes that the idea of the TPV came to the estimable Monsieur Boulanger in one of those all-embracing conceptual flashes which illuminated the work of André Citroën (of blessed memory) himself. Instead it was surely the result of a logical translation of the 5CV into the technological language of a later and much more advanced decade.

The logic itself was of that remorseless and peculiarly Gallic variety which has inspired some other Citroën models, some admirable architecture, some questionable aircraft, and some quite ghastly clothes. No clearer expression of that logic could be found than in the prototype TPV (*toute petite voiture* – another misdescription, for the 2CV was not really small, merely light) which I had the honour of driving some years ago within *la pouponnière*, within the very test-grounds where the firm nurtured its secret prototypes before the Nazi irruption. It would be vain to attempt an analysis of that logic without first invoking the times, the standards, the expectations and the prejudices of the rural French of the 1930s; and I, being old enough but probably not patient enough, do not propose to attempt it. Mr Reynolds, however, being known not only for his double-chevron qualifications but also as an historian, is welcome to try.

It is a tricky business, writing about Citroëns. One may easily get carried away, which is no good at all – the word of an enthusiast, as Mr Balfour once observed, is not to be trusted – but if he be not thus carried away, it is a sure sign that the writer has altogether missed a point somewhere. In the past I have never found the task satisfactorily done, except in the atmospheric and rhapsodic French of Jacques Wolgensinger; the lucid English of Mr Reynolds should be a very welcome addition to the bookshelves.

L.J.K. Setright, 1997

The CV of the Citroën 2CV

1935
Following the death of André Citroën and the acquisition of his firm by the Michelin tyre company, Pierre-Jules Boulanger is appointed joint managing director of the S.A. André Citroën with Pierre Michelin.

1936
Boulanger lays down the *cahier des charges* (design brief) for a *toute petite voiture* (TPV), specifically intended to be 'a simple, spartan form of transport for motorists of modest means'.

1937
André Lefebvre and his team of engineers produce the first road-going prototype of the TPV for appraisal, by Boulanger in person, at the La Ferté-Vidame test track. In late December, Pierre Michelin is killed in a car crash, leaving Boulanger in sole day-to-day charge of the Citroën organisation.

1938
August – Boulanger gains approval from the Michelin management to proceed with preparations for the series production of the TPV. During 1938, no fewer than twenty prototypes of various different types and designs are tested continually at La Ferté-Vidame.

1939
August – the final definitive prototype is submitted to the Chief Engineer of the Service des Mines (the French equivalent of the UK Ministry of Transport) for inspection and type approval, as required by French law even then.
September – a batch of 250 pre-production examples of the TPV are completed, in preparation for the car's launch at the Paris Salon Motor Show that month. The following day, 3 September, war between France and Germany is declared, and the show is cancelled.

1940
The Germans invade France, and the Citroën factory is placed under German administration. The pre-production TPVs are hidden to prevent them falling into the hands of the enemy.

1941
In defiance of German orders forbidding such activities, work on the design and development of the TPV continues in secret in occupied France.

1948
The result of this clandestine research, the 2CV, is exhibited at the Paris Salon Motor Show on 7 October.

1949
July – Production and sales of the 2CV Type A saloon commence.

1951
The 2CV Fourgonnette Type AU (light van) is launched.

1953
Sales of 2CV commence in the UK, with a right-hand-drive version built at Citroën's British factory at Slough.

1954
The original 375 cc 9 bhp engine is augmented by a 425 cc 12 bhp alternative. (The 375 cc unit continued in service until July 1959.)

1957
The original canvas boot cover is replaced by a steel panel.

1958
The 2CV 4×4 Sahara appears, powered by two 425 cc engines in tandem, one at the front and the other at the rear.

1959
A choice of colours for the body is announced – now the 2CV is available in glacier blue, as well as the plain grey of former years!

1960
The original corrugated 'ripple' bonnet is replaced by a new, five-ribbed design. At Slough, the 2CV saloon is replaced on the assembly line by the Bijou, a fibreglass-bodied version designed in England.

1962
Among other innovations and improvements, the 2CV is at last equipped with a proper instrument panel, including a conventional speedometer and fuel gauge.

1964
Assembly of the Bijou ceases at Slough, and the 2CV is withdrawn from the UK market. On the Continent, it becomes the first car ever to be fitted with tubeless (Michelin X) tyres as standard.

1965
The 2CV saloon's bodywork changes from four- to six-light style, with forward-hinged front doors. Fully homocinetic driveshafts are introduced. Hydraulic telescopic shock absorbers replace the original friction dampers on the rear axles.

1966
Production of the 2CV saloon hits its all-time high – over 168,000 examples are built.

1967
The Dyane – Type AYA – is introduced, initially in 425 cc form. The following year it arrives on the British market, now available in both 425 cc and 602 cc form.

1968
The Mehari and Baby-Brousse versions are announced.

1970
February – The 2CV's performance is uprated, and a choice of two new engines becomes available: the 435 cc 26 bhp unit (2CV-4) and the 602 cc 28.5 bhp unit (2CV-6). The original inertia dampers on the rear axles are deleted on 2CV-4 versions. The first of the great 2CV '*raids*' (or rallies) takes place – 454 assorted 2CVs and Dyanes cover the 16,500 km from Paris to Kabul and back in 28 days.

1971
The Kabul run is followed by a sequel – 1,300 cars driven by young people from eleven European nations travel the 13,800 km from Paris to Persepolis and back. The inertia dampers are deleted from the rear axle of the 2CV-6.

1972
The first 2CV Pop-Cross event is staged at Argenton-sur-Creuse in France.

1973
The year of the trans-Sahara Raid Afrique. A team of 100 young French drivers in 50 examples of the 2CV and Dyane drive from Abidjan to Tunis, crossing the wilderness of the Ténère and Hoggar regions en route.

1974
The arrival of the global energy crisis brings the 2CV family a new lease of life – combined world-wide production of all types peaks at 370,512 examples. Sales of the 2CV saloon recommence in the British Isles – right-hand-drive cars built in France and Belgium are imported into the UK. All 2CV models acquire rectangular headlamps.

1976
The first of the limited edition versions – the 2CV Spot – is announced. The inertia dampers remaining on the front axles are discontinued, and telescopic hydraulic shock absorbers replace the original friction dampers on the front axles of all models.

1978
February – The Acadiane Fourgonnette is launched.

March – Production of the 2CV-4 saloon and the 2CV Fourgonnette is discontinued.

1980
September – The 2CV Charleston special edition arrives.

1981
Front disc brakes are introduced on the 2CV models. A 2CV saloon equipped with a GS engine stars in the James Bond film *For Your Eyes Only*.

1984
Production of the Dyane-6 ceases, the Dyane-4 having already been deleted in 1975.

1987
Sales of the Acadiane and Mehari cease in France.

1988
The Paris-Levallois factory closes. No fewer than 3,418,347 2CVs had been produced there since 1949.

1990
Production of the 2CV (now confined to the Citroën factory at Mangualde in Portugal) finally ceases on 27 July.

1998
The 2CV celebrates its golden jubilee.

1999
The 2CV is listed among the top ten finalists of the Car of the Century Award, together with the Citroën DS19 and Traction Avant.

2005
Fifteen years after its production ceases, the 2CV refuses to die as, month by month, more and more examples are rebuilt and returned to the road.

INTRODUCTION

For five decades, the frugal, unpretentious 2CV has meant motoring fun and freedom for every type and class of owner – young or old, rich or poor, radical or conservative.

It's fifty years or thereabouts since the day I first set eyes on the Citroën 2CV. Since then, it seems that hardly a week has passed without my catching a glimpse of this extraordinary vehicle coming sailing around the next bend, usually leaning precariously like a yacht in a gale, but always keeping an even keel and never capsizing!

Despite the enormous changes that have occurred on the roads of Europe since the fifties, the Deux Chevaux remains an enduring and unmistakable feature of the transport scene, beloved of motorists rich and poor alike, and universally acknowledged as one of life's more agreeable certainties. With its snub nose, pert mouth and jaunty, wide-eyed expression full of character and

personality, it is still a familiar, friendly face to look out for among the queues of anonymous cars on the roads, instantly recognisable thanks to that peculiar combination of plainness and prettiness which the French call *jolie-laide*. It never seems to age – indeed, its looks have hardly changed over three human generations. Sixty years after the first prototype took to the test track in 1937, and seven years after the last example left the factory in 1990, the 2CV is still going strong, as popular as ever.

Today, now that motorists may drive from one end of Europe to the other in a day, cruising through five countries without noticing from any change in the appearance of the passing traffic that they've crossed a border, it is hard to describe the culture-shock that was experienced by British motorists when encountering the idiosyncrasies of the French way of motoring for the first time, back in the fifties. Long before the coming of the Common Market, the British driver's first Continental trip was indeed a journey into the unknown. The sights, the sounds – and the smells – that assailed the traveller driving off the ferry on to the roads of France were foreign in the fullest meaning of the word.

In the cafés on the *quai* sat rows of men wearing black berets, spongy-soled shoes and collarless corduroy jackets, and puffing pungent, yellow-papered cigarettes from bright-blue packets. At times of day and night when no English pub would be open, these chaps lounged about, quaffing their cold, gassy beer or sipping strange, milky-looking liquids that smelled of mothballs. As often as not, a radio would be playing and the sound of accordion music or a melancholy Gallic chanson could be heard against the cacophony made by the traffic in the streets. Here, a multitude of strange little grey-painted cars, seemingly constructed entirely of tin plate and canvas, whirred and wheezed about their work like a flock of asthmatic geese. Clearly, French tastes differed as much in cars as in matters of cuisine!

But if French cars seemed strangely different to the British motorist abroad, that was nothing compared to the bewildering unfamiliarity of the French road system. It was not just that visitors had to remember to keep on the wrong side of the road and give way to traffic approaching from the right. The carriageways themselves – long, straight, paved with cobbles and lined by tall, slender poplar trees – were utterly different in construction and design, and so were the vehicles running on them. The oncoming cars that *les Anglais* struggled to avoid as they dodged the potholes were evidently the product of an entirely different mentality and philosophy. And, needless to say, of all these strange Gallic designs, none were more unorthodox inside and out than the chevron-emblazoned products of the Citroën company – and in particular the unique and ubiquitous 2CV.

Today, the British happily eat snails and garlic, the French smoke filter tips (if they dare smoke at all), and both build Peugeots. Thanks to the remorseless homogenisation of cultures that has taken place, the motorists of France now look and behave more or less the same as those of other European nations – and so do their cars. The relentless steamroller of integration and standardisation has flattened individualism and ironed out national characteristics throughout the European automobile industry. And in the process, a plethora of proudly independent national marques has been compressed into a handful of multinational conglomerates, each turning out uniform, anonymous products at the rate of a thousand a day, all equally bereft of distinguishable features and recognisable identities.

Thus, of all those many fascinating, idiosyncratic Gallic motor car designs that once seemed – like the Eiffel Tower – to embody the very essence of French engineering prowess, now only the 2CV remains in any number on the roads of its native land. When the first 2CVs appeared in 1948, few experts expected the model to last for more than a few months, and yet it survived for forty-four years of constant production, thanks to its ability to undertake a whole succession of demanding motoring tasks in an ever-changing transport environment.

Yet throughout those years of change, the 2CV itself changed little. A supremely useful, practical working tool, its unique shape remained unaltered (like that of the spade or the saw) by virtue of an enduring and unsurpassed fitness for its original intended purpose.

Clearly, given its lasting aptitude for its job, the reasons for the long and active service life of the Citroën 2CV scarcely need an explanation. For this reason, as well as listing the principal events and achievements in the curriculum vitae of one of the world's most successful ever automobile designs, this book sets out to answer an even more intriguing question: how did such an uncompromisingly original and unconformist car ever come to be conceived and born in the first place? And having lived to such a ripe old age, what ultimately caused its much-mourned demise?

Part One

Autobiography

André Citroën, the founder of the Citroën marque. Born in February 1878, his career as an industrialist began with the manufacture of precision gear wheels and he did not start making cars until 1919. He died in July 1935, shortly after launching his masterpiece, the Traction Avant, and thus he knew nothing of the 2CV. This was essentially the creation of the firm's new owners, the Michelin family, who assumed control in December 1934.

CHAPTER ONE

ANCESTRY

In the history of the automobile, few cars have travelled so far, or for so long, as the Citroën 2CV. For over forty years, the unmistakable sight and sound of this extraordinary little car have been a familiar feature of the motoring landscape, as likely to be encountered in the remotest, most far-flung corners of the world as on the routes nationales of its native France.

Wherever there's a road on earth, a 2CV will already have travelled along it. And even where there is no beaten track, as long as it's a route worth following to a destination worth discovering, a 2CV will inevitably have passed that way before.

As typically French (so people say) as camembert and calvados, utterly Gallic in the logical originality of its design and engineering, the 2CV was certainly the motorised embodiment of the spirit of *Liberté*, *Egalité* and *Fraternité*. Much more than just a means of transport, it became a way of life – a cultural phenomenon that symbolised freedom from routine and escape from convention for owners, young and old alike, all round the globe.

Long before the idea became fashionable elsewhere, the 2CV pioneered the concept of the 'world car' – a go-anywhere, do-anything vehicle that was truly classless in its practicality. At home in all climates and terrain, and happy in any social situation, it helped narrow distances, broaden horizons and break down cultural and political barriers more effectively than any other vehicle before or since.

The 2CV was a motorised paradox: on one hand, its cheerful dependability brought mobility and independence to the young and impecunious, while on the other, its unpretentious simplicity and frugality brought home the value of life's cheaper pleasures to many millionaire motorists as well. Conceived as a utilitarian vehicle, it was engineered to the highest technical standards. Seemingly crude and basic, with the frailest of bodywork, it was one of the most ingenious and sophisticated designs ever offered to the motoring public, at any price. Although cheap to buy and to run, it was expensive to produce. Built to mobilise one generation of French men and women, it lived on to serve a second and third generation with even greater commercial success, transporting their children and their children's children – and millions of their European cousins too!

A style icon that was exhibited in

prestigious design collections and motoring museums, the 2CV was a constant source of inspiration for artists, sculptors, musicians, cartoonists and comics, as well as engineers. The hero of a thousand fascinating tales of exploration and adventure, it is still the butt of endless funny stories and rude jokes.

Call it what you will – 'tin snail', 'ugly duckling', 'flying washboard' or just plain 'Deux Chevaux' – the 2CV remains among the most successful motor vehicles ever produced. Manufactured continously for almost half a century and sold in over forty countries around the globe, its long-term popularity and success among European cars is equalled only by the Volkswagen Beetle, the Renault 4 and the BMC Mini, in terms of both numbers built and years in production. Between 1948 and 1990, over 6.7 million examples of all types were sold, and probably as many as a quarter of that total still survives in service throughout the world today. Remember, whereas most new motor cars can expect to survive only two or three changes of ownership, the typical 2CV passed through five or six pairs of appreciative hands in its lifetime. Although outmoded and obsolete from every conventional point of view, the timeless appeal of this remarkable design seems to go on and on – just like the vehicle itself.

Can this be due merely to its individualistic looks, its eccentric charm and its lively, fun-loving personality? On the contrary, like all survivors, the 2CV rolled on and on because it continued to do the job for which it was conceived and born – to provide maximum mobility at minimum cost. First and foremost, the 2CV was – and remains – a car in which drivers were able to set out in confidence, certain of covering enormous distances without difficulty or expense, either little by little, mile after mile around town or country, or on epic journeys of discovery around the globe.

Of course, the 2CV is not a conventional car, nor was it ever meant to be. Right from the start, it was designed and built to provide a radical answer to the problems of personal transport, by a company that revelled in its reputation for originality. When it first appeared at the Paris Motor Show in October 1948, its unexpected arrival caused uproar and astonishment. No vehicle like it had ever been seen before, not even on the Citroën stand. Although the motoring press were scathingly critical of this extraordinary little car, the public responded with enthusiasm and applause. Over 1¼ million people thronged to inspect the amazing 'umbrella on wheels', and thousands of orders were taken on the first day alone.

But in truth, the story of the Citroën 2CV goes back a further fourteen years to 1935, the date that marked a momentous turning point in the history of the Citroën company. That year saw the downfall and untimely death of its founder, André Citroën, the man who more than any other European motor manufacturer had championed the introduction of the popular, mass-produced, mass-marketed car.

The son of a Dutch-Jewish diamond merchant who had moved from Amsterdam to settle in France, André Citroën was born in Paris in 1878. Educated at the elite École

ANCESTRY

Typical of the last of Citroën's conventional rear-wheel-drive cars is this 10CV 'Rosalie' cabriolet built in early 1934. The familiar double chevrons on the radiator grille were introduced on all Citroën models in January that year.

Polytechnique (the technical academy of the French Military and Civil Services), in 1902 he abandoned the prospect of a career as an engineering officer in the artillery to establish a precision-engineering firm engaged in the manufacture and marketing of a novel type of gearwheel with V-shaped double-helical teeth, like a corporal's stripes turned upside down. The business prospered, and in 1905 was incorporated as the Société des Engrenages Citroën, the company which subsequently formed the foundation of André Citroën's fast-expanding industrial empire. This long Citroën tradition of gear-making is still symbolised today in the company's famous double chevron trademark, which echoes the herringbone-pattern teeth of those double-helical gears.

At the outbreak of the First World War in 1914, André Citroën was recalled to military service. On joining his former regiment at the front, he found that in common with other artillery units in the French Army, its fighting strength was being severely weakened by a shortage of ammunition. For every six shells fired by the Germans, the French were only able to return one – and even this was likely to be a dud. Realising that his personal contribution to the war effort would be far better directed at producing ammunition than firing it at the enemy, he quickly drew up far-reaching proposals for the mass production of ordnance, which were accepted with alacrity by the military authorities. With the active backing of the Armaments Ministry, he then acquired 30 acres of market garden at the Quai de Javel on the left bank of the Seine in Paris, and there built up a mighty ordnance factory employing over 12,000 workers and capable of producing 55,000 shells per day. By the end of the war, over 28 million shells had been manufactured there.

But with the ending of hostilities in 1918, demand for artillery shells ceased as abruptly as it had begun. Clearly, with so many jobs at risk and so great an investment in the balance, there could be no return to vegetable-growing at the Quai de Javel. So Citroën decided that his munitions plant would be converted to an automobile factory, and he would enter the motor car business. Moreover, he would do so not as a specialist constructor of elaborately engineered luxury limousines, but as the mass-producer of cars designed for the man in the street. Thus, the first generation of Citroën products were inexpensive, unpretentious *voitures ordinaires* that showed little trace of the avant-garde engineering thinking that later became the company's hallmark. Robustly built, conservatively styled and entirely conventional in concept, they followed the American pattern – so much so that André Citroën soon became known as 'the Henry Ford of France'.

The very first Citroën model – the 1,327 cc 10 hp Type A, designed by Jules Salomon – rolled off the totally reconstructed and reorganised assembly line at the Quai de Javel in May 1919. Priced at 11,000 old francs, it was not only cheaper than anything offered by Citroën's competitors, it was also more economical to run. The first European car to be built using American mass-production techniques, the Type A Citroën came to its buyer ready for the road. Unlike all the other cars available at the time, which were normally supplied as a rolling chassis plus engine for completion by a specialist coachbuilder, the Type A left the factory fully finished and fitted out. There was nothing else to buy: the car came complete with bodywork, hood, wheels, tyres, electric lights, horn, tools and even a self-starter as standard equipment. Available in a choice of three body styles, capable of reaching a top speed of 40 mph and returning 38 mpg, the Type A was an instant success. Within a fortnight of its debut, over 16,000 advance orders had been taken. At first, 30 vehicles left the factory daily, but soon this output had risen to 100 cars a day, so that by the end of 1920, 15,000 Citroëns were on the road.

In 1921, the Type A was replaced by the Type B2, equipped with a more powerful 1,452 cc four-cylinder engine. This was succeeded in turn by the Type B10, the first European car to be fitted with an all-steel body, produced, from late 1923 onwards, on a moving conveyor production line – again the first of its kind in Europe. By the end of 1925, Citroën's output of all types had reached 500 cars a day, an astonishing rate of production for that era.

But the vehicle that really made Citroën's name was the little 5CV Type C2 two-seater introduced in 1922, later made available as the three-seater Type C3 Cloverleaf in 1925. Powered by an 856 cc 7.5 hp engine and normally painted yellow in a visual pun on its maker's name, this 'Petite Citron' cost half as much to buy and run as any other car then available in France, and thus had many imitators, including the Austin 7 in England. Over 80,000 were sold at a price that never rose much above 15,000 old francs. But despite strong continuing demand, production was stopped in 1926 in favour of the new, all-steel-bodied B10 and B12 saloons. André Citroën had discovered that by using the latest American methods, he could make bigger and better cars in greater numbers for the same cost, and thus make greater profits. But by abandoning his *Petite Citron*, he left this sector of the market wide open to his rivals, a fact that led to much criticism in later years when the question of building another cheap, small car was raised once again at the Quai de Javel.

Sustaining such levels of output called for more than organisational genius, of course. And so, to expand the market

In 1924 Citroën became the first European car maker to introduce all-steel bodywork. This typically racy Citroën poster design by Pierre Louys shows the B12 open tourer of 1926.

An expert in mass-production, André Citroën was also a master of marketing and publicity. For ten years, between 1924 and 1934, he used the Eiffel Tower as a giant advertising sign. Some 250,000 lightbulbs beamed out his name in huge letters, visible for sixty miles.

for his products, André Citroën brought another of his remarkable talents to bear – his flair for marketing, publicity and promotion. A network of franchised dealerships was established throughout France, Western Europe and North Africa, the first example of this now universal method of distributing and selling cars; Citroën credit finance and insurance schemes were introduced; full-page advertising campaigns were mounted; a fleet of Citroën taxis was set up in Paris; Citroën roadsigns were erected at every crossroads in France; endurance trials and record-breaking marathon runs were staged – all kinds of novel marketing initiatives were employed to establish the Citroën marque and foster brand loyalty. Later, André Citroën was to have the ultimate bright advertising idea: for ten years, every night between 1924 and 1934, his name was flashed before the public in letters 100 ft high by 250,000 electric lightbulbs wired to the Eiffel Tower – a spectacle visible for 60 miles in all directions.

By the end of the decade, just ten years after starting up his motor-manufacturing business, André Citroën had achieved his initial objectives with spectacular success. With its annual production rate now topping 100,000, and with almost half a million Citroën vehicles having been made and sold, his company had by now overtaken all its older established French rivals to become the largest and most successful motor manufacturer in Europe – indeed, the fourth largest car company in the world, topped only by the American giants. Employing 30,000 workers and capable of turning out 400 cars and lorries every day, the Citroën company had created a service network of 5,000 agents in France, plus ten subsidiary sales companies and four independent factories abroad.

Yet to the progressive, idealistic and adventurous André Citroën, a vital factor was missing from the formula. Dissatisfied with compromise, he knew that the fight to maintain his market leadership could never be won by sheer weight of numbers alone. To stay ahead of his competitors in sales, he would need to outdistance them in technology. Ultimately, he would have to throw convention to the wind and offer his customers an exciting new model of radical – indeed revolutionary – design.

Although no man did more than André Citroën to mobilise and motorise the entire population of France, as an individual he was the personification of the urban sophisticate, born and bred in central Paris, and a habitual city-dweller with little knowledge of the ways, wants and wishes of countryfolk. His earlier attempts, in 1920, to produce an agricultural tractor had come to nought, and so, not unnaturally, in deciding on the nature of his 'new concept in motoring', he took the direction that most appealed to him personally – instead of proceeding with a scheme to build a simple, small and inexpensive four-seater design powered by an air-cooled engine, aimed for the most part at the rural population, and which would have occupied the place in the market vacated by the disappearance of the 5CV four years earlier, he decided to construct a larger, more advanced and sophisticated vehicle, powered by a 7CV engine, and restricted to the middle-class market by its greater price.

The car that he chose to produce – the immortal Traction Avant – was a truly 'clean sheet' design with a state-of-the-art specification, so dramatically new in every respect that its debut sent shock waves reverberating around the motoring world. For the very first time on a mass-produced car, such advanced features as front-wheel drive, independent front suspension, hydraulic brakes and (later) rack and pinion steering were combined in a long, low-slung, all-steel monocoque bodyshell, embodying the latest notions of graceful, streamlined styling. Rapid and responsive to drive, spacious and comfortable to ride in and affordable to

André Citroën shows off his first car, the Type A, to his family, *c.* 1919. As usual, his wife is at the wheel – Citroën was a reluctant driver!

The Citroën 2CV

André Citroën's one and only small car was the highly popular 5CV Type C 'Petite Citron' introduced in 1921. Intended specifically for lady drivers, it had a traditional wooden coach-built body, which Citroën considered old-fashioned and uneconomic, so production ceased in 1926. By then, he had developed modern assembly line methods that enabled him to build bigger and better steel-bodied cars, in greater numbers, for the same cost.

own and run, it was also an outstandingly safe, reliable and economical car, capable of returning 30 mpg while cruising at a steady 60 mph – a standard of performance unheard of elsewhere at that time.

With typical optimism, André Citroën planned to launch this audacious new product in the autumn of 1934, but by the spring of that year, certain vital technical teething troubles had still not been overcome. Solving the complex engineering problems inherent in such an unorthodox vehicle would have been enough of a challenge for most car companies of that era, yet for the Traction Avant design team there were other equally pressing difficulties to be dealt with on the manufacturing side.

After visiting Renault's new establishment at Billancourt, André Citroën had decided that in order to produce his new car efficiently and profitably, he too would have to build a brand new factory, even bigger and better than his arch rival's. Accordingly, between March and July 1933 a third of the entire Quai de Javel site was torn down and reconstructed to provide a vast, modern press shop and assembly hall, equipped with the very latest tools and machinery from America.

The huge financial burden imposed on the company's resources by the development of the Traction Avant was thus made all the heavier by the debts incurred in this massive rebuilding programme – so much so that by the

spring of 1934, the Citroën company began to experience severe financial difficulties which were compounded by a drastic fall in sales. In the bleak political and economic climate of the Depression, there could be no question of government support for André Citroën's industrial empire.

Consequently, despite the triumphal official debut of the Traction Avant in May and its sensational reception at the Paris Salon Motor Show in October, the financial collapse of the S.A. André Citroën was unavoidable. On 21 December 1934, as a result of legal action taken by an impatient minor creditor, the company was forced into bankruptcy, to be taken over by its chief creditor, the Michelin tyre company, to which André Citroën had already pledged his own personal shareholding.

Sadly, having lost his factories, his fortune and even his name, André Citroën was never to see his optimism vindicated by the resounding success of the 'new concept in motoring' that bore his double chevron badge or, indeed, by the long line of avant-garde designs which followed it. Within seven months, on 30 July 1935, aged only fifty-seven, he died a broken man in every sense of the word.

Ironically, the Citroën Traction Avant was a gamble that paid off for everyone except its creator. Hailed by the press and public alike for its exceptional stability and its exemplary handling and road-holding qualities, it quickly became

The Traction Avant was the world's first mass-produced front-wheel-drive car. Designed by André Lefebvre, it was launched by André Citroën in May 1934. It remained in production for twenty-three years, until July 1957. This is an example of the post-war 15-Six 6-cylinder version.

29

a legend. Indeed, its rapid commercial success allowed the company's new owners to repay all Citroën's remaining liabilities and debts within two years of acquiring control. Judged today to be a masterpiece of both engineering design and industrial organisation, the Traction Avant remained in production for almost a quarter of a century, during which time more than ¾ million examples of its many different variants were produced.

In one of his last public pronouncements, made in 1933, André Citroën had claimed '*L'auto n'est pas un instrument de luxe, mais essentiellement un instrument de travail*' ('The car is not a luxury article, but essentially an implement of work'). As, gradually but inevitably, it came to assume a commanding role in public transport, in a way that would prove just as indispensable as its role in transporting goods, the car would soon enter a new, popular and democratic stage in its development, he predicted. However, the big 2-litre Traction Avant was essentially a car for affluent, middle-class motorists, and priced beyond the means of the average Frenchman. What was needed to fulfil André Citroën's ambition and mobilise the masses was a smaller, lighter, cheaper car, an affordable alternative to the bus, the bicycle and the pony, a vehicle that could be driven and maintained by owners of any class or occupation, no matter how limited their knowledge of machinery. And this was precisely the kind of revolutionary product that the Citroën company's new owners, the Michelin men, set out to create, almost from the very moment of their arrival at the Quai de Javel.

What André Citroën would have thought of the result of their labours remains a matter for speculation, for although it bore his famous double chevron badge and was produced by the team of engineers that he had personally recruited, working within the tradition of engineering excellence and innovation that he had established and encouraged, the fact is that the 2CV was a car that he never saw, and knew nothing of. Indeed, it is doubtful that he could ever have dreamed of this remarkable little car and its huge, eventual world-wide success, even in his most irrepressibly imaginative and optimistic moments!

CHAPTER TWO

CONCEPTION & BIRTH

For the next forty years, the destiny of the Citroën marque was to rest in the hands of the Michelin family, the owners of the eponymous tyre manufacturing company. Normally, when car manufacturers fail financially and are taken over, it is by former rivals who lose no time in making changes, enforcing new principles and eradicating old, established practices, but in this case there was no such clash of corporate cultures. Michelin was merely a creditor, not a competitor, and with no previous car-making experience, it had no preconceived philosophy about the rights and wrongs of automobile design, providing that Michelin tyres were employed, and in great numbers! Otherwise, on gaining control the Michelin men might easily have put a stop to Citroën's progressive but risky policies, treating their new acquisition as simply a safe, captive market for their own products.

However, Michelin was itself a pioneering, research-orientated company, run by a far-sighted management which encouraged new ideas. Indeed, at the time of the take-over, it had already embarked on a course of research that was to lead inevitably to a truly revolutionary breakthrough in the technology of transportation – the steel-belt radial tyre, the technical principles of which had been mastered by Michelin even before the Second World War. Moreover, to market such advanced concepts as the low-profile Pilote tyre, which it had already developed to the point of production, Michelin needed the co-operation of an innovative car-maker – one which would help it get its new products on the road, by producing, in due course, a range of advanced vehicles with suspension and steering specifically designed to exploit and demonstrate the advantages of Michelin tyre know-how.

Although delayed by the war, the first commercial example of the steel-belt radial principle – the Michelin X tyre – was announced at the 1949 Paris Motor Show, fitted to the Traction Avant, of course. From then on, these long-lasting Michelin radials gradually became standard fitting throughout the Citroën range. During its first five years of production, the 2CV was fitted with conventional Michelin Pilote tyres, but these were superseded by the new Michelin X radials in 1953. Then, in 1964, it became the first car in the world to be equipped with tubeless radial tyres, capable of covering

How the 2CV Got Its Name

As everyone knows, '2CV' stands for 'Deux Chevaux' ('two horses'). But why?

Since January 1948, when the old RAC horsepower system of vehicle excise duty was abolished, British motorists have been subject to a fixed flat rate of car tax, with one of two bands of duty being applied to every size of private car on the road. In France, however, a variable rate of road tax, determined by a complex formula, has been applied ever since the arrival of the popular motor car, and this method of assessing duty was retained after the Second World War and is still employed today. The system originated in the late nineteenth century as a means of measuring the power output of steam-powered vehicles – hence the term '*Cheval Vapeur*' (CV – 'steam horse').

In the French *puissance fiscale* road tax system, the duty payable increases steeply with larger engine dimensions and outputs, as once was the case with the British RAC system. The rate of tax rises in stages from the small sum levied on engines under 400 cc (2CV) to that charged on medium-class 2-litre cars (11CV), but above 2.5 litres (13CV) it increases substantially. Bigger, more powerful engines above 2.9 litres (16CV) are subject to a punitive level of taxation.

The 375 cc engine of the original 2CV was designed specifically to fall into the lowest, cheapest tax category, although later models equipped with the 602 cc engine were rated as 3CVs. Thus, when the time came to give the TPV a name, it was announced simply as the Citroën 2CV or Deux Chevaux, just as Renault described its own 760 cc-engined 'people's car' as the 4CV. In any case, giving the car a fanciful name would have been completely contrary to Boulanger's principles.

100,000 km, and which, of course, are now standard on all European, American and Japanese cars.

Every car firm is bound to suffer the loss of its original creator and driving spirit sooner or later, and for many the experience proved terminal. But for the Citroën company, the demise of its founder led instead to a remarkable renaissance in its fortunes. Free to carry on its adventurous policies as before, but freed also from André Citroën's rash extravagance, the company was soon on course for a second era of success, thanks to the remarkable two-man team that the Michelin brothers chose to manage their new automobile interests and supervise this technical collaboration between the two firms.

In French, the word *pierre* means 'rock'. Certainly, these two Pierres – Pierre Michelin and Pierre-Jules Boulanger – together provided the solid foundation on which the Citroën business was rebuilt. While Pierre Michelin (son of old Edouard Michelin, the grandson of the founder of the dynasty) was put in charge of the commercial, financial and administrative side of the Citroën company, it was left to Pierre-Jules Boulanger to supervise the running of its factories and oversee the experimental work in progress at its Bureau d'Études (research and design office). Working in tandem, over the next three years the pair proved capable not only of restoring order and purpose to the tottering Citroën industrial empire, but also of leading it on to even greater levels of engineering excellence than those set by its erstwhile leader.

However, in December 1937, Pierre Michelin was tragically killed while driving from Paris to Clermont-Ferrand to spend the New Year holiday with his wife and family. Thereafter, for the following thirteen years, the burden of responsibility fell upon Pierre-Jules Boulanger alone. At first sight, Boulanger must have seemed a most unlikely person to replace the ebullient, optimistic, bon-vivant André Citroën as the master of the Quai de Javel. Completely opposite in both personality and physique, he was a dour, retiring and introspective character who disliked flamboyant self-promotion and always avoided the free-wheeling socialising and junketing that so appealed to his predecessor.

Contemporary reports describe him as a tall, austere, unassuming figure, efficient and decisive in his actions, somewhat forthright and dogmatic in his opinions, yet considerate and approachable in his dealings with colleagues. Habitually dressed in a felt hat and an enormous, crumpled raincoat, he was never to be seen without a Gitane cigarette dangling from his mouth. In his pocket he carried a succession of little black notebooks, in which he jotted down his ideas, plans and observations, plus, of course, his impressions of the constant procession of cars that he tested personally. Again in sharp contrast to André Citroën, Boulanger was a keen motorist who loved driving and who knew intuitively when a car was right or wrong, sensing its road-holding vices and virtues through the seat of his pants and then fine-tuning its handling qualities with a stream of off-the-cuff suggestions. Calm and decisive – almost to the point of seeming remote and authoritarian – Boulanger inspired respect and confidence in all who worked with him, and like a stern but fatherly headmaster he guided his school of unruly talents to new heights of achievement.

Nowadays, the rigorous evaluation of new ideas by corporate committees and customer clinics ensures that only the kind of bland, anonymous cars that promise all things to all men and women go into production. But in Boulanger's time, car design was an intensely pragmatic and individualistic process, which led inevitably to products that reflected their creator's personality and prejudices. Shaped by one man's likes and dislikes, they represented a personal statement of engineering, aesthetic and cultural values – hence that indefinable but unmistakable character that we recognise and admire in classic cars today. The spartan 2CV was to echo Boulanger's personality precisely.

Actually, Boulanger was not an automobile engineer but an architect by training. Born in 1885, at the age of twenty-three he left France to seek fame and fortune in the USA and Canada, where, after working variously as a cowboy in the Rockies and as a tram driver in San Francisco, in 1911 he established a thriving house-building business in Victoria, British Columbia. In 1914, the call to arms brought him back to Europe, where he served with distinction as a captain in the French Army Air Corps. After the war, Boulanger decided to remain in France and take up Edouard Michelin's offer of employment as supervisor of the Michelin tyre company's extensive building programme at its factory and headquarters at Clermont-Ferrand.

THE 2CV PROTOTYPES

Shortly after the outbreak of WW2, P.-J. Boulanger ordered that the batch of 250 TPVs completed thus far for the planned launch of his creation at the 1939 Paris Motor Show should be hidden for the duration. However, following the debut of the 2CV itself in 1948 he decreed that all the remaining examples of the TPV should be destroyed. But one had already escaped his purge – the prototype built by Michelin at Clermont-Ferrand. Used as a pick-up truck at the tyre factory during the war, it had been thrown out as scrap in 1946. Fortunately, it was saved from the crusher and is today exhibited in the Musée Henri Malartre at Rochetaillée-sur-Saône.

For two decades this vehicle was believed to be the only survivor, until in 1968 another complete example was discovered hidden in a barn at Citroën's test track, located at La Ferté-Vidame, deep in the countryside west of Paris. This car was then restored by Citroën for publicity purposes and attracted widespread attention throughout the 1970s.

Almost thirty years later, in 1994, 2CV enthusiasts were amazed to learn that yet another three complete examples had been uncovered at La Ferté-Vidame, where they had also been hidden in a barn on a remote part of the estate. This time, Citroën decided that the trio should be preserved in their original condition as found, and they now reside in the company's Conservatoire or Heritage Centre at Aulnay-sous-Bois, Paris. Thus, against all the odds, a total of five pre-war TPVs exists today.

This prototype, the first of the five surviving examples of the TPV to be discovered, was found in 1968, hidden away in a barn at Citroën's La Ferté-Vidame test track and restored by Citroën for the company's museum. At the time that it was designed, only one headlamp was required by French law – so to save weight, only one was fitted.

Built largely of light-alloy and canvas, with mica windows, the earliest TPV prototypes were powered by a water-cooled engine.

CONCEPTION & BIRTH

Three TPV prototypes undergoing engine trials at Citroën's La Ferté-Vidame test-track in June 1939 – a snap taken in defiance of P.-J. Boulanger's orders forbidding all photography.

Another surviving 2CV prototype, housed at the Musée Henri Malartre at Rochetaillée-sur-Saône. This example spent the war at the Michelin factory at Clermont-Ferrand, disguised as a light pick-up truck.

The three examples of the TPV discovered, untouched, in 1994, having been hidden for almost fifty-five years.

35

On assuming command of the Société Anonyme André Citroën, Boulanger's first task was to draw up a plan of operations that would determine Citroën's model range for the next decade and beyond. In view of the company's plight just two years earlier, it was a plan of remarkable courage and audacity. The middle-class Traction Avant would continue, of course, but updated and revamped with modern, streamlined bodywork – a design referred to as the AX. Above that would be an all-new luxury car of advanced specification, code-named the VGD. A completely new front-wheel-drive utility van, the TUB, would also be produced. But at the bottom of the range, Boulanger proposed to build another completely new, 'clean sheet' design, code-named the TPV ('Toute Petite Voiture') – an inexpensive, economical 'people's car' for *les paysans* and the urban working classes, to be launched in or around 1940.

This, then, was the point of conception of the 2CV. From the seminal ideas first set out over sixty years ago in Boulanger's original design brief, the vehicle we know so well today was born, to live on, modified in detail but unaltered in principle, through half a century of service. In truth, such a vehicle had first been envisaged by the Michelin firm as early as 1922, when it commissioned a vast national survey to establish the commercial viability of a French 'people's car': 'In the USA, there's already a car for every 10 inhabitants, but in France there's only one for every 150 people. There, the automobile is a working tool employed by everybody, but here its use is confined to the rich. Why should this be so?' the questionnaire demanded.

Legend has it that the idea for the TPV hit Boulanger suddenly while watching the habits of the local Auvergnat farmers on market day at Lempdes near Clermont-Ferrand, where he had his country home. Then, France was predominantly an agrarian nation, peopled by peasant farmers, smallholders and wine-growers living in widely dispersed rural comunities. And whereas the large industrial cities and departmental commercial centres were linked to the capital by the strategic *routes nationales* laid out by Napoleon, these small villages and market towns communicated via a network of rough country roads or rutted tracks, along which the farmers travelled by bicycle, pony trap or horse-drawn wagon to bring their produce to market. On arrival, the women and children would mind the market stall all day while the menfolk passed the time drinking and gossiping in the bistros, before driving the family home again at the close of day. What was needed, Boulanger observed, was a small, lightweight, all-purpose, go-anywhere car that a farmer's wife could drive and maintain – that way, she could take the goods to market while her husband stayed at home on the farm to do some useful work. What a boost such a car would bring to France's agricultural productivity. What a fillip it would bring to the Citroën firm's sales!

So runs the gospel story reverently handed down by Citroën's publicity department over the years. But the reality is less romantic. Like many other informed observers of the French auto-industry scene, P.-J.B and his Michelin masters believed that, for all his audacity, André Citroën had made only one serious mistake in his entire career: to cease production of his little 7.5 hp 5CV light car in 1926, without providing a similar vehicle to take its place. As we have seen, although the wooden-bodied 5CV was then still in great demand, it represented out-of-date design and technology to the progressive modernist, and he had no hesitation in replacing it with the bigger, all-steel bodied 11.4 hp B12 model, thus abandoning the bottom end of the market and leaving open a lucrative gap for competitors such as the Peugeot Quadrillette and the Austin 7 (built under licence in France by Rosengart) to fill.

Moreover, in making his plans Boulanger would surely have known that another of these baby cars was just around the corner – the Fiat 500 Topolino, introduced in France as the Simca Cinq in April 1936, six months before it appeared in Italy. At that point in its history, the Simca firm was solely a builder of Fiats under licence.

In fact, the true genesis of the 2CV took place not in Paris but at the Michelin plant at Clermont-Ferrand, some two or three years earlier than is generally held to be the case. In 1934 – even before the Michelin family had taken over control of the Citroën firm – Pierre Michelin instructed a Michelin engineer, Monsieur Chantaigner, to design and build a lightweight tyre testing vehicle which would also serve as a test-bed, on which to try out certain engineering ideas that he, Pierre Michelin, was currently considering.

This vehicle is known to have been in existence by 1936, and its general configuration bears a striking similarity to the platform-chassis construction, embodying projecting leading and trailing suspension arms, seen on the prototype TPV/2CVs which appeared later, in 1937. Moreover, the present head of the Michelin family, François Michelin, recalls that, as a boy aged ten, he saw his uncle Pierre make up a model from his (François') toy Meccano set to demonstrate the platform-chassis concept, saying: 'This is what I want to get the engineers to understand.'

In October 1935, only three months after André Citroën's death, Pierre Michelin issued a specification for a French People's (or, more accurately, Peasants') Car, based on the results of this early survey. The proposed vehicle, priced at 5,000 francs maximum, was to be capable of carrying four people at 70–80 km/h on a level road at an average fuel consumption of 5 litres per 100 km.

However, before any serious work on the project was embarked upon in Paris, the Michelin men commissioned a second market research study to test their hunch that a vast, unsatisfied market for such a car existed in France. Over a five-month period during 1936, a team of investigators led by Jacques Duclos and Georges Toubain (both former Michelin employees) toured the nation, asking over 10,000 members of the public about their travelling habits, to discover their wants, needs, hopes, and fears concerning car ownership. 'How far and how fast do you need to travel?' the Duclos survey asked: 'What do you have to carry with you? How much would you be prepared to pay for a car?' The results confirmed their intuition absolutely: not only farmers and country folk were interested in the proposition, but also shopkeepers, artisans, and tradesmen. The study also showed that 90 per cent of first-time French car buyers opted for a used vehicle costing less than 10,000 francs – less than half the then current price of a brand new Traction Avant.

Consequently, later in 1936 Pierre Michelin gave the go-ahead for the TPV project to begin, and a team working at the Citroën Bureau dÉtudes in Paris embarked on the task of building a prototype, based on, and developed from, the vehicle by M. Chataigner originally produced by Michelin at Clermont-Ferrand; this, the first of innumerable Citroën prototypes, appeared during the course of 1937. P.-J. Boulanger, by now heading-up the Citroën firm following Pierre Michelin's death, rapidly issued his famous *cahier des charges* for the *Toute Petite Voiture* – the design brief which has since become enshrined among the myths and legends surrounding the Deux Chevaux. In doing so, it seems that he was actually proposing a reworked version of the concept originally suggested by Pierre Michelin at least two years earlier, revised to suit his own personal inclination towards simplicity and frugality. For example, the target road-speed was reduced from 70–80 km/h to 60 km/h (40 mph) and fuel consumption cut from 5 litres/100 km (56.5 mpg) to an astonishing 3 litres/100 km (94 mpg).

Whatever its origins and criteria, Boulanger's plan was received with incredulity by the old guard at Citroën's Bureau d'Études. Its chief, Maurice Broglie, protested that it was the most unreasonable specification he had ever received in his entire career, and that the proposal was unworkable, but Boulanger was adamant that his plan could and would succeed. France was facing great social changes, he pointed out. In the future, motoring would no longer be confined to the well-to-do; the poor and underprivileged also had a right to be mobile; the arrival of a French 'people's car' was inevitable, and with the blessing of the progressive Michelin family, he was determined that it would be a Citroën.

Formulated in early 1936, Boulanger's design brief laid down that the TPV was to act as a motorised pony cart, transporting people with no previous experience of driving motor cars, or indeed of owning machinery of any kind. No more than 'four wheels under an umbrella', it was to be capable of carrying two farmers wearing clogs, plus 110 lb of potatoes or a small cask of wine at a maximum speed of 30 mph, with a petrol consumption of 90 mpg. Furthermore, it was also to have the capacity to move its passengers and cargo in the greatest comfort over the poorest roads, so that even when transporting a basket of eggs over a ploughed field, not a single egg would be broken. It should cost no more than one-third of the price of the Traction Avant. Economy, practicality and versatility were what mattered to the potential owners Boulanger had in mind; the looks and styling of the finished vehicle would be relatively unimportant. But above all, Boulanger attached the highest priority to reliability and durability: 'For the customer earning only 1,800 new francs a month, a breakdown that costs 300 new francs is a catastrophe,' he later pointed out. 'Even repairs and adjustments costing as little as 50 new francs are unacceptable. We must therefore strive to achieve perfect quality as far as the key components are concerned.'

Having identified this vast market for a radical, minimalist vehicle of a kind that had never been built before, all that remained was to design and construct it! And here again, fortune was very much on Boulanger's side. Working in a specifically French environment, without the pressure to conform to the dictates of a vast, amorphous, international market, he was free to solve specifically French transport problems in an idiomatically French way, with ideas that sprang naturally from the typical French engineering mind – highly original and inventive, yet at the same time rational, logical and philosophical in the intellectual tradition stemming from Voltaire.

Invention was certainly his aim. With the active support and encouragement of the parent company, Boulanger began to turn Citroën's Bureau d'Études into a hot-house of engineering innovation, building up a team of the best technical brains in the country. All manner of talents were engaged: intellectuals and academics (even an astronomer), artists and craftsmen, as well as scientists and technicians. Carte blanche was given to anyone with new ideas, regardless of age, seniority or qualifications. For Boulanger, motor industry experience was relatively unimportant – what mattered more was creativity and the willingness to try anything, even to the point of considering 'unreasonable' solutions. 'Even if only ten per cent of your work is finally used, you will have scored a magnificent success,' he is reported to have said. When a doubting Thomas rejected one of Boulanger's suggestions as being mechanically impossible, he was told to go away and think again. 'We are not in the business of mechanics – we're in the business of cars,' Boulanger exclaimed.

Despite this open-mindedness, the work itself was conducted in an atmosphere of obsessive secrecy, behind locked doors at the Bureau d'Études or hidden behind the 3-metre-high walls surrounding Citroën's new test track laid out at La Ferté-Vidame, near Dreux, some 130 km to the west of Paris. Here, on instructions from the Michelin family, Boulanger had acquired a 2,000-acre country estate of woods and meadows that had once surrounded a château, long since demolished. Nicknamed the *pouponnière* ('nursery'), the existence of the La Ferté-Vidame track was concealed from all but the few key personnel and test-drivers directly involved. No one from the factory was allowed to know what was going on there, let alone staff from suppliers who might inadvertently spill the beans to rival firms. And, needless to say, inquisitive pressmen and photographers were declared *persona non grata* at any Citroën or Michelin establishment.

Overall control and co-ordination of the TPV project was vested in Marcel Chinon, an old boy of the Bureau d'Études who had been with the Citroën firm since 1916. Chinon's

WHY FRONT-WHEEL DRIVE?

Today, front-wheel drive has become standard in the design of family cars, having been adopted universally by all the major volume manufacturers. But back in 1937, when the 2CV was designed, Citroën stood alone in abandoning rear-wheel drive throughout its range of products. Even by the time the 2CV was launched in 1948, the company was still unique in this respect.

The reasons for employing front-wheel drive can be summed up in just two words: stability and safety. When cornering in a front-wheel-drive car, the driving force of the car is exerted in the direction of the turn, to maintain the correct trajectory through a curve. In a rear-wheel-drive car, however, the force is exerted along the fore and aft axis of the vehicle, in the general direction being followed at the time, rather than into the curve. In other words, the driving force imparted by the rear wheels is exerted cross-wise to the required direction being followed by the front or steered axle. It therefore follows that for the same vehicle speed and for the same degree of grip provided by the tyres, a front-wheel-drive car can withstand a greater centrifugal force without loss of tyre adhesion and directional stability – this means that it can go into a turn at a higher speed without risk of skidding, or corner safely on more slippery surfaces.

To complicate matters, these centrifugal forces are magnified by factors such as the camber of the road and side winds, so that any vehicle tends to drift sideways in a turn, without necessarily losing grip and skidding. To counteract this drift, the driver must make constant steering corrections to preserve balance and maintain the set course. Moreover, as this drifting effect is greatest on the driven wheels, in a rear-wheel-drive car the back axle tends to break contact with the road before the front or steering axle, and the driver can only correct this slide by means of harsh or violent movements of the steering wheel, turning it from lock to lock, a manoeuvre that calls for experience and skill. On a front-wheel-drive car, however, the driver can correct drift easily and gently by constant slight adjustments of the steering wheel, a technique requiring much less experience and skill – so front-wheel-drive cars are far easier to control and thus inherently safer.

At its first appearance at the Paris Motor Show in 1948, the 2CV faced competition from another would-be French 'people's car' – the Renault 4CV, announced the year before, but only then coming into production. Like the VW Beetle, this was a rear-wheel-drive, rear-engined vehicle, designed according to the theories of Dr Ferdinand Porsche, which held that for optimum traction, the weight of both engine and transmission should be concentrated at the back of a vehicle, behind the rear axle. Therefore, in choosing between these two cars and their radically different design philosophies, French motorists were, in effect, voting on the future design direction of the popular French car.

Although it did not entirely lack virtues, the Renault 4CV was notoriously difficult to drive, especially when cornering fast on wet roads. So, whereas the Citroën 2CV went on for forty-two years, the Renault 4CV lasted for just fourteen, and was withdrawn in 1961, having sold just over a million examples. The following year, Renault at last forsook Dr Porsche's ideas and introduced its own version of the 2CV formula, the front-wheel-drive Renault 4, which subsequently became the most successful, biggest-selling model in the rival firm's history.

responsibilities extended to liaising with those working on the engine, running gear, suspension and body, monitoring progress and preparing for production. In fact, his work on the project extended for well over twenty years, and continued long into the service life of the 2CV. But to be his chief engineer and designer on the project, working under the overall supervision of Maurice Broglie, Citroën's head of research and development, Boulanger appointed the brilliant engineer André Lefebvre, the protégé of André Citroën who had made such a vital contribution to the design of the Traction Avant.

Born in 1894, Lefebvre had originally trained to be an aircraft designer at Paris's École Supérieure d'Aéronautique, before beginning his career in 1915, employed by the extravagant and idiosyncratic French engineering personality Gabriel Voisin, building aircraft for the French air force. After the war, when Voisin transferred his interest from aviation to the automobile business, Lefebvre moved with him, and was later partly responsible for designing a series of outlandish, streamlined grand prix cars which, in the spirit and custom of the times, he raced in person. In the wake of the Wall Street crash of 1929, the market for Voisin's luxury cars collapsed and Lefebvre joined Renault, which – not surprisingly – he found uncongenial. When, on Voisin's recommendation, André Citroën offered him a job working on the Traction Avant project, Lefebvre naturally leaped at the chance to put his ideas about front-wheel drive into practice.

Most of the great designers in automobile history have been primarily designers of engines, who sometimes had ideas on chassis design and sometimes not. But Lefebvre was

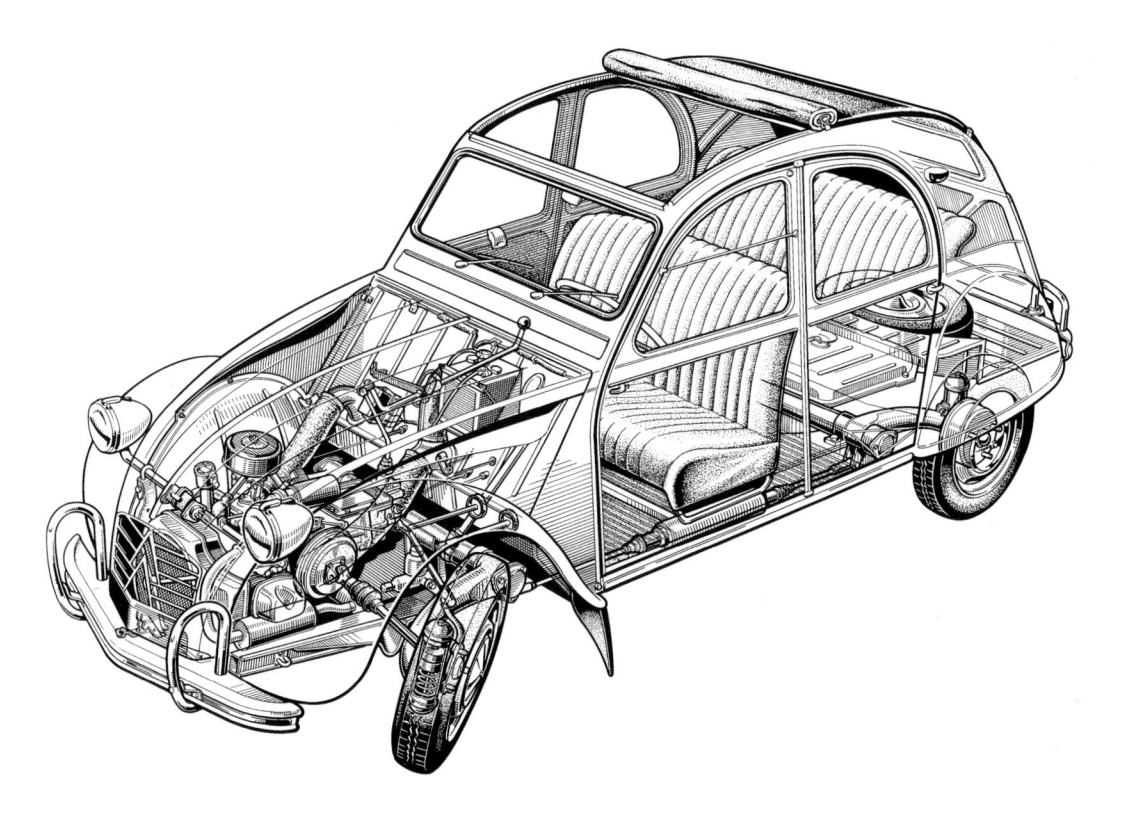

Cutaway drawing of 2CV, *c.* 1964, showing the novel arrangement of transmission and suspension.

Why the Air-Cooled Engine?

Although they powered some of the most important and technically significant cars in the history of motoring, air-cooled engines have now all but vanished from the roads. So why were they once so popular with designers and drivers alike? And, more to the point, why did Citroën choose to fit an example in the 2CV, rather than the water-cooled engine that had also been developed for it in the Bureau d'Études?

Bearing in mind the prime objective in Boulanger's design brief, the main reason for adopting an air-cooled engine for the 2CV was its lightness and compactness compared with the water-cooled alternative. Tipping the scales at just 41 kg in bare form (minus its gearbox and ancillary equipment), the 2CV's original 375 cc light-alloy engine was almost half the weight and bulk of a typical contemporary cast-iron water-cooled engine of similar performance. Not only was it made from a lighter material, it lacked the extra burden of a radiator and water pump, and also the considerable weight of water required as a coolant fluid by its rival.

But air-cooled engines saved more than weight: they also saved trouble. Hence, a second and equally important deciding factor was reliability and ease of maintenance. In those days, at least a third of engine breakdowns could be attributed to cooling system problems – overheating, icing-up or loss of coolant altogether due to failure of the water pump or hoses. Not only did air-cooling overcome these problems at a stroke – there was no water to freeze or boil – it also made for faster warming up of the engine (and hence significant fuel savings) and far more effective heating of the passenger compartment. In fact, an air-cooled engine was considered to be thermodynamically more efficient than a water-cooled engine, since far less power was wasted in forcing air over the cylinders with a fan than in driving water through the engine with a pump.

Unfortunately, one drawback was that light-alloy, air-cooled engines were very much more expensive to make. Firstly, the materials involved cost more; secondly, the process of casting the complicated finned cylinder barrels and heads was more far more difficult and costly than casting a comparable water-cooled engine. Moreover, all air-cooled engines (not just that of the 2CV) were notoriously noisy runners, mainly due to the rotation of the fan and the resonances created by the metal air ducting.

However, the technical problem that really led to their demise was the ever-increasing demand for greater power output which became a design priority for car-makers in the post-war years. It simply proved impossible to uprate the power output of air-cooled engines to produce more horsepower from the same cylinder dimensions without adopting new, more sophisticated fans and air-management systems and even more complicated and expensive finning arrangements for the cylinder heads.

Furthermore, in the post-war years, the reliability of water-cooled engines improved greatly thanks to important developments in metallurgy and materials science and a greater understanding of the process of heat dissipation in an engine. In addition, the advent of new polymers made possible strong, long-lasting, highly-flexible synthetic rubber water hoses which could withstand the extremes of temperatures encountered under the bonnet of a car without cracking or splitting. Hence, in the seventies, the two great pioneers and exponents of air-cooled motor car engines, Citroën and Volkswagen, both gave up the struggle to be different and adopted water-cooled engines like the rest of the automobile industry.

different. Thanks to his aeronautical background, he approached the problem from a different perspective to that adopted by most other leading engineers of his day. His mentor, Gabriel Voisin, was probably the first aircraft constructor to build aeroplanes for sale to private customers rather than merely for his own experiments, so Lefebvre had been made aware at the very start of his career of the prime importance of controllability as a design objective when building a plane or car. Under Voisin's influence, he formed the view that in the interests of safety, the first duty of the designer or constructor was to allow for lack of skill on the part of individual pilots and drivers. Therefore, Lefebvre always took the view that the way forward was to improve performance through greater aerodynamic efficiency and superior chassis dynamics, rather than merely maximising engine power, because this design route also led logically to greater fuel efficiency, comfort and safety through better handling and road-holding. The big Voisins that he had worked on earlier had been among the fastest cars of their time, not because their designer had pursued speed for its own sake, but because speed was the inevitable result of the overall quality of their design and construction. Thus, unlike the majority of the over-powered luxury cars built in the twenties, they could be driven safely right up to the limit of their performance. Because the

The 2CV's tiny engine and gearbox in its original 375 cc form, as manufactured from 1949 to 1959. Note the inboard drum brakes which were not replaced by disc brakes until 1981.

characteristics and capabilities of engine and chassis had been carefully matched, at 90 mph they handled with a degree of assurance and control that was noticeably missing at a mere 60 mph in most of their contemporaries.

Faced with Boulanger's design brief for the TPV – a cross-country vehicle that could be also be cruised flat-out for hours on end down the long, straight *routes nationales* – this was once again the logical design path to follow, Lefebvre concluded. After all, despite the great superficial differences in the two types of customer, the driving requirements of both playboy and peasant were determined by the same common human psychology and physiology!

In response to Boulanger's challenging design brief, Lefebvre set down three cardinal principles for the design and construction of the TPV. Firstly, for maximum stability and ease of control in inexperienced hands, the car would have front-wheel drive, with its engine and gearbox placed ahead of the front wheel axis and its wheels positioned on all four corners. This would distribute weight to the front, thus placing the car's centre of gravity both as low and as far forward as possible. Lefebvre observed that when you throw a hammer, it is the head, not the handle, that travels first. Similarly, when a car travels round a bend, it is best to have the greatest mass concentrated at the front end. To enhance this directional stability, the car would also be equipped with very positive rack and pinion steering – just 2.3 turns from lock to lock – and, moreover, it would also have a very pure steering geometry, free of bumpsteer and fightback effects.

Secondly, for maximum energy-efficiency and fuel economy, the TPV would be made as light as possible – 300 kg at the most – using aluminium alloys instead of steel. Structural strength would come not from a conventional chassis, but from a rigid, rectangular pontoon or platform, to the corners of which the suspension and wheels would be attached by means of two tubular cross-members. The all-independent suspension would take the form of swinging, crescent-shaped axle arms, leading at the front and trailing at the rear, and sprung by a system of multiple torsion bars. The engine and transmission would be fixed to mountings extending outwards at the front, and placed so that the driving front wheels would pull the weight of the vehicle along as a man pulls a wheelbarrow or a horse pulls a cart. Likewise, the rear suspension arms and wheels would simply follow on behind. The bodywork or superstructure would have no load-carrying role, but would merely act as the 'umbrella' over the wheels, a lightweight shelter with no structural function other than to protect its driver, passengers, cargo and mechanical parts from the wind and weather. To give these bolt-on aluminium body panels torsional stiffness, they would be swaged or corrugated in the manner pioneered by the German aeroplane designer Dr Hugo Junkers. Again to save weight and expense, wherever possible, waxed canvas would replace metal in the bodywork – for example, in the roof and doors and the aircraft-type hammock seats. Glass being both heavy and costly, all the windows would be made of mica. And finally, to give a soft, comfortable ride over rough terrain and poor road surfaces, the fully independent torsion bar suspension system would be arranged to give an unusually wide degree of wheel travel up and down, to absorb the shocks and vibration encountered when travelling fast over ruts and potholes.

A tall, debonair, highly strung character, who habitually drank champagne and dressed in a white silk scarf and flying jacket, André Lefebvre took little interest in engines, regarding them scornfully as nothing more than hot and oily *tournebroches* ('turnspits').

Responsibility for the design of the 2CV's power unit therefore rested entirely with the Bureau d'Études' Service Moteurs, under the direction of Maurice Sainturat, who had designed the Traction Avant's engine. The first prototype was powered by a 500 cc BMW motorbike engine, but during those four years of frenetic research and development before the war, Sainturat's team of engineers experimented constantly with various ideas involving a host of different types and sizes of engine – examples having one, two and four cylinders were all tried, but without achieving the absolute reliability and endurance in all operating conditions that Boulanger demanded.

The first official publicity picture of the post-war pre-production version of the 2CV Type A, taken in September 1948. Notice that the lower edge of the rear wing has an upward curve, not seen in series production cars.

45

The Citroën 2CV

On board the 2CV for this publicity shot were: at the wheel, Marcel Chinon, co-ordinator of the 2CV design programme; in the front seat, Madame Gaulon, secretary to P.-J. Boulanger; in the rear, left, Jacques Duclos, head of the Market Survey Department, who had carried out the initial market research survey in 1935; and in the rear, right, Jean Cadiou, Head of the Bureau d'Études.

Before the end of 1937, around twenty TPV prototypes had been built and tested at La Ferté-Vidame. The co-production of an architect and an aviator, they were strange-looking vehicles indeed. Little more than test-platforms with makeshift seats and controls, the absence of bodywork forced the test-drivers to wear leather flying suits, which further accentuated the TPV's weird, quasi-aeronautical appearance.

By this point, completion of the TPV project had become a top priority for Boulanger. On one hand, he had already informed his Michelin masters that production would commence the following year, and on the other, he was obsessed with the idea that Renault was working in the same direction, and that unless he was quick, Citroën's great rival might beat him and be first to introduce a French 'people's car'. By now, it was common knowledge that a similar project was under way in Germany. Hence the feverish round-the-clock activity at the Bureau d'Études. Brainstorming sessions would take place late into the night as the design team wrestled with technical problems in a highly charged atmosphere of urgency and secrecy. There was no longer time for methodical routine and dispassionate professional analysis.

Despite several modifications to Lefebvre's original concept, certain basic flaws were proving extremely difficult to overcome. Most worrying of all were the problems being experienced in assembling the prototypes, constructed largely from duralinox and magnesium. Given the primitive technology of the time, welding the joints of the floorpan was found to be a difficult operation, so the cars tended to split and buckle along the seams when subjected to torsional stress. Strengthening cross-members were required to keep the structure rigid, which added to the car's ever-increasing weight. Moreover, the materials themselves were inherently dangerous. One prototype suffered an electrical short circuit which ignited the petrol tank. When the flames reached the magnesium wheels and suspension arms, there was a blinding flash and the entire car literally disappeared in smoke. Worse still, these materials were scarce and expensive. At the outset of the project, Boulanger had reckoned on the cost of light alloys reducing sharply with their increased industrial use, but there was still no sign that this crucial downward price trend was taking place.

Boulanger's principal design objective – that to save fuel, the TPV should be as light as possible – was causing serious problems in another department. The difference between its weight empty (300 kg) and fully loaded (700 kg) was simply too great for its complicated interacting torsion bar suspension system to cope with. Set for a very soft ride with just the driver inside, the body sank down on to the road when the passengers climbed on board, and whenever the brake was applied, the car pitched and juddered before diving sharply downwards so that its nose hit the ground. To prevent this happening, an anti-dive modification linking the suspension to the brake pedal was necessary. But then, when the testers put the all-important sack of potatoes in the back, the car's nose pointed heavenwards.

Even the latest engine was giving trouble. Prone to icing, it refused to start in very cold weather. Worse still, its fuel economy and power output were both disappointing, well below Boulanger's original specification. Nevertheless, in the spring of 1939, after personally testing a succession of no less than forty-seven different prototypes, he declared that the TPV was roadworthy at last,

By the following year, the rear wing had acquired a straight edge, as can be seen from this rare photo of another pre-production car taken in the Levallois factory in 1949. Notice the small parking lights on the front wings; these did not appear on series production vehicles.

and authorised a pilot pre-production run of 250 cars, ready for the long-anticipated launch at the Paris Salon Motor Show in the autumn.

Had the TPV appeared that year, there can be no doubt it would have been a commercial disaster, for although it may well have satisfied the engineers, it could never have pleased the public in its current state. To the inexperienced driver, it would have been a mechanical nightmare. Routine engine maintenance such as topping up the oil required the removal of the front wing, and with no fuel gauge – not even a dipstick – it was difficult to avoid running out of petrol. Highly charged with static electricity, the mica windows attracted so much road dust that they might as well have been made of frosted glass. The steering wheel and foot pedals were badly placed, and the handbrake hardly worked. The doors and windows would not shut properly, and the roof let in rain and draughts from the slipstream, so that without a proper heater, the car's occupants were always cold, and often soaking wet as well. No one had thought of fitting a starter motor, or even a rear-view mirror. To save weight, only one headlamp was fitted, since this was all that French road traffic regulations then required. A joke went round the company that a glow-worm would have been lighter and cheaper, and would have saved on the battery too!

But then fate intervened in the story of the Citroën 2CV for the second time. On 1 September 1939, the day before the last example of the pre-production batch rolled off the line at Citroën's Levallois factory, the German Army invaded Poland. On 3 September, France and Britain declared war, and shortly after that the forthcoming Paris Motor Show was cancelled. By June 1940, the German Army had arrived in Paris, imposing a state of military occupation on the northern half of France and the unwelcome presence of a German *Verwalter* ('supervisor') on the Citroën factories, and indeed all French automobile firms in the occupied zone.

A German order dated 20 November 1940 gave these supervisors total control over all commercial transactions, including the purchase of raw materials, the payment of wages and the sale of finished vehicles. In fact, their powers extended further than just the control of production, covering the use of technical information and the direction of technical staff. At the Quai de Javel, orders were issued that the production of private passenger cars should cease forthwith, and that Citroën (in common with the Renault and Berliet firms) should concentrate on the manufacture of 3- and 4-ton lorries reserved solely for the use of the *Wehrmacht*. It amounted to a total take-over of the company. Clearly, the TPV's debut would have to be postponed for a few years, thus providing Citroën's Bureau d'Études with ample time to sort out all the minor problems – in secret!

As a war hero who had won many decorations for his valour in the First World War, Boulanger was a staunch opponent of Hitler's New European Order. Despising both the Nazis and the collaborationist Vichy regime, he avoided all personal contact with the *Verwalter*, and did only what was necessary to ensure the continued existence of the Citroën firm and protect the livelihoods of its workforce. Even when faced with the confiscation of the factory's machinery and equipment, with the full backing of his Michelin masters he refused to co-operate directly with the German military and economic authorities, and always insisted on dealing with the occupiers through his subordinates or other intermediaries. An early supporter of General de Gaulle, he was convinced that the *Wehrmacht*'s stay would be relatively short, and so, by means of a variety of ploys, he steadfastly resisted all pressure to assist the Axis war effort throughout the four years of the Occupation. By breaking all records for slowness of production, he ensured that no more than seventeen Citroën lorries a day rolled off the Quai de Javel assembly line to join the *Wehrmacht*'s transport fleet. Between 10,000 and 15,000 vehicles (including limited numbers of the Traction Avant) are thought to have been produced throughout the four years of the Occupation, but many of these were sabotaged during the course of production. A favourite trick was to put the notch on the dipstick in the wrong place, so that the vehicle eventually ran out of oil, wrecking the engine! This uncooperative stand led to Boulanger's name appearing on the Nazis' notorious blacklist of sixty-seven prominent Frenchmen known to be hostile to the Third Reich, discovered by members of the Resistance at the Gestapo's Paris headquarters, the Hotel Excelsior, after the Liberation. Consequently, he spent the war under constant threat of being arrested and deported to Germany should the Allies suddenly invade or a civil uprising break out in occupied France.

It is known that in July 1940, a technical fact-finding mission led by none other than Dr Ferdinand Porsche arrived in Paris from Berlin, to investigate rumours of a French rival to the Volkswagen. But despite promising a free exchange of information between Levallois and Wolfsburg, their enquiries revealed absolutely nothing. Questioned about the TPV, Boulanger told the German authorities that the project was a commercial secret belonging to Citroën, not the Republic, and that he would not divulge such precious information to a Frenchman, let alone a German. However, had the Nazis got their hands on the Gallic people's car at this stage, they would probably have laughingly dismissed it as no more than a soapbox jalopy, so utterly different was it in conception from its Teutonic counterpart.

In fact, on the outbreak of war, Boulanger had ordered that the 250 examples of the TPV so far completed should be hidden for the duration, either at the Levallois factory or at the La Ferté-Vidame test track. Indeed, reliable witnesses have testifed that large quantities remained under wraps at Levallois in 1943. But after the war, in 1949, with the car now an on-the-road reality (albeit in a rather different form, as the 2CV), Boulanger ordered that all remaining examples of the TPV should be destroyed, together with many other prototypes and experimental vehicles dating from the André Citroën era. Fortunately, however, a total of four examples have since been discovered, delapidated, but still intact, hidden in

The 2CV engine: rustic simplicity or refined sophistication?

A complete contrast in every way to the large and complicated lumps of metal that are normally regarded as high-points in the evolution of the internal combustion engine, Walter Becchia's tiny 2CV power plant must surely rank as one of the greatest achievements of motor car design – and certainly the most enduring. Among its contemporaries, only the engine of the fabled Jaguar XK120 (introduced in 1948, the same year as the 2CV) lasted anywhere near as long – thirty-eight years compared to the 2CV engine's unbeaten record of forty-two years in continuous production.

Brilliantly simple and utterly logical, Becchia's lightweight, air-cooled design eliminated almost all the normal electrical and cooling system trouble spots that affected the reliability of conventional engines of its era. With no radiator to leak, no hoses to burst, no fanbelt to break, no pump to seize up and no coolant to boil, freeze or cause corrosion, there was very little to go wrong. By attaching the fan to the end of the crankshaft and locating an oil-cooler in the resulting airflow, optimum working temperature was guaranteed for as long as the engine continued turning. Moreover, by dispensing with the normal distributor and placing the contact-breaker on the end of the camshaft, working in conjunction with a double-ended coil to provide a spark at both plugs for every revolution of the crankshaft, enduringly accurate ignition timing was also assured, despite the waste of a spark, and since there was no high-tension current present at the contact-breakers, the life of the points was also extended. To reduce moving parts and simplify operations down to bare essentials, even the dynamo was designed to work integrally with the crankshaft, its armature forming the spigot to which the fan was attached.

In short, the 2CV engine exhibited a sophistication and precision that completely belied its rough-and-ready sound. Manufactured and assembled to a tolerance of 1 micron, the fit between the principal components was so precise that gaskets could be dispensed with throughout. The integral crankcase and sump was an aluminium alloy casting split vertically along the centre line, and these two halves with their respective single cast-iron piston-cylinder, finned for cooling purposes, plus the alloy cylinder head with its hemispherical combustion chamber, were all bolted together in an exact, oil- and gas-tight fit without the need for the usual seals. Anticipating modern anti-pollution legislation by fifty years, Becchia provided for harmful crankcase fumes to be extracted along a vent pipe by inlet manifold vacuum action, recycled through the carburettor and burnt off with the fuel in the cylinders.

But perhaps the most interesting and unusual feature of the 2CV engine lay in the ingenious design and construction of its crankshaft and con-rod assembly. For maximum strength and perfect balance, the normal practice of using split big ends with two-piece bearings retained by bolted-on caps was rejected in favour of one-piece con-rods with sleeve bearings, fitted to the crankshaft at the assembly stage, the whole forming an extremely rigid and compact self-contained assembly. This integral five-piece crankshaft unit, comprising the crankpins, bearings, webs, con-rods and the front journal bearing, was pressed together hydraulically at the factory, the crankshaft having first been temporarily shrunk by immersion in liquid nitrogen. As the various component parts could not be stripped down and replaced independently, main bearing failure meant that the entire unit had to be exchanged, yet thanks to the low thermal and mechanical stresses inherent in Becchia's design, this was a very rare occurrence. Provided the sump contained the correct amount of clean oil at the start of the journey and the grille muff was removed when cruising at speed, the 2CV engine could always be relied upon to run flat-out at maximum revs for hours and hours on end without ever missing a beat.

At the outset of production in the forties, factory bench tests established its ability to withstand 100 hours at full throttle (5,000 r.p.m.) without damage – the equivalent of travelling 50,000 miles flat-out without a stop. It is hardly surprising, then, that on the road, under normal driving conditions, countless thousands of high-spirited 2CV drivers subsequently discovered that the harder it was pushed, the better Becchia's engine performed, and that vigorous use of the throttle had absolutely no effect on its overall fuel consumption.

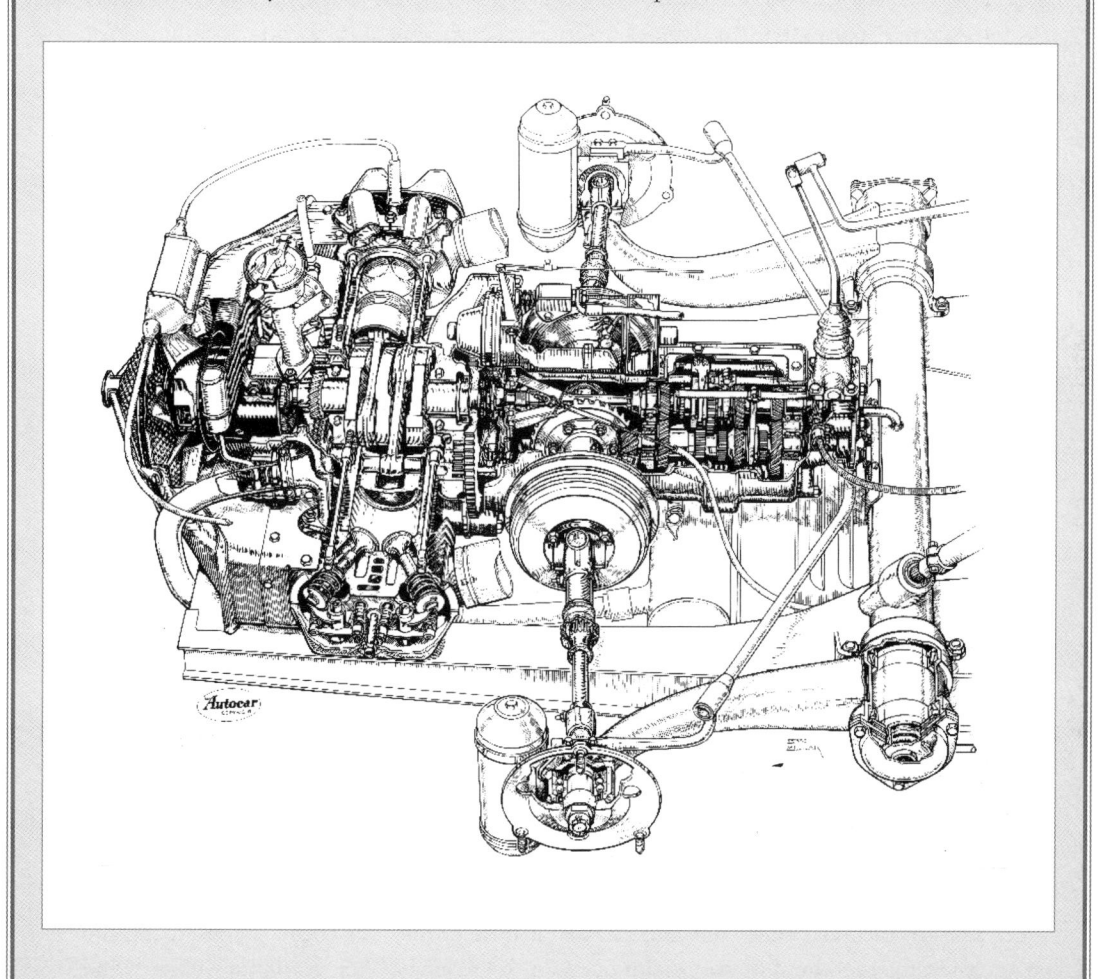

A cut-away view of the 2CV's original 375 cc engine and transmission, drawn by that master of the art, Max Millar, and published by *Autocar* in February 1953 to illustrate the Slough-built RHD car's first British road-test. The offset cylinders and two-throw crankshaft are clearly visible, as are the inertia dampers mounted to the three-stud wheel-hubs. The inherent compactness and simplicity of Becchia's design are obvious!

WHY THE 2CV SEEMS ALMOST HUMAN

Many strangers to the 2CV take fright at its bouncing gait and alarming roll angles when cornering, and assume that its soft, flexible suspension must make for a distinctly queasy ride and extremely unpredictable handling. Yet nothing could be further from the truth: the car is almost impossible to overturn. Right from the start, the 2CV's road-holding was acknowledged as irreproachable, and even today, many experts rate its ride comfort and road manners higher than those of most modern small cars.

Undoubtedly, the secret of the 2CV's outstanding comfort and security lies in its unique, interconnected, horizontally acting, all-independent suspension system, and in the fact that the spring rates of this system were carefully designed to harmonise with the natural human body rhythms of walking or running.

On a 2CV, the wheels are mounted not on axles but on crescent-shaped leading or trailing arms, attached to the corners of the platform chassis via massive roller bearings located in cross tubes. These allow the arms to swivel through a very wide arc, so permitting an unusually wide degree of wheel travel up and down. Therefore, when a 2CV's front wheel hits a bump, the deflection of the front axle arm causes a tie rod to compress a coil spring mounted horizontally in a tubular sliding housing located under the car, so cushioning the blow. But as the rear wheel is connected by the same means to a second spring in the same housing, this has the effect of transmitting the motion to the rear to force the rear axle arm downwards, thus stiffening the suspension ready for the rear wheel to meet the bump. In this way, shocks from ruts and potholes are completely absorbed, jarring and pitching is ironed out, and the travellers on board, sitting well within the wheelbase, enjoy an exceptionally smooth, stable ride no matter how rough the road below them.

The technical drawings published by Motor *in its first review of the 2CV in September 1950 to explain the mysteries of the car to British motorists. The writer reported how amazingly comfortable it was, 'even when driven over bomb-pocked pavé'.*

disused barns at Citroën's La Ferté-Vidame test track, while yet another was found in the Michelin factory at Clermont-Ferrand, where a parallel, tyre-related research project had been conducted before and during the Occupation. Examples of both the Citroën and the Michelin versions of the TPV can be inspected at museums in France today, suitably restored, of course.

Although the TPV was hidden throughout the war, it was certainly not forgotten. Free from the usual commercial responsibilities and pressures, the design and development team was able to work on without interruption, in an atmosphere of clandestine creativity. Despite the fact that French car-makers were forbidden to construct – or even to research and design – any vehicle whatsoever during the Occupation without obtaining the permission of the German authorities, Citroën ignored the order, so this was a period when imaginations ran riot, unfettered by normal business realities.

During the winter of 1940/1, Boulanger initiated a cost review of the project, so that he would be ready to revive the car the moment the war was over. Apart from the obvious political developments, economic circumstances had already changed markedly since the outset. The materials and manufacturing costs of the original light-alloy design were already 40 per cent higher, and climbing fast, Boulanger calculated. A heavier, steel-built car would now be inevitable, but that meant rethinking the suspension and even, perhaps, developing a lighter, more powerful engine. In fact, the

Conception & Birth

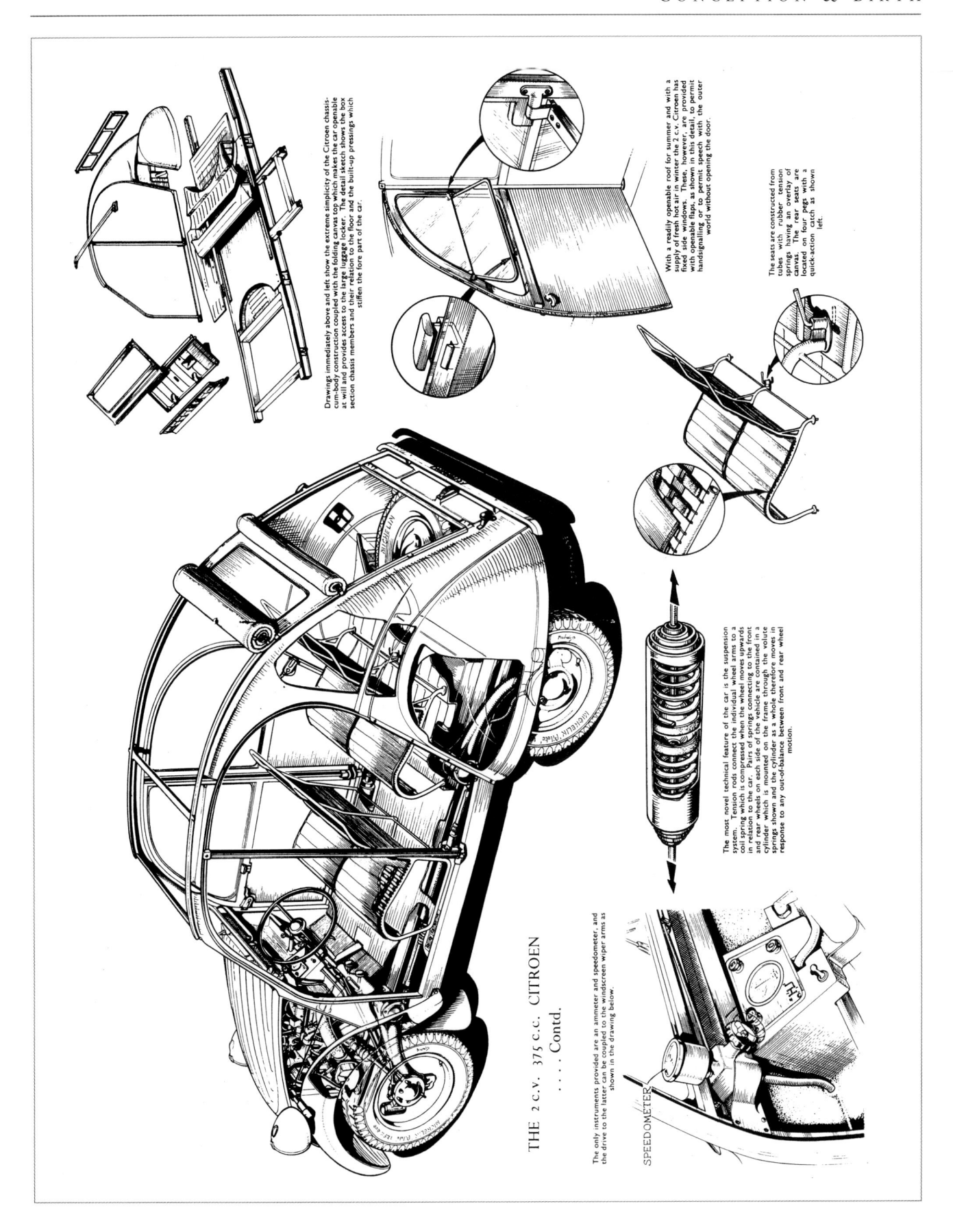

THE 2 c.v. 375 c.c. CITROEN .... Contd.

Drawings immediately above and left show the extreme simplicity of the Citroen chassis-cum-body construction coupled with the folding canvas top which makes the car openable at will and provides access to the large luggage locker. The detail sketch shows the box section chassis members and their relation to the floor and the built-up pressings which stiffen the fore part of the car.

With a readily openable roof for summer and with a supply of fresh hot air in winter the 2 c.v. Citroen has fixed side windows. These, however, are provided with openable flaps, as shown in this detail, to permit handsignalling or to permit speech with the outer world without opening the door.

The seats are constructed from tubes with rubber tension springs having an overlay of canvas. The rear seats are located on four pegs with a quick-action catch as shown left.

The most novel technical feature of the car is the suspension system. Tension rods connect the individual wheel arms to a coil spring which is compressed when the wheel moves upwards in relation to the car. Pairs of springs connecting to the front and rear wheels on each side of the vehicle are contained in a cylinder which is mounted on the frame through the volute springs shown and the cylinder as a whole therefore moves in response to any out-of-balance between front and rear wheel motion.

The only instruments provided are an ammeter and speedometer, and the drive to the latter can be coupled to the windscreen wiper arms as shown in the drawing below.

53

LOOK – NO ANTI-ROLL BARS!

Unlike most modern cars, the 2CV has no anti-roll bars to stiffen its suspension and prevent its body from leaning at an apparently perilous angle when rounding a bend. Lefebvre understood that there is no direct relationship between the force that makes a car's body roll when cornering and that which tries to overturn it. Indeed, a car that rolls a great deal may actually prove very difficult to overturn, while one that rolls little may be far more liable to overturn unexpectedly, since a vehicle's road-holding ability is governed by the grip exerted by its tyres on the road.

In designing for the straight but bumpy rural roads of France, not the twisting, snaking country lanes of England, Lefebvre took the view that anti-roll bars would tend to compromise the 2CV's finely balanced handling abilities, and would also spoil its ride. By transmitting lateral forces to the wheels and inducing them to lift off the ground when cornering, anti-roll bars might serve only to break the vital tyre–road contact at critical direction-changing moments, causing a sudden loss of steering control. Indeed, a certain degree of roll was an advantage, he believed, because it served to warn the inexperienced driver that the car was reaching the limits of tyre adhesion. Thus, although by reducing the roll he might produce a vehicle that looked safer to spectators, in reality its safety margins would be impaired, though with no corresponding gain in stability, security or ride comfort.

In short, there is no link between the 2CV's body roll and the risk of overturning, since its wide track and low centre of gravity help keep overturning forces under control by ensuring that all four wheels stay firmly planted on the road, always remaining parallel to each other to preserve optimum all-round tyre–road contact, even in the harshest turns.

Despite the alarming degree of body roll, the wheels of this swerving Dyane stay planted firmly on the road. In fact, just like all 2CVs, it was virtually impossible to overturn, even in the most violent of cornering manoeuvres.

whole scheme would have to be reconsidered.

Fortunately, the upheavals of war had caused several particularly talented engineers to change their jobs and join the Bureau d'Études, now relocated in the former Mors factory at 48 rue du Théâtre in Paris. Chief among these new recruits was the highly gifted and experienced engine designer Walter Becchia, who came from the Talbot-Lago design office at Suresnes, bringing with him the carburettor expert Lucien Girard. Another infusion of fresh ideas on the project came from the bureau's new head of research, Jean Cadiou, and also from the Italian sculptor and stylist Flaminio Bertoni, who had worked such wonders on the appearance of the Traction Avant. Cadiou instructed Bertoni, aided by other designers, to come up with designs for a new bodyshell in light-gauge steel, and this they did, basing their proposals on Bertoni's maquette for the long since abandoned AX project, or Traction Avant revamp. Once more, Boulanger decreed that this Mark II TPV must have only one headlight, which Bertoni placed at the centre of the bonnet, giving it a strange, one-eyed appearance, like the Cyclops. Its simple, flat-sided shape was due in part to the fact that the Germans had removed from the factory most of the heavy presses that would have been needed to produce a body

The 2CV at its launch at the 1948 Paris Motor Show, when it was inspected by over 1,300,000 visitors. But on this occasion, the bonnet stayed shut, because details of the engine were still undecided! On the adjacent stand is the Deux Chevaux's great contemporary rival, the Renault 4CV.

with more shapely curves. At this point, the revived TPV prototype still retained the original water-cooled engine and multiple-torsion bar springing of the pre-war version.

At that point, Boulanger had no way of knowing whether the missing presses would ever be found and repatriated after the war, and for a very good reason. During the Occupation, on learning that his machine tools and presses were about to be requisitioned and sent by train to Germany, Boulanger had arranged for the Resistance to be tipped off, in order to frustrate and disrupt the Nazi move. One night, while the railway wagons were still in the Paris marshalling yards, some members of the Resistance managed to swap the destination cards so that the freight cars ended up in the wrong places, scattered all over Europe. After the war, much time and effort was spent locating and retrieving this machinery! But either way, with or without the presses, this plain, functional styling with its absence of adornment and ostentation appealed to Boulanger's aesthetic sensibilities. Although it would be stretching things to describe him as an intellectual, as a former architect he was strongly influenced by le Corbusier and the thinkers of the Modern Movement who attempted during the twenties and thirties to lay down comprehensive criteria of design covering all the products and artefacts of a modern industrial society. If, as le Corbusier claimed, a house was simply a machine for living in, then it followed that a car was just a machine for travelling in, and that all design aims or considerations other than the purely functional were superfluous.

After the Liberation in 1944, work on the TPV was resumed in earnest, with a view to commencing production as soon as possible. Initially, a detailed cost and

The following year, on 7 October 1949, all is revealed at last!

P.-J. Boulanger proudly explains the technical details of the 2CV's air-cooled flat-twin engine to the French government ministers, MM. Robert Lacoste and Antoine Pinay.

viability analysis was carried out by M. Bercot (later to head the company), following which a radical third redesign programme was commenced by the Bureau d'Études. This engineering project was headed by Jean Muratet, with the overall body design work being carried out by Maurice Steck, the bodywork specialist of the Méthodes Techniques department, while questions of detail and styling remained the responsibility of Flaminio Bertoni.

For several years after the Liberation, the economic situation in France remained just as parlous as it had been during the war, if not more so, for now the difficulties caused by continued shortages of raw materials, machinery and fuel were compounded by political instability and industrial unrest. However, by the end of 1946 the Citroën firm was well on the road to recovery, having turned out over 10,000 examples of the Traction Avant saloon since production at its Quai de Javel factory had been resumed in June 1945. By now, plans to bring out a revised post-war version of the TPV were well advanced, and already the design was beginning to resemble the car which would eventually appear in 1948, especially since it had now acquired its unique and justly famous air-cooled, light-alloy flat twin engine. The work of Walter Becchia, this marvel of compact, weight-saving design and high-quality precision engineering was intended to run flat-out for hours on end, even in especially arduous conditions. Designed within the space of a week, to the same 375 cc capacity and overall layout as Sainturat's earlier water-cooled design, this perfectly balanced engine combined extreme simplicity and reliability of operation with great fuel economy and efficiency. It could also be depended

WHY THE SKINNY WHEELS?

To reduce unsprung weight to the minimum, the front brakes of the 2CV are mounted inboard, and the wheels themselves are lightweight and of very narrow cross-section, giving better road-holding in wet conditions than wider-rimmed wheels with fatter tyres which are less effective in cutting through surface water to grip the tarmac when it rains. As well as reducing the rolling resistance of the tyres to the minimum, these skinny narrow-section wheels also help mimimise the gyroscopic forces induced when rotating at the extreme points of their suspension travel, which would otherwise cause handling problems. Again, to damp out rebound and prevent wheel hop, early 2CVs were also equipped with friction dampers located at the suspension arm articulating points and by inertia-weight dampers fitted on all four wheels. By 1975, however, all types and models were equipped with conventional hydraulic, telescopic shock absorbers, not fitted directly on the axle arms, but underslung beneath the car and working in a horizontal plane in conjunction with the mechanism that interconnects the wheels.

Another interesting feature of the 2CV's suspension system is the way that it allows for the car's steering geometry to vary with the load on board. When weighed down with, say, four passengers and their luggage, the car's wheelbase is lengthened by 2 inches and its steering castor angle is increased by 8°. This has the effect of neutralising any adverse influence the added load might have on the car's handling and road-holding qualities.

With the added advantage of its light, sensitive and extremely accurate rack and pinion steering, full or empty, a 2CV tends to corner in the same safe and predictable way and to cruise with remarkable straight-line stability, as if on rails.

The platform layout of the 2CV's chassis revealed in plan view. The unorthodox curved axle arms, facing outwards front and rear, together with the inter-connected suspension springs, can be clearly seen.

upon to start first time, whatever the weather, although with no built-in self-starter, this could only be achieved manually, with a starting handle.

Up to this point, it had always been intended that the TPV, as conceived by Boulanger, should have a three-speed gearbox, but Becchia could not resist rethinking this too, giving it four forward gears. When Boulanger noticed this departure from his brief, he was furious. The farmer's wife would have enough problems mastering three speeds, let alone four, he maintained! In the end, a compromise was reached. Becchia succeeded in convincing Boulanger that the fourth ratio was not just another gear, but an 'overdrive', so on the gear-selector only three standard ratios plus reverse were indicated, the fourth position being marked with an 'S' for *Supermultipliée*. Boulanger might have had a point – even today, many novice drivers find gear-changing a complicated business and say that the simple push-pull action of the 2CV's dashboard-mounted gearshift is far easier for beginners to master than the floor-mounted, stick-type levers of modern cars.

The one remaining trouble spot was the suspension, which, after revisions by Marcel Chinon, now featured compressible coil springs, mounted horizontally and interlinked front to rear. A great improvement on the expensive and complicated torsion bar arrangement used on the earlier prototypes, this system prevented pitching and gave the car a very comfortable ride, but at the expense of its road-holding ability: some form of damping was still required to keep the wheels in contact with the road on rebound. The problem was that Boulanger refused to countenance fitting shock absorbers, which he felt would destroy the purity of his conception. Matters were finally resolved when Léon Renault revived his famous pre-war idea of inertia dampers, fitted to the ends of the axle arms, next to the wheels themselves. By describing these modifications as *batteurs* ('beaters'), Boulanger's objections were finally overcome, and the system remained in use on the car for many years, until it was phased out between 1965 and 1975, by which time conventional telescopic dampers were finally fitted on all models.

Throughout 1945 and 1946, the car was subjected to constant, almost non-stop testing at La Ferté-Vidame, under Boulanger's personal supervision. By this point, Lefebvre's involvement in the TPV project had diminished: his creative energy was now focused on another major research project in progress at the Bureau d'Études, the so-called 'Voiture de Grande Diffusion' which was eventually to evolve into the revolutionary Citroën DS19. From then on, the TPV was entirely Boulanger's baby, and as a result, the *patron*'s personality and physique somehow became imprinted on to the car, evident forever in its unique characteristics and appearance. In contrast to the average Frenchman, Boulanger was tall and lean, and he wore a trilby hat, not a beret, so to accommodate him, the car had to be given much more headroom and legroom than provided in other contemporary small cars. On Sundays, he would even take his wife and family for a test drive,

The first publicity shot of the 2CV taken on the public highway. The headlamps of the first few hundred series production vehicles were painted black. On board are members of the Bureau d'Études staff.

each time driving over the same route at the same speed, to check that the petrol consumption never fell below 55 mpg.

Boulanger was a perfectionist, and he always found something to worry about. By now it was the car's weight that was causing him concern. With all the changes and modifications that had taken place, this had now reached over 400 kg – 25 per cent more than laid down in his original design brief. The story goes that in an effort to reduce this, he ordered a prototype to be stripped down completely and the parts weighed one by one, to see if each item could be made smaller, lighter, thinner, or simply eliminated altogether. To monitor the precise weight of every component manufactured from then on, a special department called the Service des Poids was set up, and Citroën's draughtsmen were instructed henceforth to specify a nominal weight for even the tiniest, most trivial part shown on their drawings.

But Boulanger's efforts were in vain – the weight kept increasing regardless, as more and more extra but essential items were incorporated into the design, such as proper window glass, a second headlamp and a rudimentary heating system. Even so, Boulanger still drew the line at an electric starter motor, and refused to countenance any device other than a lawnmower-type recoil starter, worked by a cord pulled from the driver's seat. Later, this directive was reversed in panic just weeks before the launch, when a panel of Citroën secretaries was asked to try out the prototype and succeeded only in hurting their fingers in their futile attempts to get it started. Boulanger demanded an electric starter immediately, and against the odds, he got it. Walter Becchia had foreseen the inevitability of such a volte-face some years earlier, and had designed his engine so that a starter motor could easily be bolted on.

At the first post-war Paris Motor Show, held in September 1946, the newly nationalised Renault firm revealed that it had also been engaged in the secret development of a French 'people's car' during the war. This vehicle, the Renault 4CV, was to be built

The Type H van introduced in 1948 was the first commercial vehicle to feature front-wheel drive, torsion bar suspension, and a forward-control driving position. It was developed from the pre-war TUB prototype of 1937, commissioned by P.-J. Boulanger. This is a 1964–69 example.

The 2CV was essentially a Michelin-inspired project, and was therefore developed at Michelin's Clermont-Ferrand factory in parallel with Citroën's Bureau d'Études in Paris. Here, an early example is seen undergoing tests chez Michelin, circa 1949.

in its factory on the Ile de Séguin in Paris, destroyed by Allied bombing during the war, but presently being rebuilt and re-equipped by state funding. A conventional four-door, four-seater car, the Renault 4CV was powered by a 757 cc engine mounted in the rear behind the axle, as on the VW Beetle. Indeed, the earliest prototypes of the 4CV, built in 1944, showed a very strong overall resemblance to the German car, production of which was by now under way at Wolfsburg.

Sales of the Renault 4CV commenced one year later, in August 1947, under the provisions of the so-called Plan Pons, a five-year plan for the re-establishment of the French motor industry, introduced by the socialist government after the Liberation, in late 1944. This was the work of a certain Paul-Marie Pons, deputy director of the Confederation of French Mechanical Engineering and Electrical Industries, who had produced a study of the pre-war French auto industry published in the left-wing political journal *Cahiers Politiques*. Pons' paper criticised the inordinately wide variety and duplication of models offered by the prinicpal French car producers before the war in comparison to their British and American competitors, and also the frequency with which these models were unnecessarily and uneconomically replaced purely to allow their makers to announce some novelty at the annual Paris Salon. Thus the Plan Pons was intended to rationalise production and increase efficiency through eliminating all unnecessary competition, duplication and change, which the socialist government considered undesirable. Among other measures, the plan stipulated that Citroën should continue to confine itself to constructing the Traction Avant in its 11CV and 15CV forms, so giving Renault a virtual monopoly of the cheaper end of the market. The production of approximately 1,300,000 passenger cars and 630,000 lorries and vans over the five-year period of the plan was envisaged, in steadily increasing numbers, the cars to be manufactured principally by Renault, Peugeot and Citroën, with each firm keeping strictly to its alloted quantity and market sector; 4CV or below, 6–8CV, 10–12 CV, and 12CV and above.

Although he was a member of the committee formed to supervise the implementation of this somewhat

Naturally, the 2CV was designed from the outset to run solely on Michelin tyres and wheels. In fact, no other company manufactured the correct size. These photographs show clearly the 125×400 cross-ply Pilote tyres that were fitted on the earliest examples, before the new Michelin X steel-braced radial tyre was introduced across the range in the early 1950s. The tread pattern on the Pilote and X tyres was identical.

restrictive and bureaucratic plan, in February 1948 Boulanger responded to the arrival of the Renault 4CV by finally approving the much-revised TPV prototype for series production, with the intention that its existence should be revealed to the public at the next Paris Motor Show that coming autumn. Sales were to commence as soon as the end of the five year Pons plan was reached, in the autumn of 1949.

It only remained to choose a name for the little car and to take some pictures for a sales brochure – and, needless to say, Boulanger supervised that job too.

THE CITROËN 2CV

British registered but French made, a very early – and very rare – 2CVAZ, built in the mid-1950s.

This is a 2CVAZL of 1957, distinguished from the AZ by the aluminium trim strips on its doors. 'L' indicated 'Luxury'!

For the first few years of its life, the only publicity pictures taken of the 2CV were monochrome. But then, during the late 1950s, Citroën began to advertise the Deuche using colour photography and employing attractive female models. This glamour photo was shot in 1957.

THE CITROËN 2CV

By the early 1960s more and more French families could afford a car for leisure and holiday use, so the market for the 2CV widened to include urban as well as rural buyers. This charming advertising photo emphasises its appeal for town-dwelling owners by highlighting its suitability for picnic trips into the countryside, a favourite activity of the newly-motorised population …

In December 1960 the 2CV received the first in a new range of colour schemes (Panama Yellow, as seen here), to replace the dingy grey that had been the only option until then. A wider choice of colours was introduced the following year.

This shot of a 1961 2CV shows another of the new range of colours that became available that year – *Vert Embrun*, or Mist Green. It also shows off the new bonnet and grille introduced towards the end of 1960.

66

THE CITROËN 2CV

By the 1970s the 2CV had become an essential part of the Gallic way of life, an ever-present feature of France's urban and rural landscape. Although not quite so ubiquitous today, the car is still regarded by the French as a cultural icon.

This is the 2CV-6 of 1975, equipped with a 602 cc engine (actually rated as a 3CV) plus the rectangular headlamps introduced that year.

67

The 2CV Special introduced in 1979 was the basic model of the three-car range available that year. It had the 435 cc engine and round headlights.

The 2CV-6 Club of 1980 had a slightly higher level of trim than its counterpart, the 2CV-6 Special, and cost 22,000 francs as opposed to 19,800 francs. It was overtaken in popularity by the 2CV-6 Charleston which arrived that year, costing 27,600 francs.

The 2CV-6 Special in its 1985 guise. There had been few noticeable external changes since this model first appeared in 1979, and no more would be made before its production at the Levallois factory ended in 1998.

THE Citroën 2CV

This publicity shot from 1964 was clearly intended to attract more customers from amongst the increasing number of youngsters and students who were discovering the 2CV as their ideal form of transport. 'Not just a motor car – more a way of life', was the claim.

Sun, sand and sex in a 2CV. In 1984, this familiar advertising theme was repeated once again to demonstrate the Deuche's credentials as the fun car par excellence for a new generation of drivers.

69

The 2CV-6 Charleston first appeared in October 1980 in a limited edition of 8,000 cars, painted in this red and black colour combination. This version, the first of three, became so popular that it was adopted as a standard model, remaining in the catalogue until production of the 2CV ended in 1990.

This yellow and black version of the 2CV-6 Charleston, the second to appear, is the rarest of all three types, as it remained in the catalogue for just one year, from July 1982 to June 1983.

The two-tone Art Deco look of the 2CV Charleston was an instant hit with the younger generation. Two-thirds of customers were under 35 years old.

The Charleston was always fitted with round headlamps, initially painted but chromed from September 1981 onwards.

The Citroën 2CV

The 2CV light van or *fourgonnette* as introduced in 1951. The little oval rear windows lasted until 1963. These vans accounted for nearly a third of total 2CV production – ultimately 1¼ million were built.

Just in case anyone should have forgotten the original rural purpose of the 2CV van, in 1964 Citroën produced this atmospheric farmyard shot of the AZU to show that it was still the ideal vehicle for taking goods to market.

A side window reappeared on the AKS van in 1977 by popular demand. The AKS had a taller roof than its counterpart the AK, but both had indentations instead of corrugations to strengthen their lower body sides, with no ripples on the roof in order to facilitate sign writing.

72

CHAPTER THREE

LIFE & DEATH

If the Citroën firm had been attempting to launch a musical rather than a motor car at the 1948 Paris Salon Motor Show, held at the Grand Palais d'Exposition just off the Champs-Elysées on 7 October, there's no doubt that its creation would have been a disastrous one-night flop, for the smash-hit design which was destined to stay on the motoring stage for forty-two years and to sell almost seven million copies was cruelly panned by the critics of the motoring press at its debut. 'Grave error' ... 'a fiasco' ... 'a total misreading of the market' ... 'the ugliest car in the world' – these were some of the kinder comments. With the sole exception of a perceptive Swiss motoring journalist writing in the *Revue Automobile Suisse*, not a single reviewer had the foresight to predict that, in the hackneyed show-biz phrase, the 2CV was a production that would run and run.

Even Citroën's own dealers thought that Boulanger had made a big mistake. At a preview two months earlier, they had begged him to change his plans, or at least to do something to beautify the car, but *le patron* was adamant – the 2CV was not meant to be a status symbol or object of prestige like other cars, and the launch would go ahead regardless. He could hardly do otherwise. An enterprising photographer from the newspaper *La Presse* had given its readers a sneak preview of the 2CV by penetrating the security screen surrounding La Ferté-Vidame and snatching a shot of a prototype on the test track. It made headline news – Citroën could no longer deny that the car existed, even though the vehicle shown in the picture was not the final version about to be introduced.

As it happened, the 2CV turned out to be the star of the show, which was attended by over 1,300,000 visitors, all of them anxious to catch their first glimpse of France's new 'people's car'. When Boulanger proudly unveiled the three first examples before the President of the Republic, Vincent Auriol, crowds surged on to the stand to get a closer look. Security guards had to be called in to prevent the public forcing open the sealed bonnets to inspect the engines and to stop them bouncing the cars up and down to see the novel suspension in action. In fact, the bonnets were empty: the final design and specification of the engine had not yet been settled! No matter: thousands of orders were taken on the first day alone, and by the end of the proceedings over 1¼ million visitors had flocked to the stand.

A publicity shot from the early fifties, showing the remarkable spaciousness of the 2CV compared with the Renault 4CV. Although hardly a true seven-seater, the Deux Chevaux offered ordinary French families their first taste of mobility and independence.

It was hardly surprising. Here at last was the means by which the ordinary Frenchman and his family could eventually become motorists. For little more than the price of a motorbike-engined cyclecar – 185,000 old francs – Citroën was offering a spacious and extremely comfortable four-door, four-seater saloon which, as a bonus, converted instantly into a removal van or pick-up truck. Its great advantages as a load- and people-carrier over its main French rival, the rear-engined Renault 4CV, were plain for all to see!

But despite all this interest and excitement on the part of potential customers, almost another whole year was to pass before a single 2CV was built and sold, in July 1949 – production actually commenced on 23 June that year. For in the aftermath of the Second World War, France suffered an economic crisis of far, far greater severity than that which occurred after the First World War. During those grim post-war years, virtually every commodity, including food and fuel, was in short supply, especially the raw materials and equipment needed to build cars. Following the depredations of the Occupation, during which the factories of the French auto industry had either been pillaged by the Germans or damaged by Allied bombing, machine tools were virtually non-existent. Moreover, a severe shortage of foreign currency meant that it was difficult for both Citroën and its suppliers to import new plant to re-equip their production lines. Thus, even though the Plan Pons had by now been abandoned and, theoretically, a free market in cars and car components was in the course of being re-established, components of every kind were still severely rationed, especially tyres and batteries, not to mention petrol and steel.

When the 2CV made its second public appearance, at the Paris Salon motor show of October 1949, the bonnet was opened, with the tiny flat-twin engine in place and exposed for all to see. Yet production was still beset with problems, and only 924 examples were completed by the end of the year. By now the price had climbed by some 28 per cent, to 228,000 old francs – almost half the annual income of the average French household – but it seems that this did not present a deterrent that depressed demand, so great was the urge among the peasantry and *petit-bourgeoisie* to join the motoring classes. Whereas in the USA one in four families owned an automobile, in France the figure was still only one in seventeen.

But although there was nothing to stop these would-be owners from putting their names down on a waiting list of inter-planetary proportions, very few were given the chance to consummate their passion to possess a car, for it was almost impossible for private drivers to obtain a permit to purchase one. Indeed, the paltry total national output of 5,000 vehicles built on the resumption of automobile manufacture in France during 1947 had only been raised to 20,000 vehicles per year by the beginning of 1950, and most of these cars were earmarked for export.

Thus the Paris streets on to which the first examples of the 2CV emerged in the early fifties were almost completely empty of motor traffic and quite devoid of the bustling atmosphere that characterises the city today. Although the war had been over for the French for almost five years (Paris had been liberated in August 1944), wartime conditions still prevailed. It was a time not just of universal restrictions and shortages, but also of industrial unrest and political uncertainty. Of the several million cars that had existed in pre-war France, less than 100,000 had survived the Occupation in working condition, and of these, many had been converted to run on town gas or charcoal fumes, using gazogene equipment. In Paris and

The 2CV was produced in large numbers at Citroën's Belgian factory at Brussels-Forest for almost thirty years, from 1952 to 1980, for service in various export markets as well as the Benelux countries. This Belgian-built example, recognisable by its extra brightwork, appeared in a Swiss advertisement.

By the mid-fifties, the 2CV was becoming a familiar sight amongst the traffic, not just in Paris but throughout France. Yet after five years of production scarcely 100,000 had so far been built – less than two month's output by Citroën's present-day standards!

the other major cities, horse-drawn cabs had reappeared on the streets, while in the country, horses, donkeys and oxen had returned to work in the vineyards and fields.

Observing this austere economic situation as a visitor during the particularly severe winter of 1946/7, the American writer Arthur Miller reported: 'The sun never seemed to rise over Paris, the winter sky was like a lid of iron.' Although physically undamaged, the city had been all but destroyed, both morally and economically, by the war, and 'a doomed and listless silence' prevailed, he affirmed. There were few cars on the streets – just occasional trucks running on wood-burning gazogene engines, rumbling past old women riding ancient

bicycles. The whole sombre picture was composed of a thousand subtly different shades of grey – a chiaroscuro effect formed by the stone-paved streets, the shabby, peeling stucco and louvre-shuttered windows of the apartment houses and the gaunt, bare plane trees lining the boulevards.

Two years later, the grim atmosphere of '*les années grises*' had still not lifted entirely, so that when the first examples of the 2CV appeared in numbers on the streets of the capital, in 1950, its subfusc paint introduced a further shade of grey to this depressing, monochromatic scene, enlivened here and there only by posters pasted to the walls, or by the Tricolore flag fluttering dejectedly from public buildings. Even so, across the

Seine, on the other side of the city from the Levallois factory, in the left bank cafés and clubs of Saint Germain des Prés, the old *ésprit* was at last returning to revive the body of France. Here the first flames of the Existentialist movement, led by Jean-Paul Sartre, Albert Camus, Simone de Beauvoir and Juliette Greco, were already alight, restoring the intellectual vigour and vitality of the past. For these free-thinkers, the utilitarian 2CV became part of the sparse furniture of their bohemian life. Later, a whole new generation of French youth whose idols included such stars as Brigitte Bardot, Jeanne Moreau and Jean-Paul Belmondo followed their example, adopting the 2CV as a symbol of their new-found liberty and mobility.

Towards the end of 1951, the economic situation in France had improved somewhat, and Citroën was now able to turn the 2CV out at the rate of over 100 per week. Almost 15,000 examples were built that year, with output climbing to more than 21,000 in 1952. Nevertheless, throughout that era, the Levallois factory still could not make enough cars to satisfy demand. As export markets continued to take precedence, the supply of vehicles to French customers remained strictly rationed, with top priority given to those who, in Boulanger's words, 'have to travel by car because of their work and for whom ordinary cars are too dear to buy'. Citroën's dealers were permitted to make provisional contracts only, and after signing these, the would-be buyers were visited by special inspectors, to check that they fulfilled Boulanger's social criteria and that they would undertake to supply Citroën with a written report on their experiences with the 2CV.

For the first few years, cars went only to the most deserving cases, such as country vets, doctors, midwives, priests and, of course, the small farmers and

The first major up-date of the 2CV's specification took place in October 1953, when amongst other improvements new seats covered with tartan fabric were introduced.

horticulturists for whom the 2CV had originally been designed. Owners' and drivers' enthusiastic tales of 2CV ownership alone were sufficient to advertise the car. Their word-of-mouth accounts were so favourable that second-hand 2CVs regularly commanded a far higher price than new cars of other marques, which ensured that the waiting list got longer and longer all the time. Although by 1952 production was nudging 400 cars a week, an eighteen-month-long wait was still unavoidable for every customer without exception, no matter how prominent or influential he or she might be. There was to be no queue-jumping – the incorruptible Boulanger had seen to that. A government minister wrote to Citroën requesting one for his daughter, a member of the Chamber of Deputies applied on behalf of a friend, but to no avail. Demand outstripped supply to such an extent that Citroën could choose its own customers, and the rich and powerful were given no priority.

So what precisely did those very earliest 2CV-buyers get for their money in 1949? Much the same as those of 1989! There's no disguising the reality that the last cars made differed so little from the first that apart from noticing a marked contrast in engine power, the modern-day 2CV owner feels immediately at home at the wheel of a model of early fifties vintage – a measure of the enduring 'rightness' of André Lefebvre's design. On closer inspection, however, both drivers and mechanics find dozens of subtle differences, all bearing witness to the fact that the 2CV underwent a constant process of improvement and enhancement throughout its long lifespan, but these refinements were always minor revisions of detail, never major rethinks of construction or design.

The earliest Series A 2CV of 1949 (fitted with the original 375 cc 9 bhp

The earliest publicity for the 2CV emphasised its rural roles, as in this shot designed to appeal to hunting and shooting enthusiasts. The oval-ring badge on the grille shows that this car was built before 1953.

Perhaps the archetypal 2CV, this AZL built in 1956 represents the essence of motoring minimalism. The colour was grey and grey only – a choice of colours was not available until 1959.

engine) was a four-door, four-seater saloon capable of 54.7 mpg, a maximum speed of 40.9 mph and a 0–40 mph acceleration time of 42.4 seconds. Yet even with this feeble performance, very good average speeds could be maintained on uncrowded country roads, thanks to the car's excellent road-holding and cornering ability – just like today. Available only in a matt metallic-grey finish, its bodywork featured detachable tubular-framed seats and a fully-opening canvas roof extending right down to the rear bumper, instead of the opening metal boot lid seen today. In later years, this roll-back top was advertised as a sunroof, but its original purpose was to allow the carrying of awkward, oversize loads.

Despite the similarities between early and late examples of the 2CV, there are some internal and external differences. The most noticeable of these are the early swaged 'ripple' bonnet with its slatted front grille and side louvres, the lack of rear quarter windows, and the fact that the front doors opened backwards. The rudimentary instrumentation of the earliest cars consisted only of an ammeter and a speedometer fixed to the windscreen pillar (the speedo cable also drove the windscreen wipers) and the car lacked direction indicators, electric windscreen wipers, a heater and a fuel gauge (the fuel reserve was measured by a dipstick). But even so, the experience of travelling in a 2CV didn't change much over the years, despite the successive improvements achieved in performance. When cruising at its typical speed of 40 mph on the open road, the earliest 'tin snail' feels just as easy, pleasant and comfortable to drive, and be driven in, as its modern counterpart.

The AZL again, unmistakable thanks to the alloy enjoliveur (trim strip) running down the centre of the bonnet.

In short, then – as now – the 2CV's basic engineering strengths and virtues more than compensated for its lack of superficial polish. Hence, very soon, the ugly duckling had become a golden goose for its makers. By 1953, Citroën was rolling out 400 examples a week, both saloons and the newly introduced 2CV Fourgonnette (light van). By 1954, production was up to almost 1,000 vehicles a week – yet even so, throughout the mid-fifties, the waiting list of would-be buyers was never less than two years long. Manifestly the right car in the right place at the right time, demand for the 2CV was insatiable.

To enhance its popularity further still, Citroën began to introduce a series of gradual improvements, embellishments and modifications, both technical and aesthetic, to uplift its performance on the road and in the showroom. This process of evolution began in 1951, when the car was equipped with an ignition key and locking door handles for the very first time. It continued in 1954, when a new AZ version was introduced as an option to the basic 2CV Type A, offering a larger 425 cc 12 bhp engine which, with 33 per cent more power, boosted the top speed to almost 50 mph. A centrifugal clutch which disengaged automatically at low revs was also provided (as standard until February 1961, and as an alternative to a conventional clutch thereafter), making driving easier in town traffic and allowing coasting to save fuel – although it also prevented the car from being push-started in the event of a flat battery. For the first time on a 2CV, this version had flashing direction indicators, but fitted only on the rear quarter panel, a single lamp unit shining both fore and aft – an improvement subsequently fitted to the basic Type A versions the following year, when tartan seat covers were also introduced to help relieve the austerity of the interior. Even so, the door trim panels remained just plain, flat boards, unadorned by armrests. In 1953, the frontal aspect of all 2CV models was changed slightly by the removal of the oval surrounding the double chevrons on the grille.

By 1956, a luxury Type AZL model with a heater and demister and a larger rear window plus a choice of higher-quality seat coverings had appeared in France, inspired by a similar version currently being produced by Citroën's Belgian factory at Brussels, where 2CV assembly had commenced in 1952. Externally, Belgian-made 2CVs of that era could easily be distinguished from the French-made cars by their alloy wheel embellishers and wingspats. By 1957, an AZLP version with a metal boot lid replacing the standard canvas covering was also available on the French market; this improvement was fitted across the range for the following 1957/8 model year. In late 1959, a choice of body colours was offered for the first time: now the 2CV could be ordered in glacier blue as well as in the traditional light- or dark-grey paint which had replaced the original metallic grey in 1952. And if that was not choice enough, the option of a Radioën factory-fitted radio was offered as well!

Notwithstanding all this extra performance and luxury, the 2CV remained the ideal transport for

In December 1960 the familiar face of the 2CV saloon was given a make-over, when the old 'ripple' bonnet was replaced by a completely new hood and grille. The van was likewise improved in July 1961.

THE CITROËN 2CV

The AZAM introduced in March 1964 was a deluxe model that featured many extra refinements including bright-metal wheel trims and elaborate bumpers with tubular overriders.

country-dwellers, farmers and working people – and for explorers and adventurers too. No other car of its time could be relied on to travel so cheaply, so reliably and so comfortably over poor or non-existent roads. So, with the 2CV's reputation as an indefatigable workhorse spreading right round the world, Citroën began to set up manufacturing operations abroad, to bring it to a wider public in those foreign markets that demanded a low-cost utility car that would perform well in difficult conditions and across rough terrain. Consequently, the 2CV and its derivatives eventually came to be assembled in no fewer than fourteen countries besides France. Belgium, Spain, Portugal, Yugoslavia, Romania, Iran, Tunisia, the Ivory Coast, Chile, Argentina, Madagascar, Cambodia, Vietnam and the UK all produced versions at various times.

Having amply demonstrated the standard 2CV's capabilities as a go-anywhere, do-anything, off-road vehicle, in 1958 its manufacturers decided to exploit this cross-country potential to the full by producing a specialist all-terrain version for mountain and desert use. In the true Citroën tradition of never doing things by halves, the result was the 2CV 4×4 Sahara, the world's one and only two-engined, four-wheel-drive car. With a separate 425 cc power unit and gearbox located at both front and rear, running either in tandem or front-only, the Sahara was certainly a concept way ahead of its time. Much lighter than conventional off-road machines, it was widely regarded as one of the best-performing all-terrain vehicles ever developed. However, only 694 were ever produced, of which only a handful survive today.

December 1960 (July 1961 for vans) saw the first major facelift to the 2CV saloon's exterior appearance when the old one-piece 'ripple' bonnet was replaced by an entirely new pressed steel panel having five ribs running fore and aft along its surface, with, beneath it, two further panels on either side having recessed longitudinal ventilation slots opening into the engine bay, instead of louvres as before. At its first appearance, this bonnet also featured a new aluminium grille with the double chevrons set into five horizontal alloy strips, but this feature, unlike the bonnet itself, was destined to be changed a number of times. The spare wheel continued to be stowed in the rear luggage area except on commercial versions where it was located under the bonnet. On the inside of the car there were further changes, including better seats and seat covers, together with stronger door locks, while outside, the familiar dingy grey paint was finally discontinued, replaced by a vibrant Panama yellow. Before very long, the

The 2CV of the late sixties was characterised by a new style of grille, first seen in October 1965. This had three prominent bars, without chevrons – the Citroën badge was now relocated on the bonnet. The rear quarter windows were introduced at the same time. During 1966 production of 2CV saloons reached its all-time high of 168,357 units.

The seventies saw another small change – in October 1975 the grille was revised again and more powerful rectangular headlamps were introduced.

2CV's previously limited choice of colours had expanded beyond recognition to include a wide palette of fresh, bright, youthful Mediterranean shades, including red, beige, green and Monte-Carlo blue.

In September 1962, improved trim, controls and instrumentation finally arrived – at last the car had a real fascia with a modern steering wheel and a proper instrument binnacle boasting a conventional speedo and fuel gauge, plus electric windscreen wipers! Indeed, the early sixties witnessed a host of improvements to the 2CV range, together with the introduction of several new variants offering much higher performance and trim specifications. Most notable of these models were the AZC Mixte or Combi, a commercial version equipped with folding rear seats and a rear door that hinged above the window rather than below it, and the AZAM, a luxury, top-performance 2CV, the letters AM standing for '*améliorée*' ('improved'). Fitted with an extra third side window let into the rear quarter panel, its body boasted brightwork galore, such as stainless steel hubcaps and alloy bumper overriders. Inside, there were further lavish touches to the trim, such as a vanity mirror and sunvisor for the passenger.

To meet newly-introduced EEC safety regulations, during the course of 1964 all three saloon models then on sale – the AZL, the AZA, and the AZAM – received new hinges for their front doors, repositioned from the B to the A pillars so that they opened in the proper way, towards the front. They also got new individual single front seats to replace the double bench type previously fitted, and also lap-type seatbelt mountings. With minor improvements, this three-car range continued through to the end of the decade, although by 1970 a 12-volt electrical system supplied by an alternator had been also fitted. It was also in 1964 that the 2CV made motoring history by becoming the first car ever to be fitted with 125×380 Michelin X tubeless radial tyres as standard; in 1960, tubed Michelin X 135×380 radial tyres had already replaced the cross-ply Michelin Pilote 125×400 type originally fitted across the range.

At the Paris Motor Show in October 1965, a further major facelift for the 2CV saloons was put on public display. For the 1966 model year, all models were equipped with six-light bodies with a glazed rear quarter panel, plus yet another new grille, again made from alloy, but this time having just three, thicker, bars running laterally across the trim surrounding the fan aperture. The double chevron badge was now to be seen mounted on the bonnet, while the bumpers and overriders were fitted with a protective rib of black plastic material, said to be resistant to minor parking impacts or traffic accidents. On the technical side, fully homocinetic driveshafts replaced the simple universal cardan joints formerly used, while conventional telescopic hydraulic shock absorbers superseded the old friction dampers, though on the rear suspension only.

In August 1967, the 2CV family was enlarged by the arrival of a sister model, the Type AYA or Dyane saloon. Although it shared the same platform chassis, suspension and other mechanical components as the standard 2CV and was roughly equivalent in performance, the Dyane featured a larger, wider, stronger, more modern-looking body structure boasting up-to-date styling details such as faired-in headlights. At first available only with the 425 cc 21 bhp flat-twin 2CV engine, but shortly after with either an uprated 435 cc 26 bhp unit or the 602 cc 28 bhp engine from the Ami-6, then the 33 bhp unit and finally the 35 bhp engine, the Dyane was Europe's first true volume-production hatchback car.

With its full-length, fully opening tailgate and fold-back sunshine roof (which could be opened from the inside and fixed in a half-open position), it offered even greater versatility and practicality than the

To satisfy the purists, for the 1976/7 season Citroën introduced a back-to-basics version of the 2CV-4, the Special, available only in France. As well as losing its rear quarter windows, this economy model reverted to the old round type of headlamps. Some progress!

The changing face of the 2CV

How can you tell the age of a 2CV at a glance?

Throughout the production life of the 2CV, the official Citroën model year ran from 1 September through to 1 August, with little or no production taking place during the factories' annual holidays in August. Major changes to the range therefore normally occurred with effect from 1 September each year, with all models listed in the catalogues for that season remaining available through to 31 August the following year. These changes were usually revealed at the Paris Motor Show held in October, with the new models arriving at the dealerships shortly afterwards. However, some important changes were made halfway through the model year, being introduced after the Christmas and New Year holidays, at the beginning of the calendar year.

The principal changes to the frontal appearance of the 2CV saloons were introduced in the following sequence, arriving on the streets in the year and month given.

October 1948   When launched at the Paris Motor Show, the 2CV had a grille bearing the traditional Citroën badge of double chevrons surrounded by an oval ring, mounted on horizontal slats. But on pre-production vehicles built earlier that year, the grille had diagonal slats which echoed the oblique angles of the chevrons.

October 1953   The oval ring of beading surrounding the double chevrons on the grille was deleted, and the chevrons were increased slightly in size.

October 1955   A bright-metal trim strip running down the centre of the bonnet was added, together with a further strip along the sills, on the AZL model only.

December 1960   The original one-piece swaged 'ripple' bonnet was replaced by a new pressing having five ribs running fore and aft along its surface, with, beneath it, two separate side panels having recessed longitudinal ventilation slots opening into the engine bay instead of louvres as before. This bonnet also featured a new detachable aluminium grille with a large double chevron emblem set into five horizontal bars.

October 1965   The alloy grille was revised once again and given three larger, thicker bars extending over the edge of the surround, but with the chevrons removed to a new position above it, on the bonnet.

October 1970   New front direction indicators appeared, inserted in recessed roundels on the wings.

October 1974   Rectangular headlamps were fitted on all models, together with yet another new style of grille made from plastic, having a small pair of chevrons mounted on four horizontal bars set within a thicker surround. This grille came in three interchangeable versions, according to the individual model concerned: plain grey all over, grey with a black surround, and grey with chrome-effect surround.

October 1975   Round headlamps reappeared on the 2CV-6 Special but rectangular headlamps remained on the Club and other variants.

October 1980   Round headlamps were reintroduced on the new Charleston special edition, initially painted black but chromed from September 1981 onwards.

October 1982   Rectangular headlamps disappeared entirely, replaced by round headlights on the 2CV-6 Club. On all versions the grille remained the same pattern as that introduced in 1974, until the end of production.

1949–1953. The original grille with an oval badge featuring large double chevrons.

LIFE & DEATH

1953–1960. The oval surrounding the double chevrons disappears, but the grille remains an integral part of the bonnet.

1960–1965. A completely new bonnet with a detachable aluminium grille is introduced. The large chevrons remain prominent.

1965–1974. A second type of grille appears, without chevrons – the Citroën badge is reduced in size and moved to a new position above the grille, on the bonnet. This car is an export version having rectangular front direction indicators, not fitted in France.

1974–1990. The third and final version of the grille with the chevrons restored to the centre but remaining small. The surround of this plastic grille could be either plain grey or chrome-effect, according to the model.

In the shape of the 2CV-6 Club of 1976/7 the Deux Chevaux – now thirty years old – finally evolved into its modern-day form, with the appearance and features it kept until the end. But another thirteen years of steadfast service still lay ahead of it!

2CV, if not quite the same degree of character and charm.

Regarded as something of a heresy by 2CV purists and fanatics, the Dyane-4s and 6s came in two levels of trim, Luxe and Confort, with both a centrifugal traffi-clutch and a folding rear seat for extra load space available as optional extras. Instead of having the 2CV's upward-hinging front windows, the Dyane's opened by sliding fore and aft, just like those of the Ami-6. The first examples of the Dyane-4 produced had four-light bodies, with six-light for the Dyane-6, but from March 1968 onwards, six-light bodies were fitted on both variants. During its production life, the Dyane underwent few changes. In September 1974, its front grille was changed from the original stainless steel mesh to a plastic version featuring horizontal bars, first grey, then black after 1980. In 1977, front disc brakes were introduced on the Dyane-6.

By now, the unmistakable sight and sound of the Citroën Two-Pot in all its various forms had become a familiar feature of city life in France, to be seen and heard in towns and suburbs as well as country villages. During the 1960s France's economy – and the living standards of its citizens – had been spectacularly transformed, so that the ownership of household appliances and consumer durables, such as washing machines, refrigerators, and television sets, had become the norm. Even the possession of a modest motorcar like the 2CV was now well within the reach of the majority of the population, which had moved from the land to live and work in an urban environment. Between

1954 and 1975, the number of peasant farmers in France declined from 20 per cent to 7 per cent of the active work force, while from 1960 to 1975 the number of private vehicles on French roads increased from 5 to 15 million.

Yet the older and more ubiquitous it became, the more the 2CV seemed to appeal to the young and the young-at-heart, so that throughout the sixties its erstwhile agricultural image gave way to a newfound classless status as the ideal cheap car for students, teachers and professionals, as well as peasant farmers. In 1967, its production rate peaked at 146,395 units – an average of 765 a day – but still the 2CV was only just approaching its adulthood, let alone its middle age.

In fact, the coming of the Dyane was meant to signal the beginning of the end for the Deux Chevaux, so, from February 1970, the range was consolidated with just two standard saloon models, the AZL 2CV-4 and the AZL 2CV-6, each incorporating all previous improvements and powered by 435 cc (26 bhp SAE) and 602 cc (33 bhp SAE) engines respectively. On both models, the bumpers were sheathed with grey plastic, instead of black as before, while the front direction indicators (formerly located together with the rear indicators in a single unit mounted on the rear quarter panel) were set into recessed roundels on the front wings. The rear lamp clusters were also enlarged and improved to house the rear

In April 1976, Citroën – the pioneers of front-wheel-drive and countless other engineering innovations – invented another important feature of modern automobile design: the Special Edition, a clever device for giving old models a new lease of life. The first example, the 2CV-4 Spot, was actually limited to a mere 1,800 units.

The most popular of all the special editions was the Charleston. First seen in April 1981, it remained in the range until the end of production.

direction indicators, and to improve the lighting system, a 12-volt electrical system was adopted for the first time, incorporating an alternator and a 25-amp-hour battery. Inside, an entirely new instrument binnacle was fitted, plus a more modern twin-spoke steering wheel. Outside, identifying letters on the boot lid distinguished the 2CV-4 from the 2CV-6, the first time such badges had been used.

This was the basic two-level range that endured until the end, with only minor visible changes, such as the switch to rectangular headlamps in 1974, and then back again to the original round shape in 1982, and the introduction of the final style of grille, also in 1974. Made of plastic, this had four thin lateral bars on which were mounted the Citroën double chevron badge, now returned to its original location. In September 1975, telescopic hydraulic shock absorbers replaced the inertia dampers on the front wheels also, while the following year a twin-circuit braking system was adopted, with a tandem master cylinder, and the original 14:1 ratio of the rack and pinion steering was changed to 17:1 on the 2CV-6. By April 1977, this improvement, made in the interest of lightness, had been extended down to include the 2CV-4 Special base-level model as well.

By 1970 the 2CV had been on the roads for well over twenty years, and more than 1,716,000 examples had already been built, although sales were slowly declining, as was only to be expected of a car on the point of retirement after a hugely successful career. But just as the final curtain appeared to be in sight for the 2CV family, fate intervened once again to save the show from closure and keep its already long-running act in business for another two decades. The global oil crisis of the early seventies sent shock waves through the motor industry as customers stopped buying big cars and searched for smaller, less thirsty vehicles instead. Suddenly, the 2CV was back in demand again – not just in France and Belgium, but also in Germany, Holland, Italy and the UK – as a new generation of drivers rediscovered its frugal, rustic virtues. Once again, the 2CV was the right car for the time – a dependable, durable vehicle that would cover maximum distances with minimum effort and expense. And not only was it economically sound, it was also respectable from the ecological standpoint!

With the blessing of environmentalists and the radical intelligentsia, its European sales took an upward turn to give the 2CV a new lease of life as the only real alternative for the alternative society as far as personal transport was concerned. By 1974, production levels had climbed back to over 163,000 cars per year again, and to boost its popularity higher still among trendsetters, Citroën embarked on another marketing innovation – the idea of bringing out special editions of the 2CV, produced in limited numbers, usually for one season only, and aimed at fashion-conscious buyers looking for extra individuality and style.

The first of these – equipped with a 602 cc engine for the UK market – was the orange-and-white-coloured 2CV-6 Spot of April 1976, followed by the 2CV-6 007 five years later in 1981. Painted in brilliant mimosa yellow, this was built to celebrate the 2CV starring

The 2CV Dolly special edition followed in 1985, produced in recognition of the fact that over 40 per cent of current buyers were women. It was so well received that it duly became part of the standard range.

Dating from 1978, the FAF (Facile à Fabriquer) was intended to be an easy-to-make version of the 2CV for the Third World. Based on the Dyane, its simple folded steel bodywork required no expensive press tools.

role in the James Bond film *For Your Eyes Only*, screened that year. Next, in April 1983, came the 2CV-6 France 3, known as the Beachcomber in the UK. Limited to just 2,000 examples, this was painted in the blue-and-white livery of the successful French challenger in the Americas Cup yacht race that year. In 1989, the 2CV-6 Special Bamboo arrived, painted appropriately in a vivid shade of jungle green, while finally, in 1986, came the jokey red, white and blue 2CV-6 Cocorico, but sold on the French market only.

But in October 1980, Citroën launched the most successful 2CV special edition of all, the art deco style 2CV-6 Charleston – so successful that it became a standard model, remaining in the catalogue for ten whole years, until the end of production. Available initially in a two-tone burgundy-and-black colour scheme, then later also in canary yellow-and-black, and finally in a dark- and light-grey combination also, the Charleston was rivalled in popularity only by the 2CV-6 Special Dolly first seen in April 1985. Introduced in recognition of the 2CV's loyal following of women drivers (over 40 per cent of latter-day buyers were women), the Dolly was so well received that it also became a standard model, and it continued in production through to the end, alongside the Charleston, the normal Special and the more lavishly equipped Club versions of the 2CV-6 by then remaining in the catalogue.

Initially, the Dolly came in no less

than seven colourways – grey-and-red, grey-and-buttermilk, grey-and-white, red-and-white, burgundy-and-buttermilk, buttermilk-and-midnight blue and, finally, green-and-white – but the first three combinations were deleted at the end of the 1985/6 season.

Unusually among the 2CV saloons, all six of these special editions were fitted with small, stainless steel wheel embellishers covering the central dome and wheelnuts only; the outer surface of the wheels remained exposed, painted with a colour-coordinated finish, either burgundy, yellow or silver. Three special editions of the Dyane were also produced: the Caban, Capra and Côte d'Azur.

By the beginning of the eighties, the 2CV had arrived at last in the form and specification that was to prevail until the end. In September 1978, in response to a pressing need for greater power to keep up with ever-rising traffic speeds, the 435 cc engine had been phased out and a version of the 602 cc engine (producing 33 bhp) fitted throughout the range, even on the budget-priced 2CV Special. From September 1981, front disc brakes were fitted as well, as they had been on the Dyane-6 from 1977 – a sensible improvement, for it was now possible to exceed 120 kph in the 2CV, twice the top speed possible in 1948. In June 1981, a special economy version was introduced, the 2CV Special E, fitted with a centrifugal clutch of the type last used in the early seventies, but this car remained in the catalogue for two seasons only. On all other models, a

The 2CV-6 Special E introduced in autumn 1983 was an economy version intended for town use. It reintroduced the centrifugal 'traffi-clutch' last seen ten years earlier.

diaphragm clutch replaced the toggle-type dry plate clutch previously used.

Ironically, the Dyane-4 – the 2CV's intended replacement – was phased out at the end of 1975, with deletion of the Dyane-6 following in 1984, by which time over 1,400,000 examples had been built. In 1978, the 2CV Fourgonnettes also came to the end of the road, replaced by the Acadiane van, which used cab and bonnet pressings from the Dyane grafted on to a lengthened and strengthened version of the current AKS 2CV-6 van platform.

All in all, over thirty different versions, variants and direct derivatives were produced and sold around the world during the 2CV's 42-year lifespan. Two particularly interesting yet relatively unknown examples were the Baby Brousse and FAF (Facile à Fabriquer) models, the latter being specially designed for easier construction or CKD assembly in developing countries. A total of over 33,000 of these two types were assembled overseas, mostly between 1968 and 1982.

Another Citroën A Series model rarely seen outside France was the Mehari variant. First introduced in 2×4 form in 1968, with a 4×4 version following in 1979, this innovative vehicle was, strictly speaking, a Dyane-6. Powered by the 602 cc 28 bhp engine, it combined the Type AY's rugged, robust chassis and mechanical components with a virtually indestructible open-topped, doorless plastic bodyshell, moulded from semi-flexible, impact- and corrosion-resistant ABS (acrylonitrile-butadiene-styrene). Its body (which came in a choice of three colours – green, red and ochre) could be hosed down inside and out, a practical virtue that made it highly popular as a fun car or runabout in its home country, especially in the warmer climate of the Midi, although front doors and a folding canvas hood with plastic windows were available as an option, for protection in less sunny regions.

One of the last 'Tin Snails' to arrive in the British Isles was this 2CV-6 Club imported in 1989. Over 100,000 examples of the various A series Citroëns were sold in the UK between 1974 and 1990.

The special edition 2CV-6 Beachcomber, which arrived on British shores in the summer of 1984.

Throughout production, the design of the Mehari was changed only once, in 1978, when the grille was revised to incorporate new metal headlamp mounting panels with integral direction indicators. However, a special edition version, the Azur, intended as a beach buggy and thus equipped with a bright-blue body, white hood and blue-and-white-striped seats, was produced in 1983, while a fully enclosed version with a plastic hard top was marketed by the ENAC company around the same time. In its 4×4 form, the Mehari also saw service with the French Army, as a lightweight, air-portable jeep. All in all, 144,953 Meharis were produced, of which 1,213 were civilian 4×4s.

By the mid-eighties, total Citroën 2CV and Dyane production was fast approaching a staggering 6½ million vehicles, of which almost 3½ million had been built at Levallois. With CKD and Mehari output figures added, the total production tally for the 2CV family was reaching almost 7 million. Parked bumper to bumper, they would have formed a line nearly 17,000 miles long; drawn up in rows with just 1 foot between them, they would have filled a car park covering 24 square miles.

The 2CV had now reached the summit of its international success; scarcely a street in Europe could be traversed without encountering an example. But familiarity breeds contempt among the car-buying public, and inevitably the falling order levels for the 2CV in its own country gradually began to be overtaken by the strong demand still being shown in its principal export markets – Germany, Belgium, Portugal and the UK. So, regrettably, the unavoidable decision was made to close

THE CITROËN 2CV

In December 1964, the 2CV was given new front doors that were hinged on the A pillars, to open the safe way rather than the suicidal way.

Happy family motoring in the 2CV circa 1966. The lockable metal boot-lid and large glass rear window introduced as standard on all versions that year can be clearly seen, though this feature had been available on the AZLP variant since 1958.

LIFE & DEATH

Between 1965 and 1974, the 2CV wore this third type of grille, but the round winkers on the front wings were not introduced until 1970.

In September 1979 the saloon range was reduced to just two models, the 2CV-6 Club (left) with rectangular headlamps, and the 2CV-6 Special (right) with round headlamps. Both were equipped with the same 602 cc engine.

A right-hand-drive 2CV-6 Club photographed in France for a British-market brochure in 1982. The Deux Chevaux was now more popular with *les étrangers* than in its native land.

down the old, outmoded Paris-Levallois plant and concentrate production at Citroën's more modern facility at Mangualde in Portugal.

Thus, on 25 February 1988, well over fifty years since the very first pre-war TPV prototypes had been built there, the last French-built Deux Chevaux, a grey 2CV-6 Special, rolled off the assembly line at the ancient Levallois factory, the 3,418,347th car to have been assembled within its walls. Constructed a hundred years earlier for the Clément bicycle company, and a Citroën factory since 1921, the Levallois building now possessed more profit potential as a property development site than as a museum of car manufacture, so it was promptly and unceremoniously demolished to capitalise on its valuable suburban location.

But although the threatened death sentence seemed at first to have been commuted to the lesser penalty of permanent exile, already the end of the road was in sight for Citroën's seemingly immortal 'tin snail', now reduced to a three-car range – the 2CV-6 Special (round headlamps), the 2CV-6 Club (rectangular headlamps) and the 2CV-6 Charleston (round, chromed headlamps), all powered by the final 1978 version of the 602 cc (33 bhp SAE) engine, distinguishable from its predecessors by its 8.5:1 compression ratio and additional emission control measures. After a mere two years' further production at Mangualde, during which time another 42,000 or so cars were made, that assembly line was also condemned. Like the proverbial cat with nine lives, the 2CV had dodged the Grim Reaper before; a succession of fortuitous turns of fate and twists of providence had spun out its career and given it a string of successful roles on the motoring stage. But this time there could be no escaping the final curtain.

Thus, at precisely 3 pm on Friday 27 July 1990, after almost forty-two years of continuous production, the very last example of the Deux Chevaux, a grey 2CV-6 Charleston, left the Portuguese production line. The final score had reached the staggering total of 6,956,895 vehicles, made up of 5,114,966 2CV saloons and vans plus 1,443,583 Dyane saloons, 253,393 Acadiane vans, 144,953 Meharis and other assorted derivatives – not bad for a design condemned as a disaster on its first appearance!

Part Two

Family Relations

For over twenty-five years the 2CV Fourgonnettes or light vans performed a thousand and one commercial tasks in France, including delivering the post in rural areas.

CHAPTER FOUR

THE SAHARA, THE MEHARI & THE FOURGONNETTE VANS

THE 2CV SAHARA

To ease the difficulties of overland transport in the roadless desert terrain of French North Africa, where extensive oil and mineral exploration work was then under way, in 1958 Citroën introduced a four-wheel-drive version of the 2CV, appropriately named the Sahara.

Naturally, in the true Citroën tradition of never doing things by halves, this was no ordinary 4×4 design. Uniquely, the Sahara had two engines, one for each axle, front and back. These were controlled in such a way that the two could be run together in tandem to provide double the motive power for cross-country work or, alternatively, the front engine operated solo during normal road use. Each of the two standard 425 cc power units developed 12 bhp, so that this twin-engined 850 cc 24 bhp cross-country 2CV was in effect a 5CV. With both engines in use, the Sahara could reach a top speed of 62 mph on the flat, consuming petrol at a rate of between 28 and 35 mpg; 47 mpg was claimed with only one engine running.

But the Sahara's most impressive feature was its truly exceptional climbing ability. Due to its very light kerb weight (650 kg), optimum 50/50 weight distribution, low ground pressure and excellent traction, the Sahara could easily outperform most conventional, heavy-duty 4×4 vehicles, sure-footedly ascending treacherous, steep, loose-surfaced slopes where bigger, more powerful vehicles would merely slip and slide. When crossing soft sand, snow or mud in which heavier designs would normally get bogged down, its performance was even more impressive. In July 1961 a Sahara became the first all-wheeled motor vehicle to climb to the top of the great Pyla sand dune on France's south-western coast, a 360 foot climb over three miles of dry sand, with slopes as steep as 1 in 6.

Mounted on a specially strengthened platform-chassis, the body of the Sahara differed from that of the standard 2CV in a number of quite noticeable ways. From the front, the bonnet-mounted spare wheel, reinforced bumpers and the fatter 155 section tyres can be clearly seen at a glance; from the back, the fan air-intake of the reverse-mounted second engine located in a compartment behind the rear seats and visible through the boot lid are unmistakable; while from the sides, the widened cut-away rear wings and the petrol filler caps poking through the front doors also give the game away immediately (the Sahara's twin petrol tanks – one for each engine – are located under the front seats). But the chances of spotting a Sahara are today few and far between. Only 694 examples were built and sold between 1960 and 1966, eighty of which saw service with the Guardia Civil in Spain. No more than twenty-five are believed to remain in existence today, two of them in the UK.

Although the prototype was fitted with centrifugal clutches to disengage the respective transmissions when either engine was switched off, or when the revs fell to idling speed, this feature was not included in production models. Even so, despite the fact that the two engines are not linked or synchronised in any way, driving a Sahara is far less complicated than you might imagine. A single common accelerator pedal and gearshift lever (mounted on the floor) control the speed of the vehicle during simultaneous running, while clutch engagement both fore and aft is actuated hydraulically, jointly by a single pedal, rather than by the normal mechanical linkages. But to isolate the rear engine during normal on-road use, a manual gearbox disengagement lever is also provided. Therefore, when pushing as well as pulling power is required, it's just a matter of stopping briefly, engaging neutral, switching on the ignition of the rear engine and pulling this lever to engage the rear transmission before driving off. Conversely, if the

This shot of the Sahara prototype reveals most of the 2CV 4×4's unique exterior features, including the cut-away rear wings, the spare wheel on the bonnet and, of course, its two engines.

petrol tank serving the front engine runs dry, the rear engine alone can be used for a limited period to reach a filling station, by engaging a hook which holds the clutch of the front engine in the disengaged position. To help the driver determine the direction and angle of the front wheels when crossing slippery mud or loose sand, the Sahara has a steering lock indicator, fitted on the steering column.

The Mehari

Although it was a simple and uncomplicated design in comparison with the Sahara, Citroën's next off-road car, introduced in 1968, was no less interesting and innovative technically. Named after the dromedary favoured by Berber tribesmen for long-distance travel in the desert, the Mehari was the first series-production vehicle in the world to feature a lightweight body made of flexible, durable, non-corroding ABS thermoplastic. The prototype originated from the SEAB company at Villejuif, which subsequently produced the first pilot run of cars by forming the ABS bodies and attaching them to running chassis supplied by Citroën. Thereafter, for the rest of its production life, the vehicle was assembled by Citroën at the Panhard factory at Ivry, with body components supplied by SEAB.

This second generation of Citroën cross-country vehicles was intended to be a very much more versatile design than the Sahara which it replaced, and to offer a far greater load-carrying

Only 694 examples of the Sahara were built and sold between 1960 and 1966, of which 80 – such as this one – went to the Guardia Civil in Spain.

A 4×4 Mehari, distinguishable from the 2×2 version by the spare wheel on the bonnet.

capacity. More a pick-up truck than a car, the Mehari was designed to serve a wide variety of tasks: agricultural and forestry work, light construction site duties, as a public service vehicle and as a practical, economical fun car in the newly emerging leisure vehicle and beach buggy market. For this reason, it was initially fitted with two seats only, in order to qualify as a commercial vehicle for taxation purposes.

The Mehari was derived from the Dyane-6 rather than the 2CV, sharing both the Dyane's 602 cc 33 bhp SAE twin-pot engine and its platform chassis, strengthened to PO ('*Pays d'Outre-mer*' – 'overseas markets') specification to allow a 400 kg payload to be carried. For cross-country work, a protective undershield was fitted beneath the engine compartment.

Attached to the platform chassis by its supporting tubular steel framework, the Mehari's bodywork comprised thirteen separate panels, including the floorpan, wheel arches, dashboard, bonnet, tailgate and the optional doors, all vacuum-moulded from sheets of robust, impact-resistant Cycolac ABS. Fastened to the frame by screws or rivets, these panels were coloured by pigments added to the thermoplastic mix during processing, and so required no subsequent painting, polishing or maintenance, except in the case of vehicles destined for service in hot countries: as ABS is sensitive to heat and ultra-violet light, cracks and stress lines tended to appear in cars exposed to strong sunlight for long periods, so in this case polyurethane-based UV-resistant paints were used for protection. At first, a choice of sage green, red and ochre bodies was available, but later, yellow and white versions were also offered. Only the protection of a simple canvas folding roof with sidescreens was ever provided by Citroën, but a closed hard top, also formed from ABS, was eventually made available as an optional extra by the specialist French firm ENAC.

From July 1978 the Mehari received the 33 bhp engine of the current 2CV-6.

In 1979, a four-wheel-drive version of the Mehari was added to the range, but this time powered by one engine only through a conventional transfer reduction gearbox and a propshaft drive to the rear wheels. In this optional 4×4 mode, three of the four main forward ratios could be geared down, giving a total of seven forward speeds. For additional traction in rough conditions, a differential lock was also provided. The 4×4 Mehari could be recognised by its cow-catcher bumpers, different grille and bonnet-mounted spare wheel, similar to that of the Sahara. A total of only 1,313 examples had been built when sales were suspended in 1982, after only three years of production. The reason for this stoppage may well have been the large order for 5,000 4×4 Meharis placed by the French armed forces in 1981, but these were steel-panelled vehicles, powered by the 652 cc air-cooled engine fitted to the Citroën Visa.

Although no less than 144,953 examples were made, the Mehari was, in effect, a pioneering feasibility study, to evaluate the economics of thermoplastics body parts technology. It was found that although ABS offered the advantage of very low tooling and production costs compared with conventional pressed steel panels, in high-volume production situations this benefit was rapidly cancelled out by the very high price of the material itself. Citroën persevered with the experiment for nineteen years, until 1987, when production ceased. Needless to say, the Mehari was never offered on the UK market at any point in its lifespan, since in several ways it did not comply with British Construction and Use and National Type Approval Regulations.

THE 2CV FOURGONNETTE

Although rarely seen in the UK, the 2CV Fourgonnette (light van) played as important a part in the long-running success story of the 2CV as did the familiar saloon. Over the years, almost 1¼ million were sold throughout the world (nearly a third of total 2CV production) to serve in hundreds of different ways – as delivery vans for

In its original Type AU form, the Fourgonnette was powered by the 375 cc engine from the 2CV saloon, and could carry a payload of 250 kg. In its final AKS form, powered by the 602 cc engine from the Ami-6, it could handle 400 kg.

105

every conceivable type of trade and occupation, as ambulances and campers, and even as the official transport of the French rural postal service.

Between March 1951 and March 1978, four successively improved and updated versions were produced – the Type AU (1951–4), the AZU (1954–78), the AK (1963–70) and the AKS (1970–8) – although latterly, from February 1978 until May 1985, the basic design continued in the form of the Acadiane van, which combined the body of the 2CV Fourgonnette with the cab and mechanics of the Dyane-6.

The Fourgonnette was never just a 2CV platform chassis and engine with a van body hastily grafted on to its back, however: although the chassis dimensions were identical, the chassis structure of the van was strengthened and its ride height raised, to cope with the greater loads that would be carried, so it was always a slightly wider and taller vehicle overall. Structurally, it also differed in that its floor was a flat pressing throughout its length. To give maximum unobstructed load space, the spare wheel was stowed outside in a neat compartment located on the left-hand side, while the petrol tank was hidden away in a similar recess on the opposite flank. Nor did the mechanical improvements successively made to the Fourgonnette follow exactly the evolutionary development of the saloons, at least initially. On some occasions, van changes (such as the fitting of more powerful engines and the introduction of an alternator in February 1966) actually preceded those made to the passenger car.

The first 2CV-based Fourgonnette, the 375 cc-engined AU with a payload of

The 2CV AU van – which first appeared in March 1951 – was as much of a success as the saloon, at least in France, where almost one and a quarter million examples found customers.

THE SAHARA, THE MEHARI & THE FOURGONNETTE VANS

The early 2CV AU van even served as an ambulance – surely a testament to the comfort provided by its suspension. The distinctive rear door windows of the AU can be clearly seen here.

This page from an early brochure suggests a variety of other uses for the 2CV Fourgonnette. The use of the double chevron badge is typical of Citroën brochures of the fifties.

107

The Citroën 2CV

An export version of the 3CV AK van, as produced between 1963 and 1965, equipped with the new bonnet and grille. The rectangular front direction indicators on the wings are an export-market-only feature.

Throughout the sixties, the ANWB (the Dutch equivalent of the AA) used a large fleet of yellow-painted 2CV vans for its Wegenwacht road patrols throughout the Netherlands.

The Sahara, the Mehari & the Fourgonnette vans

The 3CV Type AK van, as seen between 1965 and 1970, distinguishable by the absence of ribbing on the upper body and the presence of a side window. The spare wheel is stowed in a compartment beneath it.

The Fourgonnette in its high-roofed AKS form, as produced for the 1970/1 model year. Note that the grille and the panelling of the lower body sides have both been changed, and that the direction indicators are now in the front wings. Also the headlamps are rectangular, not round, in keeping with similar changes made to the saloons.

250 kg, was indeed the mobile tin shack celebrated in countless cartoons and jokes – a small, windowless hut on wheels, with grey corrugated metal walls and roof and twin back doors pierced by tiny, oval peepholes. With the arrival of the larger 425 cc engine in 1954, this design duly became the AZU, but it was not until July 1961 that its bodywork received the new bonnet (and successive grille variations) which had earlier been fitted to the saloons. In March 1963, the body design was finally revised and modernised by the fitting of large, rectangular windows to both the side and the back doors, and by eliminating the swaged ribbing above the waistline.

A demand for greater carrying capacity led to the introduction of the 350 kg payload AK model the following month, powered by the 602 cc engine from the Ami-6, and immediately recognisable by its longer body overhanging the rear wheels. These two basic versions, the AK and AZU types, continued to be offered side by side until the end, although in 1970 the AK was replaced by the 400 kg payload AKS. Initially, both were available in high-roof configuration, on special order. After the consolidation of the saloon car range as the 2CV-4 and 2CV-6 in 1970, the evolution of the *camionnettes* continued in step with these vehicles, so that the vans received the improvements introduced on the corresponding saloons simultaneously.

A special 'combi' version of the AZU was also available for a number of years in the early sixties. Called the Weekend (even in France), this featured larger, panoramic side windows on both sides, plus two removable extra seats in the back. An ideal all-purpose touring or holiday car for long-distance tourists travelling on low budgets, even complete camper versions were offered, equipped with a gas stove and washbasin stowed in the back doors. Two converted 'after-market' pick-up versions were also produced in limited numbers in France around the same time – but not by any Citroën factory; the only standard 2CV pick-ups ever made were those produced by Citroën Cars Ltd at Slough. These French pick-ups looked just like standard 2CV vans with the top half of the body cut off and a flat panel welded in to close the cab, unlike the Slough-built pick-ups, which had rounded cab bodies built from specially manufactured pressings.

In September 1969, the AZU received a completely new high-roof body in which the strengthening corrugations took the form of indentations rather than protruding ribs or ripples, and this style of body was also introduced on the AKS the following year. In 1972, the AZU's specification was revised yet again, and this, the smaller of the two Fourgonnette options, was offered with the 435 cc 24 bhp engine from the current 2CV-4 saloon, mated to the gearbox from the 2CV-6, in an economy version specifically intended for public service or *grandes administrations* use. For the 1976 and 1977 model years, plain upper-body sides minus side windows were introduced on both types, but due to customer pressure, the side windows reappeared in September 1977 for the new model year. In March 1978, both the AZU and the AKS Fourgonnettes were finally deleted and replaced by the 480 kg payload Acadiane van.

CHAPTER FIVE

THE AMI-6 & AMI-8

By the late fifties, Citroën's Continental dealers and concessionaires had begun to find themselves in something of a quandary. Although they had in their showrooms two of the best-selling cars in France – the cheap, practical 2CV and the costly, sophisticated DS19 or ID19 – these highly successful designs, both produced by André Lefebvre, were completely opposite in character, having been produced to cater exclusively for the needs of either the most affluent or the least well-off of motorists. Between these two extremes, a great new middle-income market was opening up, consisting of drivers who demanded comfort with economy and space without expense, and who found the DS or the 2CV either too big or too small for their needs. What was needed was a new car which would end this polarisation and plug the large gap in the centre of the Citroën range through which much valuable business was escaping.

The answer was to be that most individual of vehicles, the Ami-6. Launched in 1961 as 'the world's most comfortable medium-class car', this versatile and popular town and country saloon was the first Citroën model to be built at the company's brand new factory at Rennes-le-Janais in Brittany, opened by General de Gaulle the previous year. A kind of super-2CV, based firmly on the mechanical conception of the 2CV but fitted with an all-new body of a very different design and appearance, the Ami-6 saloon and its successors and derivatives shared so many features and components with their 2CV cousins that they were always classed as members of the Type A family of vehicles in Citroën parlance, so they rightly deserve a mention in this, their family album.

Although rarely seen outside its native land, the Ami range was to be another smash hit for Citroën. Between 1961 and 1971 1,127,649 Ami-6 saloons and estates found customers in France, and at the high point of its popularity in 1966, when 180,000 were sold, the Ami ranked as the country's best-selling car by far. Later, between 1969 and 1979, healthy sales of the more powerful Ami-8 and Ami Super continued to bear witness to the design's enduring virtues.

An outstandingly comfortable and capacious small family car for its time, the Ami opened up the possibilities of cheap, long-distance holiday or recreational motoring to a great many

Introduced in April 1961, the Ami-6 marked Citroën's entrance into the middle-income market. In France its remarkable combination of space, comfort and economy made it a huge success – ultimately almost two million examples of its various versions were sold. But its Gallic looks did not travel well, and elsewhere in Europe it was far less popular.

One of a famous series of publicity shots of the Ami-6 taken in Paris, for a superb brochure designed by Robert Delpire. From the outset, the Ami-6 was marketed as a woman's car – the ideal vehicle for shopping, for taking the kids to school, or for travelling on family holidays.

To some eyes, the sheer originality of the Ami-6's appearance is strangely attractive. But for others, it is simply the ugliest car ever made.

The Citroën 2CV

The Ami-6 was essentially a re-bodied 2CV, powered by an enlarged 602 cc version of the flat-twin air-cooled engine (later also fitted to the 2CV), and having a similar form of interlinked all-independent suspension.

Gallic parents and their children. And yet, unlike the 2CV, its attractions never really caught on among British or German motorists.

Derived directly from the 2CV, the Ami shared its principal component systems – its unburstable, air-cooled, twin-cylinder boxer engine, its four-speed front-wheel-drive transmission, its rack and pinion steering, its interconnected, all-independent suspension system, and its platform-type chassis. Styled by Flaminio Bertoni, the stylist of the DS range, the Ami-6 shared numerous trim and styling features with this famous car, such as its unique single-spoke steering wheel, door handles and switchgear, and its use, initially, of an unpainted, translucent matt-white fibreglass roof panel. To save weight, maximum use of aluminium was made – for example, in the bumpers, grille and trim-strips – which made its appearance seem stranger still. Yet the aesthetics of the Ami had little in common with the DS's elegant shape and style, and the car resembled a pop-eyed frog rather than a slinky shark! For some people, the Ami represented Citroën's attitude to design at its most unorthodox and original: the raw, uncompromising result of engineering logic and integrity. For others, the Ami-6 was quite simply the ugliest car ever made!

There was no distinguishing badge on the front, not even the small double chevron sign fitted to the 2CV. The Ami's quirky appearance so obviously labelled it a Citroën that fitting this emblem was considered superfluous by its makers. No other company but Citroën could have built a car remotely like it. But besides its bizarre frontal aspect, which presented a grotesque, tortured, grimacing expression to oncoming traffic, the Ami-6 saloon had another most unusual and unconventional visual detail – its reverse-sloping rear window. According to Robert Opron (who succeeded Bertoni as Citroën's chief of styling in 1975), this was no superficial gimmick, but the only logical alternative: 'Cadiou, the boss of the Bureau d'Études, had specified a classical three-box layout in his *cahier des charges*, although the overall dimensions really called for an estate layout. Bertoni found it impossible to divide up the space available to accommodate both a large boot and a passenger compartment providing sufficient headroom for the rear-seat passengers. The only answer was to gain cabin length at roof level by putting the window in the wrong way round.' As a bonus, this solution also kept the large glass surface of the rear window clean and dry in wet weather. A distinct improvement on those of the 2CV, the side windows on the Ami's front doors were of the sliding type; a similar arrangement was later fitted to the rear doors too. The spacious interior accommodation made possible by this layout was also enhanced by the car's flat floor and its wide bench seats, removable for even greater flexibility in loading, as with the 2CV.

The first examples of the Ami-6 saloon, introduced in April 1961, were

The Ami-6 was styled by Flaminio Bertoni, the creator of the Citroën DS19, and it was his favourite among all his remarkable designs. The unusual rectangular Cibie headlamps represented the very latest in lighting technology at that time.

THE CITROËN 2CV

A true family car, the Ami-6 brought mobility to urban dwellers, just as the 2CV had put the country folk of France on the road! And with a turning radius of only 18 feet, its manoeuvrability in towns was exceptional.

In the UK the Ami-6 was marketed as the most comfortable medium-sized car in the world – and compared to its British-made competitors such as the Ford Anglia and the Morris Minor, this claim was not without foundation!

CITROEN ami 6
The world's most comfortable medium-sized car

equipped with an uprated version of the current 2CV engine, enlarged to 602 cc and producing 22 bhp at 4,500 rpm, so, strictly speaking, the car was a 3CV. This gave the early Ami a top speed of 65 mph, slightly greater than that of the 2CV, with no loss in fuel economy, which was claimed to exceed 50 mpg. In September 1963, its engine power output was increased to 26 bhp, and then raised again to 32 bhp in May 1968, bringing the top speed up to almost 70 mph. This gave the Ami-6 a surprisingly fast yet economical long-distance cruising ability. Just like the 2CV, the Ami-6 was far superior to the majority of small family cars of its era in the standards of comfort, road-holding and general ride quality it offered.

Despite displaying an alarming degree of body roll when cornering, its stability and handling were always entirely predictable and forgiving, whatever the conditions, while its tight turning circle (18 feet) made for outstanding manoevrability when parking.

The Ami was truly driver-friendly in both name and nature. Regardless of its weird looks and eccentric styling, French motorists took it to their hearts, and by 1962, the Ami-6 was rolling off the assembly lines at the Rennes-le-Janais factory at the rate of over 600 units a day; by 1965, the production rate had overtaken even that of the 2CV. The ever-growing number of French women drivers on the roads (a market at which the car had been specifically aimed) formed a significant proportion of this clientele. But another important reason for the Ami's popularity was the instant success of the Break or Estate version (Type AMB), which arrived in 1964, accompanied by the Ami-6 Commerciale, which differed from passenger versions only in that it had a large, unobstructed load space with no rear seats, since the glass side windows of the estate car were retained. At a stroke, the improved rear-end arrangements of these two new variants eliminated all aesthetic objections to the unusual lines of the saloon, and widened the Ami's sales appeal by offering an unrivalled amount of load-carrying space – 53 cubic feet.

One of the first inexpensive, small estate cars ever offered to the motoring

The remarkably spacious and comfortable interior of the Ami-6 is fully revealed here. The raked-back rear window (also seen on the contemporary Ford Anglia) was no styling gimmick; as well as improving rear-view visibility in bad weather, it also allowed far greater headroom for backseat passengers. The inspiration for both cars came from the 1957 US Ford Lincoln Capri.

As on the 2CV, the absence of a transmission tunnel made possible by front-wheel-drive allowed an unusual amount of space for driver and passengers, thanks to a bench seat and a flat, unobstructed floor. Notice the push-pull gear shift lever from the 2CV and the single-spoke steering wheel from the DS19. The seats were normally upholstered with jersey-nylon cloth rather than vinyl, while the heating and ventilation system was exceptionally efficient for that era.

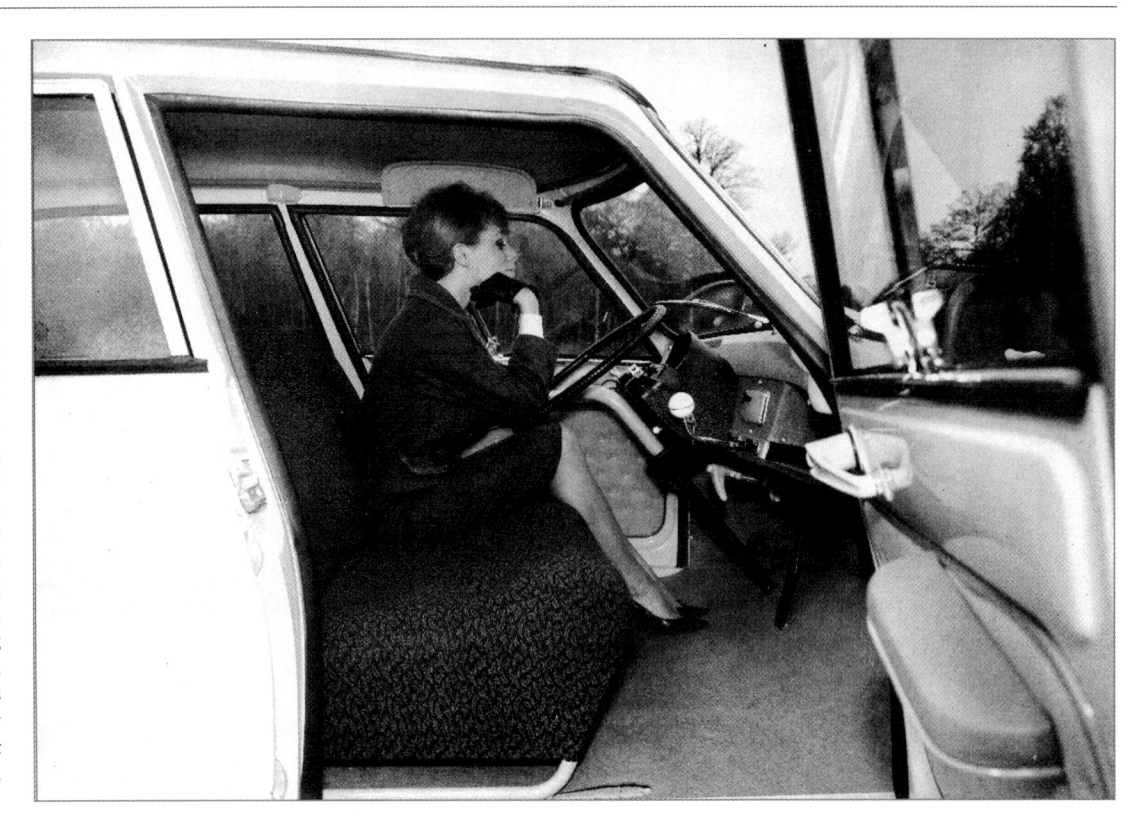

public, the Ami-6 Break turned out to be the ideal vehicle for small families, small businesses and small farmers alike. Boasting a payload of 660 lb and 15 sq feet of load floor (with the folding rear seat removed completely, a 5 foot 5 inch long object could be transported), the Ami-6 Estate offered all the qualities of reliability, simplicity, versatility and economy provided by the 2CV, but with the bonus of a much greater load-carrying capacity, so it duly replaced the 2CV as the universal workhorse of France. Like the saloon, it was also offered with the option of a centrifugal 'traffi-clutch'.

For the 1968 model year, introduced in September 1967, two levels of trim were available on both the saloon and estate: a standard Tourisme and a more luxurious and expensive Confort grade. Vinyl upholstery could be fitted on both, but jersey nylon cloth was seen on the Confort version only. Individual front seats were also offered as an alternative to the normal bench arrangement, plus various other extras, such as windscreen washers and a proper fan-assisted interior heating and ventilation system. A 12-volt electrical system was also introduced on all Ami models at this time, powered by an alternator.

In May 1968, the range was augmented by a further new estate variant, known as the Ami-6 Break Club, a more upmarket version immediately distinguishable from its fellows by its twin round headlamps. The following October, for the 1969 model year, this was joined by a similarly upgraded saloon model, the Ami-6 Club. Then, finally, in December 1968, the range was completed by the arrival of the Ami-6 Enterprise or Service Van, available in two forms, with or without side windows for the load compartment, which was particularly commodious thanks to its broad, flat, unobstructed floor and wide rear door aperture. Relatively few of these vehicles were made, for in the spring of 1969 the Ami-6 series was replaced by the Ami-8, launched in saloon form at the Geneva Motor Show that March. The Ami-8's name was slightly misleading, however, as the Ami's engine capacity and fiscal rating remained exactly the same as before: all that changed was the appearance of the car, which was given a major (and some say much-needed) face-lift to rejuvenate its time-worn looks. Inside, a completely revised dashboard was installed. Outside, at the front, the grille and headlamp treatment was tidied up (though the single rectangular headlamp units rather than the twin round versions were retained), and the overhanging bonnet line was smoothed out so that the Ami lost its toothless mouth and beetle-browed expression. At the back, the reverse-rake window was replaced by a more modern, sloping, fast-back look, though this improvement did not extend to providing a hatchback door to the rear luggage compartment.

In the autumn of 1969, the Ami-6 Estate and Van versions were also upgraded to Ami-8 status, with the same frontal styling modifications. As with the Ami-6, two different trim specifications of the Ami-8 Saloons and Breaks were offered; the upmarket Club version having a higher level of seating and equipment (with proper winding windows from September 1970), and the more spartan Confort grade. Although the first examples of the Ami-8

The Ami-6 Break or estate car, introduced in September 1964, offered yet greater space and load-carrying flexibility, thanks to its fully opening tailgate and folding rear seats. The elaborate bumpers with tubular over-riders indicate that this is the more expensive Club version, available during the 1968/9 season only; this also featured twin round headlamps.

In April 1969 the Ami-6 was replaced by the Ami-8, immediately recognisable from its predecessor by its fastback (not hatchback) styling. The name was misleading, for though the new car boasted many improvements, its engine remained unchanged. The first examples had no Citroën badge on the grille.

Apart from the obvious alterations and improvements to the bodywork, little else was changed. The early examples of the Ami-8 still had sliding windows – but wind-down windows came later, in the summer of 1970.

saloons retained an all-drum braking system, from the time of the launch of the Break versions in September 1969, all models were fitted with inboard-mounted disc brakes.

Finally, in January 1973, the Ami family was enlarged and augmented by the arrival of three new and very muscular cousins, the Ami Super Berline (saloon), Break (estate) and Enterprise (service van). Rated as 6CVs, these were powered by a 55.5 bhp version of the 1,015 cc air-cooled flat-four engine from the recently launched Citroën GS range. With four times the swept volume of the original 2CV engine, this power unit was capable of propelling the Ami chassis up to a top speed of 87 mph! A four-speed all-synchromesh gearbox was fitted, operated by a floor-mounted stickshift rather than the traditional push-pull 2CV-type dashboard-mounted lever. To cope with all this extra performance, the Ami Super models were equipped with disc brakes and a completely revised suspension layout, minus the front-to-rear interlinking seen on other 2CV and Ami types.

Although the Ami Super offered Citroën customers a lot of car for their money, it was probably somewhat overpowered. Not surprisingly, production was stopped in late 1976 after just three years, with only 42,000 or so examples having been built. But the 602 cc Ami-8 saloon continued on sale for another two years, until it was eventually replaced by the new Visa model which arrived in early 1978. The Ami-8 Estate model survived for a further year, until 1979.

During its seventeen-year career the Citroën Ami had made friends with over 1,840,000 Continental customers, but

A right-hand-drive example of the 1972 Ami-8 Break photographed in a typically British suburban location. This version sold well in Britain among discerning motorists – there was no other small estate car of comparable abilities on the market! Note the slightly extended roofline of the estate version, compared to the saloon.

From January 1973 onwards the Ami was offered in a new 'sports' version, the 6CV Ami-Super, powered by the 1,015 cc four-cylinder air-cooled engine from the recently introduced Citroën GS. Capable of 87 mph it could be distinguished from the two-pot Ami-8 by its different grille and extra engine air intakes.

The Ami-Super shared the same saloon, estate and van bodywork as the Ami-8, so the two are hard to distinguish. The big difference lies under the bonnet and inside the cockpit – for the Ami-Super had a floor mounted gearchange, just like the GS. In profile the two are virtually identical, save for the rubbing strip fitted to the Ami-Super.

initially, its British admirers were rather less numerous, so plans to build the car in the UK were never implemented. Despite some reports to the contrary, there was never an assembly line for the Ami series at Citroën's UK factory at Slough, although between 1961 and early 1966, when the Slough works closed, 95 French-built Ami-6 vehicles (38 saloons and 57 Breaks) were imported into Britain by Citroën Cars Ltd on a special-order basis.

However, from October 1966 onwards, when both the Ami-6 Berline and Break were included as a standard offering in the Citroën Cars range, the Ami proved rather more successful with the British motorist, and between then and 1969, a total of 750 examples of both kinds were sold, mostly estates, all of them built at Rennes.

Thus, with the arrival of the new Ami-8 in the autumn of 1969, a more concerted effort was made to market this most Gallic of designs to British motorists, who were by now becoming rather less insular in their tastes. As on the Continent, two versions of the Ami-8 saloon were initially available, the Luxe and the Club, until the Luxe was renamed Confort for the 1974 model year. The Ami-8 estate was offered in Confort trim from the start, along with the Ami-8 service van, and remained available until the end of 1977; but from August 1976, the cheaper saloon was dropped, leaving just three Ami-8 versions on sale by 1978, when the entire Ami range was dropped by Citroën Cars, a year before it was deleted in France. After the introduction of British National Type Approval

The Ami-6 & Ami-8

The back view of the two cars was also virtually identical except for the badging. But for the 1974 model year, shown here, the Ami-Super also featured ventilated wheels and a painted coachline on its flanks. Note that the door hinges from below the window, not above it.

Regulations that year, no more Ami models could be imported: unfortunately, the design of their seat anchorage points did not conform to the new regulations and could not be modified without unacceptable cost.

As for the Ami Super, the first imports of both saloon and estate versions arrived in April 1973 and continued until May 1976, although the 1,015 cc service van was dropped from the catalogues in August 1974.

The exact total of British sales for the Ami-8 and Ami Super is unrecorded, but as deliveries are known to have ranged between 2,000 and 4,000 units per year, it could have amounted to as many as 20,000 vehicles. Where are they now?

CHAPTER SIX

THE DYANE & ACADIANE

THE DYANE SALOONS

In August 1967 (some months after the French motoring magazine *l'Auto Journal* had first revealed the existence of such a project), Citroën announced the arrival of a new addition to its A Series range: the Dyane saloon. Designed by Louis Bionier, who had joined Citroën's Bureau d'Études from Panhard when the firm took control of this most ancient and illustrious of French marques in 1953, the Dyane was clearly intended to be a successor to – and perhaps eventually a complete replacement for – the 2CV. Combining the engine, suspension and underlying platform chassis of the 2CV with a completely new and enlarged body, it was thus a fully fledged member of the 2CV family, as is indicated by its official designation: AYA.

Determinedly modern in appearance, the Dyane's stronger, heavier, slightly wider bodywork featured integral wings with recessed headlights and larger windows, which, in the case of the front doors only, opened by sliding action. Inside, the usable load and passenger space was far more generous, making for greater versatility, although the unused spare wheel well in the floor of the rear load area was retained, as were the enclosed rear wings, a characteristic common to all contemporary Citroëns. Perhaps the first true hatchback car to be produced by any motor manufacturer since the Citroën Traction Avant Commerciale of 1953, the Dyane was also fitted with a full-height, fully opening, glazed tailgate. As on the 2CV, the roof was a folding fabric panel, but in this case the front part could be folded back and left in a half-open position without the driver leaving his seat, although attempting to do this when on the move was not advisable!

At first, a 425 cc 21 bhp air-cooled flat-twin engine was fitted, coupled to an Ami-6 transmission, but after just seven months' production, this was soon replaced by a new, enlarged 435 cc version, developing 26 bhp and the vehicle was renamed Dyane-4. In January 1968, however, the original design was joined in the showrooms by a sister car, the Dyane 6, equipped with a 602 cc 28 bhp engine, again using the Ami's transmission plus larger, more powerful drum brakes. Henceforth the two variants were referred to as the Dyane-4 and Dyane-6 respectively until September 1975 when the Dyane-4 reverted to Dyane. Now it was possible

Originally intended as a complete replacement for the 2CV, the Dyane saloon was launched in August 1967. But it remained on sale for only eleven years until it was phased out in favour of its elder sister, the 2CV-6, in 1978.

At its first appearance in 1967, the Dyane-4 had a four-light body, but a rear quarter window was added in March 1968. The Dyane-6, introduced in January 1968, had a six-light body from the start. The numbers relate to the engine, not the windows!

to exceed 69 mph in a 2CV, while retaining the same frugal fuel consumption of an average 50 mpg (Dyane-6). Later the same year, in September 1968, the Dyane-6 was re-equipped with the redesigned and uprated 602 cc engine from the 2CV-6, producing 33 bhp and, finally, in February 1970, with the Ami-8 engine of 35 bhp.

The very first examples of the Dyane-4 had four-light bodies, the rear quarter panel being left unglazed, but the Dyane-6 always had six-light coachwork, with an extra quarter window at the rear, just like contemporary versions of the 2CV. From March 1968, though, identical six-light bodies were fitted to all the Dyanes. Both versions were always made available in a choice of two trim levels, Luxe and Confort, while a commercial variant featuring a fully folding rear seat was also supplied as an option. A centrifugal traffi-clutch was also available on both types, at least initially.

Technically, the Dyane saloons went through the same process of mechanical evolution and improvement as the traditional 2CV saloons, with revisions to their respective specifications being made more or less in parallel. However, in September 1977, the Dyane-6 became the first of the 2CVs to receive disc brakes, four years in advance of their introduction on the ordinary Deux Chevaux.

From the styling point of view, though, the Dyane underwent very few revisions, all extremely minor. For example, in September 1972 the position of the door handles was inverted, while in September 1974 the treatment of the front grille was changed from the original stainless steel mesh to

A right-hand-drive Dyane-6 of 1972 shows off its half-opening fabric roof. Unlike the 2CV, the Dyane was always fitted with wheel trims.

The special edition Dyane-6 Caban, announced in April 1977. Only 1,500 examples were built.

a plastic fitment featuring horizontal bars, coloured grey at first, but black after September 1980.

The Dyane saloon was produced in three special editions only, the first being the Dyane-6 Caban of April 1977. This was a limited series of 1,500 vehicles, painted dark-blue with white wheels and a white roof, plus white coachlining or decals on the bonnet, wings and doors. The second was the Dyane-6 Capra of 1980–1, intended for the Spanish and Italian markets, and easily distinguished by its GSA wheel trims, while the third was the blue-and-white Dyane-6 Côte d'Azur of 1982–3, which was imported into the UK.

Although in many ways a better, more practical vehicle than the original 2CV, the Dyane failed to equal the long-term popularity of its cousin. Indeed, many enthusiasts regarded it as an interloper in the 2CV family, entirely lacking the character and integrity of the true, authentic Deux Chevaux. Thus, by late 1975, the Dyane-4, once intended as the 2CV's replacement, had been deleted from the catalogues, superseded entirely by the Dyane-6. This was now available in two forms, the Dyane-6 Confort and the Dyane-6 Weekend, the latter distinguished from the former by its standard folding rear seats and removable covering panel over the wheel well in the luggage area. But inevitably, at the end of the model year in July 1984, the Dyane-6 was also finally discontinued, having been made redundant by the arrival of Citroën's new Visa model in October 1978. Initially, in its 3CV Special form, this car also made use of the latest high-compression version of the 2CV's 602 cc air-cooled flat-twin engine, now producing 35 bhp at 5,750 rpm, a 25 per cent increase in power output. In

The Dyane & Acadiane

The Dyane first arrived in the UK in 1968, well before the re-introduction of the 2CV saloon on the British market, in 1974.

The Acadiane van, first seen in March 1978. Notice that it is fitted with the second type of Dyane grille.

total, 1,443,583 examples of the Dyane saloons were built during its eleven-year lifespan, which turned out to be no less than thirty years shorter than that of the venerable vehicle it was originally intended to replace!

THE ACADIANE VAN

The familiar face of the Dyane did not vanish entirely from the roads of France at that time, for its front doors, wings and bonnet pressings continued in service as the cab and bonnet of the Acadiane van. A hybrid vehicle formed by grafting the fore end of the Dyane on to a lengthened and strengthened version of the current 2CV AKS van, the Acadiane could carry an increased payload of 480 kg in its 2,270 cubic metre interior. Its name was derived from a marriage of the terms AK and Dyane.

Introduced in October 1977, the Acadiane was powered by the 602 cc 35 bhp 2CV-6 engine, gearbox and other mechanical elements inherited from the AKS. Produced at Citroën's Spanish factory at Vigo, it remained available until May 1987, when it was phased out in favour of the new C15 light van, based on the Visa. Total production numbered 253,393 units, with 49,679 being assembled during 1979, the high point of its career.

PART THREE
PARENTAGE

THE CITROËN 2CV

Pierre-Jules Boulanger, 1885–1950, the architect-turned-industrialist who was in charge of the Citroën firm from 1935 until 1950. His austere personality and ascetic mentality inspired and infused the 2CV. The man and the motor car were virtually indissoluble.

CHAPTER SEVEN

THE FOUR FATHERS OF THE 2CV

Even in firms as unusual as Citroën, the work of designing and constructing cars always was – and always will be – a team game, calling for the efforts of a number of players, all contributing their differing skills and expertise, rather than the genius of a sole individual.

The 2CV was no exception. Among the many gifted people who played a part in its conception and birth, no fewer than three are now acknowledged to have been engineers and designers of truly outstanding ability and integrity, as was proved by their work on other cars, while another was an industrialist and manager of the very highest calibre.

The band of four prodigious talents principally responsible for the composition of this masterwork – two Frenchmen and two Italians – were indeed a quartet of virtuosi: an engine designer, a chassis expert, a stylist and bodywork designer, and the 'captain of industry' who brought the ensemble together and directed its activities, like a conductor.

PIERRE-JULES BOULANGER

As the progenitor of the TPV project, P.-J. Boulanger was undoubtedly the father of the 2CV, guiding its early development so closely that his personality was forever imprinted upon it. But even so, he cannot be said to be among the designers of the car in the accepted sense of the word. Boulanger was an administrator, not an engineer, and in drawing up his celebrated design brief upon which the car was based, he was obliged to call on the assistance of a Michelin engineer at Clermont-Ferrand, a M. Chataigner. Nevertheless, as a man who had a genuine love of cars and an enthusiasm for driving, by representing the interests of the motorists for whom the 2CV was intended and by personally testing prototypes continually throughout all stages of its development, he played a vital, active part in the creative process which produced this milestone in automobile design.

Pierre-Jules Boulanger was born on 10 March 1885 at Sin-le-Noble, a village on the outskirts of Douai in the Nord *departement* of France, and educated at the Chaptal College in Paris. Forced by family circumstances to abandon his academic studies and earn his own living, in 1908, at the age of twenty-three, he emigrated to the USA to seek his fortune in this land of opportunity. But already an event had occurred which was to determine the path of his future career and, ultimately, to lead him back in an unexpected direction and make him famous in his native land. When serving the two-year period of national service then compulsory for all young Frenchmen (from 1906 to 1908 he was stationed at Satory in the French Army's 25th Balloon Observation Battalion), he won the friendship of Marcel Michelin, André Michelin's son.

Then a family-owned firm (as it remains to this day), the Michelin company of Clermont-Ferrand had its origins in the 1830s, when the Englishwoman Elizabeth Pugh-Barker, niece of Charles Macintosh (who first discovered the secret of dissolving natural rubber in benzine) married Edouard Daubrée, the part-owner of a sugar refining business in the Auvergne, known as Barbier & Daubrée. Elizabeth brought with her to France the know-how for making toy rubber balls and other domestic articles, and by 1863 the company was fully established as a manufacturer of rubberware and agricultural machinery. In 1889, however, it was reconstituted as Michelin & Cie, a *société comandite* (private limited company), entirely reorganised and recapitalised to concentrate almost exclusively on the development and manufacture of pneumatic tyres for bicycles and motor cars.

In 1891, Edouard and André Michelin (the grandsons of co-founder Aristide Barbier) patented the world's first fully-detachable pneumatic bicycle tyre, which they followed four years later by inventing a similar pneumatic tyre for automobiles, the first of its kind. A development of John Dunlop's idea, the Michelin beaded-edge tyre consisted of a flexible rubber inner tube containing air under high pressure, protected by an outer cover of canvas coated with harder rubber moulded with a tread. This cover had wire rings bonded into its inner edges, which allowed the tyre to be secured firmly, but not permanently, to the wheel rims. Now it was possible to ride and drive on a cushion of air, instead of a solid, circular block of rubber, and if it punctured, to rapidly remove and repair it!

Enterprising and astute, the Michelin brothers prospered greatly in the motor car boom which took place before and after the First World War, and soon became figures of great importance in the French economy. Despite being cunning and secretive (so much so that they were known in Paris as 'the old foxes of the Auvergne'), they were certainly not backward or old-fashioned in their outlook. On the contrary, like a good many other entrepreneurs from a rural background, they proved to be extremely go-ahead in their business methods, and embraced modern technology with enthusiasm. And although they were undoubtedly secretive to the point of paranoia, they also possessed a flair for publicity rivalling that of André Citroën himself. In 1898, they created their famous 'Michelin Man' trade mark, 'Monsieur Bibendum', and then went on to launch the renowned series of road maps and guides which, with their coveted stars, still represent the ultimate test of the standards of cuisine and accommodation provided for motorists travelling on the roads of Europe today.

Arriving on the west coast of the USA in 1908, Boulanger was forced to work his way up in the world the hard way. Starting off at the bottom as a ranch-hand in the Rockies, and later working as a tram driver in San Francisco, by 1910 he found himself employed as a draftsman with a firm of architects in Seattle, where his practical knowledge of building methods and his skill at organisation and administration brought him rapid promotion. By August 1911, at the age of twenty-five, he was his own boss, having founded a building and construction firm called Modern Houses Ltd in the Canadian city of Victoria, on the island of Vancouver, British Columbia, just across the water from Seattle.

But three years later, on the outbreak of the First World War in August 1914, as a reservist, Boulanger answered the call of duty and left his business to return to France, rejoining his former unit as a corporal. In November 1914, however, he was transferred to the MF36 reconnaissance squadron of the Service Aéronautique (the French Army Air Corps), where he became a specialist in aerial photography, flying behind enemy lines in spotter aircraft to observe German troop movements and artillery positions. By the end of the war, Boulanger had won promotion to the rank of captain, having been shot down by anti-aircraft fire in 1917, sustaining injuries that kept him in hospital for six months. For this exploit, he won a citation for bravery and the award of the Légion d'Honneur. Ultimately, he was decorated eight times for bravery and meritorious service, winning, among other medals, the Belgian Croix de Guerre, the American Distinguished Service Medal and the honorary Order of the British Empire.

Pierre Michelin (the youngest son of the patriarch Edouard Michelin), born in 1903. Following the demise of André Citroën, he was Managing Director of the Double Chevron firm until his untimely death in 1937.

During the war, Boulanger renewed his friendship with his boyhood friend, Marcel Michelin, and made such an impression on the Michelin family that Marcel's uncle, Edouard Michelin, invited him to postpone his return to the USA in order to supervise a programme of building work planned for the Clermont-Ferrand headquarters and factory. Boulanger accepted, and on the ending of hostilities in 1919, he joined the staff of the Michelin tyre firm. By 1922, now aged thirty-seven, he had worked his way up into the top management echelons of the company, having gained the respect and confidence of Edouard Michelin and his only surviving son, Pierre, then the principal active executive directors of the company, who made him their trusted right-hand man. Clearly, his responsibilities now extended well beyond matters of bricks and mortar.

When, at the end of 1934, the Michelin family acquired the Citroën organisation, together with its debts and difficulties, it was Boulanger who was sent to Paris to sort out the problems and supervise its reorganisation. As Citroën's new managing director, he reported to Pierre Michelin, who remained at Clermont-Ferrand, assisted by his cousin, Marcel, who was then in charge of research and development at the tyre factory.

Unfortunately, in December 1937, while rushing home for the New Year holidays, Pierre Michelin was killed in a car accident at Montargis, on the road between Paris and Clermont-Ferrand. Boulanger was immediately appointed chief executive of the S.A. André Citroën and later, in 1938, as a co-director of Michelin et cie also, in conjunction (and on an equal footing) with Edouard's son-in-law, Robert Puiseux, another long-standing employee, friend and confidant of the Michelin family. On the death of Edouard Michelin in 1940, these two faithful lieutenants together inherited the custodianship of the combined Michelin and Citroën business empires which together formed one of the largest and most important industrial and commercial organisations in France at that time.

A profoundly serious man who set himself the strictest moral standards, Boulanger brought high ideals to the motor industry. At Citroën, he revived the culture of technological excellence created by André Citroën, establishing there a research department that, for thirty years at least, was certainly unrivalled by any other French car firm and, perhaps, by any other automotive company in the world. By encouraging its staff at all times to avoid imitation and reject dogma in their search for new ideas, he fostered a remarkable *ésprit de corps*. But despite this commitment to scientific progress, his approach was always pragmatic. Being self-taught, he preferred to employ those with a similar background, especially people who had studied part-time at evening classes (particularly at the Arts and Métiers technical colleges), believing that engineers trained at the universities and *grandes écoles* were blinkered by their formal education and incapable of truly original thought.

In Boulanger's scale of values, simplicity was never to be equated with poverty, nor frugality with deprivation, and his abhorrence of the glamour and ostentation so often associated with the automobile industry was reflected in the car that he created. Somewhat aloof and austere, he deplored egotism and self-promotion, and was completely disinterested in the material rewards of achievement that normally motivate motor industry bosses, preferring to work in a sparsely furnished office devoid of the normal trappings of executive prestige. An admirer of flair and self-expression in other men, for his own part he was the model of sobriety and restraint, and always wore a quasi-uniform of subdued grey suits, shirts, ties and hats bought off-the-peg from an outfitter at Clermont-Ferrand. Punctilious in his personal habits, he hated routine and inactivity. Formal and conservative in his demeanour, he was far from being a traditionalist: he never looked back at the past, and thought only of the future. Although lacking personal ambition in the

This 2CV AZAM, built in 1965 and exported to the USA that year, has only 35 miles on the clock, having spent the past forty years immobile in an auto museum.

Now resident in California, it presents a perfect unmarked example of the 2CV AZAM's special interior and exterior features, including its elaborate alloy bumpers. But note the non-standard direction indicators, fitted to comply with US regulations, and also the double chevron badge on its side that conceals the bolt-holes where the original single indicators were located.

THE CITROËN 2CV

Initially, the Mehari was classed as a commercial vehicle and had no rear seats, side doors, or hard-topped roof. Protection from the weather was provided by a canvas hood and transparent plastic side-screens.

Based on the Dyane's chassis and powered by a 602 cc version of the familiar air-cooled flat-twin engine, the Mehari came in LHD form only. None were sold in the UK.

This is the 4×4 version of the Mehari. It is recognisable by the spare wheel housed on the bonnet and the cow-catcher bumpers.

138

The Citroën 2CV

Only a few styling changes were made during the evolution of the Dyane between 1967 and 1983. This is the Dyane-6 of 1973, distinguishable by its stainless steel mesh grille.

This is the Dyane-6 of 1975 with a horizontal bar-type grille.

The earliest examples of the Dyane-4 had a four-light body, but windows in the rear quarter panels were introduced on the Dyane-6 in 1970.

The Acadiane van, first seen in 1978, was a combination of the Dyane-6 saloon and the 2CV AKS van. Its cab and bonnet came from the saloon and its chassis and engine came from the 2CV *fourgonnette*.

The Acadiane boasted a 2,270 m³ body which could carry 480 kg. It remained available until 1987.

The Citroën 2CV

Introduced in April 1961, the Ami-6 was based on the 2CV and shared the Deuche's air-cooled flat-twin engine (enlarged to 602 cc) plus its chassis and suspension.

The Ami-6 was exceptionally light, thanks to its thin-gauge steel panels and its aluminium bumpers and trim, which gave it a remarkably high cruising speed and fuel economy for its class.

The reverse rake rear window was the Ami-6's most controversial feature. Designed by Flaminio Bertoni, it permitted extra headroom for rear seat passengers as well as a more commodious amount of boot space.

THE CITROËN 2CV

The Bijou's plastic panel-work comprised eleven separate mouldings fixed to a tubular steel framework and then mounted on a 2CV platform chassis.

The Bijou was the only Citroën model to have been designed and constructed entirely outside of France, with no French equivalent.

THE CITROËN 2CV

The unique polyester-bodied Bijou built at Slough between 1960 and 1964. A total of just 211 examples were constructed.

Its aerodynamic bodywork shared many interior and exterior design details with the DS19, including its door handles and single-spoked steering wheel.

The Bijou came in a wide choice of striking colour schemes, including Sherwood Green, Dove Grey, Regal Red, Coral Pink, and Daffodil Yellow, as in this example. The wheels were painted a standard cream throughout.

143

The design of the roof also had the effect of lengthening the glass house, to give the Ami-6 a big-car feel. The absence of a transmission tunnel and central console also helped to increase interior space.

The frontal aspect of the Ami-6 was original to say the least, but it came about through purely practical considerations. Similarly, the unusual swaging of the side panels was intended to give stiffness to the bodywork, as well as contributing to its form and style.

material sense, he pursued his own ideals and goals with a relentless concentration and determination to overcome all obstacles in his path. His spartan philosophy is best summed up in the words he wrote himself: 'Certes la vie de chaque jour ne nous épargne pas les difficultés de toutes sortes. Il est stérile de s'étendre sur ce sujet. La seule chose qui compte, c'est l'effort à faire pour vaincre ces difficultés.' ('It is pointless to dwell on the difficulties of everyday life. The only thing that counts is the effort to overcome them.')

Evidently, more than a few members of the Bureau d'Études considered Boulanger's high moral standards excessively severe, and confessed to finding his hair-shirt mentality oppressive, or even priggish. Some recalled that during the Occupation, Boulanger forbade his wife buying bread, meat or butter on the black market or obtaining any other articles, such as children's shoes, for which she did not have the appropriate ration coupon. By virtue of his position as Director-General of SA Citroën, Boulanger was one of the few citizens of Paris entitled to use a car for his personal needs, even at weekends. But he refused to exercise this privilege: when going home on Friday evenings and returning to work on Monday mornings, he travelled on the Métro. Only when it came to deceiving the Germans was this rectitude relaxed, it seems. As a consequence of its work in constructing lorries, the Citroën firm was allowed unlimited supplies of petrol throughout the war – but only for the purpose of fuelling these lorries. By order of the Nazi administrator at the factory, all passenger cars in use by the firm had to be powered by gas, which was obtained from a wood-burning gazogene apparatus towed in a trailer behind the vehicle. The cars that travelled daily about Paris on Citroën business under the noses of the Germans appeared to be conforming to this rule, but with Boulanger's full knowledge and approval, in reality they were running on petrol, with their tanks full of liquid fuel!

In December 1950 Boulanger was also killed on the road between Paris and Clermont-Ferrand, at a point on Route National 7 just south of Moulins known as Brout-Vernet. Driving a Traction Avant fitted with an experimental engine and gearbox, he somehow left the road at high speed and struck a tree. Exactly what caused this terrible accident was never established by the police, although it was believed that Boulanger had suffered a heart-attack, brought on perhaps by the strain of propelling the Citroën firm forward through its difficulties by the sheer force of his extraordinary personality. He was succeeded as *chef* of the Quai de Javel by his deputy Pierre Bercot, who for the next twenty years shared the reins of power with Antoine Brueder, the latter being responsible for purely administrative and personnel matters. It was Bercot, therefore, who gave the go-ahead for the important avant-garde models that were to follow the 2CV, including the DS and ID, the GS, and the Citroën-Maserati SM.

ANDRÉ LEFEBVRE

André Lefebvre, the genius principally responsible for the engineering thinking behind the 2CV, was born on 19 August

André Lefebvre, 1894–1964, the automobile engineering genius who created the Citroën DS19 as well as the Citroën 2CV. Besides Vincenzo Lancia, he was the only man ever to reach the highest levels of achievement in both motor racing and car design simultaneously.

1894 at Louvres on the northern outskirts of Paris. Educated at a *lycée* in Nantes, in 1911 he entered the École Supérieure d'Aéronautique in Paris, gaining an engineering diploma in 1914. The École was situated in the Montmartre *quartier* of Paris, a village-within-a-city that had long supported a bohemian community and which was renowned even then as a centre of French artistic life. Peopled by poets, writers and painters such as Picasso, Braque and Derain, the *quartier* exuded an atmosphere of radical creativity. As he sat with his friends in the cafés and bistros of Montmartre, discussing *la vie*, *l'amour* and *les autos* late into the night, the young Lefebvre would doubtless have mixed with such men and become deeply affected by their progressive ideas, soaking up their spirit of iconoclastic inventiveness.

Eventually, on 1 March 1916, aged twenty-two, Lefebvre joined the firm of

Gabriel Voisin, remaining there for fifteen years until 30 April 1931. Here he became the protégé, deputy and right-hand man of this famous aeronautical pioneer (a former associate of airman Louis Blériot), at first designing military aircraft, but then, after the First World War, a number of very advanced luxury automobiles and racing cars, all showing a strong aeronautical influence.

An all-rounder, Gabriel Voisin experimented in a wide variety of fields, including architecture. During the twenties, when at the height of his fame and prestige, he collaborated with le Corbusier in sponsoring a visionary plan for the redevelopment of the city of Paris. Based on a grid pattern designed to cater for the demands of the motor car, this Plan Voisin was first revealed to the public in le Corbusier's celebrated Pavillon de l'Esprit Nouveau at the 1925 Exposition Internationale des Arts Decoratifs et Industriels, the birthplace of the Art Deco movement. Fortunately for the historic buildings and architectural treasures of Paris, however, the proposal was eventually rejected by the authorities as nothing more than futuristic madness, and abandoned. Most probably, Lefebvre would have met the famous architect while working with Voisin; certainly, like his mentor, he was greatly influenced by the ideas of le Corbusier and the Modern Movement, as was Boulanger.

With the sole exception of Vincenzo Lancia, Lefebvre was the only automobile engineer ever to have competed in motor sport at the highest level, and often drove for the Voisin racing team himself. Most notably, in 1923 he finished fifth in the Grand Prix de l'Automobile Club de France held at Tours, at the wheel of a 2-litre six-cylinder Voisin, a highly aerodynamic machine with a revolutionary monocoque body built almost entirely of light alloy, which he had helped to design. Later on, with César Marchand as his co-driver, he took part in a famous series of high-speed, long-distance endurance runs held at Montlhéry. Staged by Voisin and sponsored by the Yacco Oil Company, these runs set many enduring world records, most notably that for forty-eight hours of non-stop driving, during which the Voisin covered 10,560 km at an average speed of 220 kph, to international acclaim.

The economic problems of the Depression had a severe impact on the makers of luxury cars in France – and, being avant-garde, the Voisin firm was hit harder than most. The market for Voisin's expensive and eccentric products suddenly collapsed, almost bringing down his company, so, in 1931, André Lefebvre and Gabriel Voisin were obliged to part company, although the pair were to remain close friends for the rest of their lives, consulting each other on every technical and automotive issue.

After an unproductive and uncongenial two-year stint with Renault, Lefebvre joined Citroën on 12 March 1933, having been recruited personally by André Citroën, on the recommendation of Gabriel Voisin, specifically to take overall technical control of his Traction Avant project. Lefebvre had already developed proposals for a front-wheel-drive car while working with Voisin, but Louis Renault had rejected his suggestions as

André Lefebvre at the wheel of the Voisin racing car he helped to design, photographed shortly before the start of the 1923 Grand Prix de l'Automobile Club de France, held at Tours. The Voisin's lightweight, chassis-less, all-alloy body marked the first use of the monocoque construction principle. Lefebvre finished fifth.

idiotic. 'I won't waste five minutes on such nonsense,' Renault is said to have told him. Being opposites in every conceivable way, inevitably the two men quarrelled, and Lefebvre walked out – straight to Renault's great rival on the Quai de Javel. Here, over the next twenty-five years, Lefebvre was to create that succession of radical, revolutionary cars which gave Citroën the world-wide reputation for technical excellence, innovation and unconventionality that it still enjoys today – the Traction Avant, the 2CV and the DS19.

During his years as *de facto* chief engineer and designer at Citroën's Bureau d'Études, André Lefebvre held no official rank or title in the company's hierarchy, yet he was regarded as the supreme authority and source of policy on all technical matters. After the demise of André Citroën in 1935, he reported directly to the Michelin family at Clermont-Ferrand, who gave his advanced theories and adventurous principles their total support and endorsement. 'He's formidable – he thinks like us and does things our way,' *les patrons* are reported to have said. Even Boulanger (no engineer himself) was known to bow before Lefebvre's judgement on questions of automobile technology. Moreover, Boulanger's successors as managing director were happy not to question or disturb this arrangement, and continued to allow their resident genius *carte blanche* to follow whatever lines of research seemed most interesting and promising to him personally, almost regardless of their cost or ultimate commercial viability.

Bored by administrative and organisational matters and totally uninterested in the symbols of power

The winning Sunbeam, driven by Henry Segrave – the first British-built car to win a Grand Prix race. But as it was designed by two Italians working for the Sunbeam-Talbot-Darracq company in France, the ex-Fiat engineers Walter Becchia and Vincenzo Bertarione, some continental commentators claimed it was no more than a Fiat in green paint! In 1942 Becchia joined Citroën – to produce the tiny engine of the 2CV.

and status that motivate lesser men, Lefebvre concentrated his energies and talents entirely on producing new engineering ideas, working at all hours and in all places. The archetypal artist-engineer, he worshipped novelty for its own sake, taking a perverse delight in doing things differently, and refusing to copy proven techniques and methods used successfully elsewhere. Nothing seemed impossible to him. The more audacious, unconventional and complex a solution, the greater was its appeal.

Throughout his career, both with Voisin and with Citroën, André Lefebvre was obsessed with the idea of adapting the principles of aeronautics to the automobile. Yet he never went in for the phoney streamlining that was so fashionable in the thirties, and which, as often as not, was aerodynamically unsound and merely cloaked a crude chassis with a thin veneer of spurious sophistication.

A tall, dark, elegant figure who dressed with style and drank nothing but water or champagne, he was evidently extremely attractive to women. Three times married (unusual for his era, even in France), his life was one long, passionate love affair with the motor car, punctuated by countless much shorter liaisons with innumerable pretty females. But the intense, good-looking Lefebvre was not always so successful in persuading men to acquiesce to his wishes and desires. Like many other brilliant minds, he was highly strung, and could often seem temperamental and impatient with those who simply could not keep up with the furious pace of his inventiveness. Consequently, he was confined in an isolated inner sanctum in the Bureau d'Études, surrounded by a small staff of carefully chosen research assistants who could be trusted to understand his thinking and to carry out his instructions without contradiction, no matter how far-fetched they might appear at first sight. His draftsman during the fifties, Georges Sallot, said that Lefebvre would come to his drawing board almost every day with a new idea or device that he had just thought up and wanted to have produced and tried out. Another assistant of that period, Hubert Seznec, claimed that his boss had just too many new ideas for the means available at the time.

Clearly, the exciting opportunities then being opened up by the wealth of novel methods and materials (such as the new industrial plastics which first appeared in the early fifties) fascinated the forward-thinking, revolutionary Lefebvre. According to the journalist Jacques Borgé, he was one of the first men in Paris to buy a drip-dry nylon shirt, delighted by the fact that it could be washed through and worn without ironing. One day he turned up at his office clutching a plastic bag. Turning to one of his assistants, a M. Lecoultre, he suggested that the principle should be used for developing a flexible, shock-proof petrol tank which could be inserted into the cavity under the driver's seat of a car, where its weight would least affect the vehicle's balance, and where it would be least likely to be ruptured in an accident. Only today, fifty years on, is this particular concept being adopted as a practical proposition by the motor industry.

But to understand exactly what André Lefebvre achieved at Citroën – and to explain how it was that his Michelin bosses allowed him sufficient leeway to realise those remarkable achievements – it is necessary to remember that above all, he was a man who loved driving. As a highly skilled and experienced former grand prix racing driver who had risked his life countless times on the track, no matter whether it was the little 2CV or the big, powerful DS19 that he was designing, he approached the task entirely from the owner-driver's point of view, rather than that of the production engineer or cost accountant.

For Lefebvre, the question of chassis dynamics was the key to all the other conflicting design considerations. From Voisin he had learned that lightness, aerodynamic efficiency and good road-holding and handling qualities were all far more important in determining performance than outright engine power. But what ultimately determined the speed and safety of a car was *'la liaison au sol'* – the relationship between its moving wheels and the ever-changing road surface passing beneath it. In this approach, all design objectives were held subservient to achieving optimum contact between the tyre and the road, at all speeds and in all situations. Since that all-important tyre–road contact governed the traction, acceleration, steering and braking abilities of a vehicle, under Lefebvre's perfectionist approach, no effort was spared to develop sophisticated new suspension and steering arrangements that would guarantee this continuing contact, no matter what happened to the driver or the car. The intention was to improve the *liaison au sol* of Citroën vehicles to levels of refinement and security never before achieved by any other motor manufacturer.

It is no coincidence that throughout Lefebvre's period of involvement on the 2CV (and later also on the DS), at Clermont-Ferrand the scientists and engineers of the Michelin tyre company were working towards the same objective. Even before the war, the Michelin firm had decided to abandon rigid cross-ply tyres and to concentrate its resources on the development and manufacture of a safer-running, longer-lasting replacement: the revolutionary, flexible, steel-braced radial tyre. Committed to this policy, the Michelin family was aiming at an ultimate commercial goal that involved its two companies co-operating in synergy. Citroën vehicles of advanced design equipped with Michelin steel-belt radials would demonstrate the superiority of French automotive technology to the world. With global domination of the automobile tyre market the ultimate objective, in matters of research and development there existed a complete concurrence of intentions and policies between the two Michelin-owned companies, and hence a constant exchange of information and personnel between Paris and Clermont-Ferrand. It was this long-term strategy on the part of the Michelin management then controlling Citroën that gave André Lefebvre his power and prestige at the Bureau d'Études, and allowed him to pursue his adventurous ideas no matter what the cost.

In fact, André Lefebvre continued in the service of the Citroën marque until the end of his life, having been forced to retire through illness in July 1958. Even so, partly paralysed, he went on designing for Citroën, working from his home, until he died on 4 May 1964, aged seventy. Long after his demise, however, the spirit and influence of André Lefebvre lived on at the Quai de Javel. Later cars, such as the SM and the GS (both launched in 1970) and the CX (which appeared in 1974), were all designed according to the principles and philosophy bequeathed by Gabriel Voisin's spiritual heir.

The other great joint creation of André Lefebvre and Flaminio Bertoni was the Citroën DS19 of 1956, as photographed by Robert Doisneau.

FLAMINIO BERTONI

Although he was responsible for the shape and style of three of the most individual and instantly recognisable cars ever produced, the stylist of the Citroën 2CV, Flaminio Bertoni, remains virtually an unknown and unrecognised talent in the English-speaking world, not least among those who own and admire the very cars that he designed. Even in his adopted homeland of France, Bertoni continues to be regarded as '*un génie encore trop méconnu*' ('a misunderstood and undeservedly neglected genius').

Today, popular interest in automotive styling is such that even those motorists with just a passing interest in cars can recognise the names of the leading Italian automobile stylists of the fifties and sixties, such as Farina, Ghia, Michelotti and Bertone. But Bertoni (with an 'i')? Surely some mistake!

Far from it: experts on automobile and industrial design now acknowledge that Flaminio Bertoni must be ranked among the most gifted and influential stylists ever to have worked in the motor industry, on either side of the Atlantic. His achievement was to create the visual appearance of a quartet of completely original and radical designs – the Traction Avant, the Citroën 2CV, the Citroën DS and the Citroën Ami-6, all now hailed as cult cars and icons of creativity. On this evidence alone, Flaminio Bertoni surely deserves a place in the pantheon of heroes of twentieth-century automobile styling alongside such figures as Raymond Loewy and Harley Earle.

Born on 10 January 1903 at Masgano Varese in northern Italy, the son of a stonemason, Bertoni began work at the age of fourteen as an apprentice carpenter in an aircraft factory, but soon developed an interest in automobile body styling and construction, and qualified as a sheet metal worker. A gifted self-taught draughtsman, painter and sculptor, who at that point in his career lacked only formal academic qualifications, he was unable to establish himself in Italy, so, in 1923, now aged twenty, he made his way to Paris, then the centre of both the artistic and the automobile engineering worlds. Here, over the next ten years he earned a precarious and bohemian living in a number of ways – as a freelance book jacket designer and illustrator, as a consulting inventor and engineer, and as a sculptor.

Eventually, having attracted the attention and patronage of André Citroën and his wife, on 8 July 1932, aged twenty-nine, he joined Citroën to work on the development of the Traction Avant, initially as a maker of plaster styling models. But as the full extent of his talents became apparent to his colleagues and superiors, he gradually assumed overall responsibility for all matters of exterior styling and interior design at Citroën, working directly under successive chiefs of coachwork in the company's Bureau d'Études. He remained at Citroën for the next thirty-two years, until his death in 1964, aged sixty-one.

During this period in the history of Citroën, the company pursued a policy of absolute self-sufficiency in every aspect of engineering and body design, undertaking all such activities in-house. No outside consultant stylists or design studios were ever employed. Consequently, Bertoni can safely be held solely responsible for the innovative appearance of all the notable Citroën cars of his era. In addition, he was also involved in a number of important styling studies, prototypes and unproduced designs. His influence also extended to matters of graphic design and corporate identity – it was he who reworked André Citroën's original double chevron trade mark into the modern form employed today.

But because research and development activities at Citroën were conducted in total secrecy, and an absolute ban on personal publicity for employees and their achievements was rigidly enforced, throughout his career there Bertoni worked in virtual anonymity. During the development of both the 2CV and the DS19, research work at the Bureau d'Études was just as closely guarded as at a Russian atomic weapons base, and the rue du Théâtre building became known as the *'maison de mystère'* ('house of secrets'), as impenetrable as the Kremlin. As a result, Bertoni's contribution to the reputation of the double chevron marque – indeed, even his presence at Automobiles Citroën – remained largely unknown to the outside world until many years after his death. So complete was this ignorance of his work, even among motoring journalists, that as recently as ten years ago, when knowledge of his talents at last began to leak out, his contribution to the DS was still being attributed to Bertone (with an 'e') due to an elementary confusion over names, if not styles!

Bertoni's direct involvement in the design of the 2CV can be traced back with certainty to 1942, when he produced drawings for a series of prototypes upon which the lines of the post-war production model were eventually based. Among these was the so-called 'Cyclops' version, on account of its single headlamp mounted centrally in the bonnet hood. But surviving pictures of his maquette for the AX project produced in 1936–7 (intended as a replacement for the Traction Avant, but later abandoned) reveal a close and distinctive resemblance to the unique overall shape we recognise so well today, especially when viewed from above.

In truth, Bertoni's role in the production of the 2CV was somewhat smaller than the part he played in the design of the Traction Avant, DS19 and Ami-6. In fact, to a certain extent he was kept out of the project by Boulanger, who was anxious that the conceptual purity of his car should not be corrupted by spurious embellishment or beautification of any kind. Its lines were to be determined entirely by rational criteria, such as the position of the wheels, the height of the engine and the optimisation of space in the passenger compartment. The unscientific, aesthetic obsessions of a stylist, however gifted and imaginative, carried little weight with *le patron*.

But one day, feeling rather put out at not having been consulted on such an important project, Bertoni was bold enough to present his boss with a full-scale mock-up demonstrating several improvements he was proposing, to soften the stark outline of the approved prototype. Not only was this maquette sculpted with more rounded curves than Boulanger's austerely angular version,

Flaminio Bertoni, 1903–1964, seen here working on a plaster maquette of the Traction Avant, the car he helped to style shortly after joining the Citroën company in 1932.

but it was also painted in a pretty shade of primrose yellow! When he saw this outrage, Boulanger exploded. '*Quelle horreur!* What have you done? Take it away! I never want to see this again!' he raged at the poor, misguided Italian, according to Jean Muratet, an old boy of the Bureau d'Études who witnessed the scene.

Small, dark and extremely energetic, with a large, square head framed by thick sideboards, Bertoni was a workaholic who never stopped creating things, beavering away late into the night and throughout weekends once an idea took hold of him. He certainly didn't confine himself to designing cars: during his years at Citroën he kept up an impressive output of highly accomplished works of art – architectural drawings, charcoal sketches, clay statuettes and busts of his family and friends, including his boss, Boulanger. Colleagues described him as working like a demon, with a wicked gleam in his eyes, keeping them amused with a constant stream of witty remarks delivered in his Italian accent, which he never lost even after living for forty-three years in France. According to one leading French journalist, he was a 'force of nature', an 'intuitive genius', blessed with an 'electronic eye' for shape and form, and who toiled at a 'madcap pace'. He could visualise the finished appearance of a car, or part of a car, from every angle, down to the tiniest detail, and sculpt it out of a solid mass of clay in less than a day. Another contemporary witness said he looked like a sorcerer in his cave, bustling round his trough of plaster and constantly chewing aspirins to fend off the incessant migraines caused by the motorbike accident that he had suffered during the war.

In June 1940, shortly before the invading German Army reached Paris, the Citroën factory was bombed by the *Luftwaffe*. Although the company's production facilities were scarcely damaged, its administrative buildings (which also housed the Bureau d'Études) were totally destroyed, with the loss of all the company's records, including its engineering drawings and technical archives. Immediately, the management and research staff moved south to Niort, near La Rochelle on the Atlantic coast, until the political and military situation was stabilised, whereupon the Bureau d'Études returned to new accommodation in the old Mors car factory, located at the rue du Théâtre in the 15th Arrondissement of Paris, just off the Quai de Grenelle, a few steps away from the main Citroën factory on the Quai de Javel.

As the German Occupation spread inexorably southwards throughout France that autumn, communications between Paris and Niort became ever more difficult. But because of his Italian passport, Bertoni was able to travel without restriction, so, using his motorcycle, he became a sort of despatch rider, carrying vital parts and messages, until he suffered a severe road accident which almost cost him his life and which left him crippled and subject to severe headaches for the rest of his days. While convalescing from his accident, Bertoni took a leave of absence from Citroën to study architecture at the École Nationale des Beaux Arts in Paris, gaining a diploma – the formal qualification he had always sought.

Later, in 1953, he was awarded the distinction of Chevalier de l'Ordre des Arts et des Lettres for his work as a sculptor. Bertoni actually lived just a few doors away from the Bureau d'Études with his son, Serge, and his Italian wife, who was a talented dancer, having once been a leading member of the *corps de ballet* at La Scala in Milan.

Throughout the greater part of his time at Citroën, Bertoni's role in the scheme of things was to translate André Lefebvre's avant-garde thoughts on styling and body design into three-dimensional form, while adding his own personal vision to their joint creations. Both being artist-engineers of exceptional talent, one highly sophisticated and a perfectionist, the other a more primitive and pragmatic personality, the two men complemented each other perfectly and formed a

Flaminio Bertoni pictured in 1950 at the age of 47, with his second son Serge, born the previous year.

remarkable partnership. Lefebvre was never short of ideas, and moreover could set them down on paper as sketches and diagrams, but to make them work in reality, he needed practical craftsmen and mechanics who could transform his idealistic conceptions into objects that could be produced economically in large volume.

Bertoni had this gift – rare among visual artists – and was able not merely to appreciate the problems and preoccupations of engineers, but actually to assist them in their work. The exceptional originality and individuality of his imagination is obvious to even the most casual and uninterested observer; what seems all the more remarkable today, thirty years after his death, is his deep, practical understanding of the mechanical capabilities of the materials at his disposal, both new and old. As one of the very first designers to work with thermoplastics and glass-reinforced polyester resins as well as the traditional aluminium and steel, his grasp of the opportunities was total.

The Citroën DS has often been described as a masterpiece of engineering and aesthetics; if so, then it was entirely Bertoni's achievement that in this car, as with the 2CV, form and function were united with such unsurpassed inventiveness and skill.

Walter Becchia

If Walter Becchia had ever been his own master, with his name proudly cast on the many marvellous sporting and racing engines that he created, then today his work would surely be ranked with that of those other great Italian engineer-entrepreneurs – Ettore Bugatti, Vincenzo Lancia and Alfieri Maserati. But although a supremely gifted designer, Becchia was just not the frontman or figurehead type, and was content to devote himself to building cars for other men, rather than establishing a marque of his own. Modest, discreet and unassuming, he chose to spend the greater part of his career at Citroën, working out of the limelight in comfortable obscurity. Here, in post-war years, his reputation undoubtedly suffered as a result of the policy of secrecy and obfuscation that surrounded activities at the Bureau d'Études, so that by the end of his life, his talent was recognised and remembered only by his colleagues and a few knowledgeable connoisseurs.

Born in 1903, Becchia began his career with the highly successful Fiat Racing Department in Turin, but in 1922, accompanied by his colleague Vincenzo Bertarione, he moved to Paris to join the Anglo-French Sunbeam-Talbot-Darracq firm, having been recruited by its famous managing director and chief designer, Louis Coatalen, a Frenchman who had taken British nationality. Working at Suresnes on the outskirts of Paris, the pair designed the 2-litre six-cylinder double overhead cam engine which powered the British-entered Sunbeams, built at Wolverhampton, that won both first and team prizes in the 1923 Grand Prix de l'Automobile Club de France at Tours. Described by some experts as one of the most successful British racing cars of all time, and by others as merely a Fiat painted green, this car (driven by Henry

Segrave) was the first ever British entrant to win a major grand prix race, an achievement that, unfortunately, was not to be repeated for another thirty-five years. By a strange coincidence, André Lefebvre also competed in this race, driving a Voisin.

When the British side of the Sunbeam firm retired from racing in 1926 to concentrate on land speed record attempts, Becchia and Bertarione remained at the Sunbeam-Talbot-Darracq design office, and eventually found themselves employed by a fellow Italian, the distinguished engineer Antonio (Anthony) Lago, who took over the French side of the business when the Rootes brothers acquired its British interests in 1934. Intent on re-creating a sporting image for the Talbot marque, Lago set up a new competition department and promoted Becchia to be its chief engineer; Bertarione left to work for Hotchkiss. Later, in 1937, Lago engaged the carburettor expert Lucien Girard from Zenith-Stromberg to work with Becchia, and the two formed a partnership that was to endure for over twenty years.

Becchia's greatest contribution to the revival of the Talbot name was to design a new 3-litre straight-six engine with a novel type of cylinder head, having hemispherical combustion chambers aspirated by twin overhead valves set at a V angle and operated by rockers driven by a complex arrangement of cross-over pushrods. This 2,996 cc T120 engine was soon enlarged to 3,996 cc and 140 bhp. Thus equipped, Talbot Lago's T150SS sports car duly showed itself to be the equal of those from Bugatti and Delahaye, both on the track and as a *grande routière* – and not just in price. A further version, uprated to 4.5 litres and 250 bhp, powered the Talbot Lagos that won the first three places in the 1937 French Grand Prix at Montlhéry, a sports car event. These cars were capable of over 150 mph.

Unfortunately, due to the harsh economic climate of the times, this sporting success did not translate into sales, and soon the firm began to experience severe financial difficulties. In 1939, Pierre Boulanger invited Becchia to join Citroën, but he refused, saying that he could not desert a company that was in trouble – a remark that only increased Boulanger's determination to secure his services. So, in 1942, Becchia, the designer of powerful racing car engines, found himself at Citroën's research department at the rue du Théâtre, designing a tiny 9 hp engine for the 2CV. Here, Becchia employed the same hemispherical combustion chamber technique used on his Talbot Lago engines, but with the valve gear of the horizontally opposed cylinders driven by pushrods from a single central camshaft. The following year, he was joined at Citroën by Lucien Girard.

Endowed with the creative, Latin temperament in full measure, Becchia was not the slow, methodical type of engineer who ponderously weighs up the alternatives for weeks on end before coming to a decision. On the contrary, like his great friend and compatriot Bertoni, he was a kind of poet-mechanic, who worked intuitively, constantly improvising and inventing just for the fun of it. He never got bogged down in detail or minutiae, or lost in endless calculations. His gift was

The 4.5 litre Talbot Lago sports car co-designed by Walter Becchia, which took the first three places in the 1937 French Grand Prix, held at Montlhéry. The man wearing overalls and a felt hat is Becchia's colleague, the carburettor expert Lucien Girard who helped to design the engine of the 2CV.

that he always saw a problem in its entirety and from a new angle – hence the bold originality and verve of his designs. One of his colleagues, a M. Dupin, described him as simply bursting with astute and audacious ideas that, more often than not, were also perfectly viable from a commercial and production point of view. According to an eye witness, the entire 2CV engine and gearbox unit was designed within six days. Evidently, engines were not just in Becchia's head, but in his blood!

Besides this masterpiece, designed immediately after the war, during the early fifties Walter Becchia was also responsible for a series of highly original flat-six engines, both air- and water-cooled, originally intended for the DS19, and modelled closely on the 2CV design. Sadly, none of these prototype engines ever went into series production, due to lack of funds for the necessary retooling. Instead, the DS came out in 1955 fitted with a version of the old Traction Avant engine, modified by an all-new alloy cross-flow cylinder head, again incorporating hemispherical combustion chambers and valves in V formation – designed by Becchia, of course.

His service at Citroën extended into the sixties, when he produced a new five-bearing four-cylinder water-cooled engine for the DS based on the old Sainturat design and introduced in 1965. Yet his influence at the Bureau d'Études persisted longer still, as can be seen from the air-cooled four-cylinder boxer engines fitted to the GS and GSA models produced from 1970 to 1984. Walter Becchia retired from Citroën in 1968, and died eight years later, in 1976.

PART FOUR

FOREIGN AFFAIRS

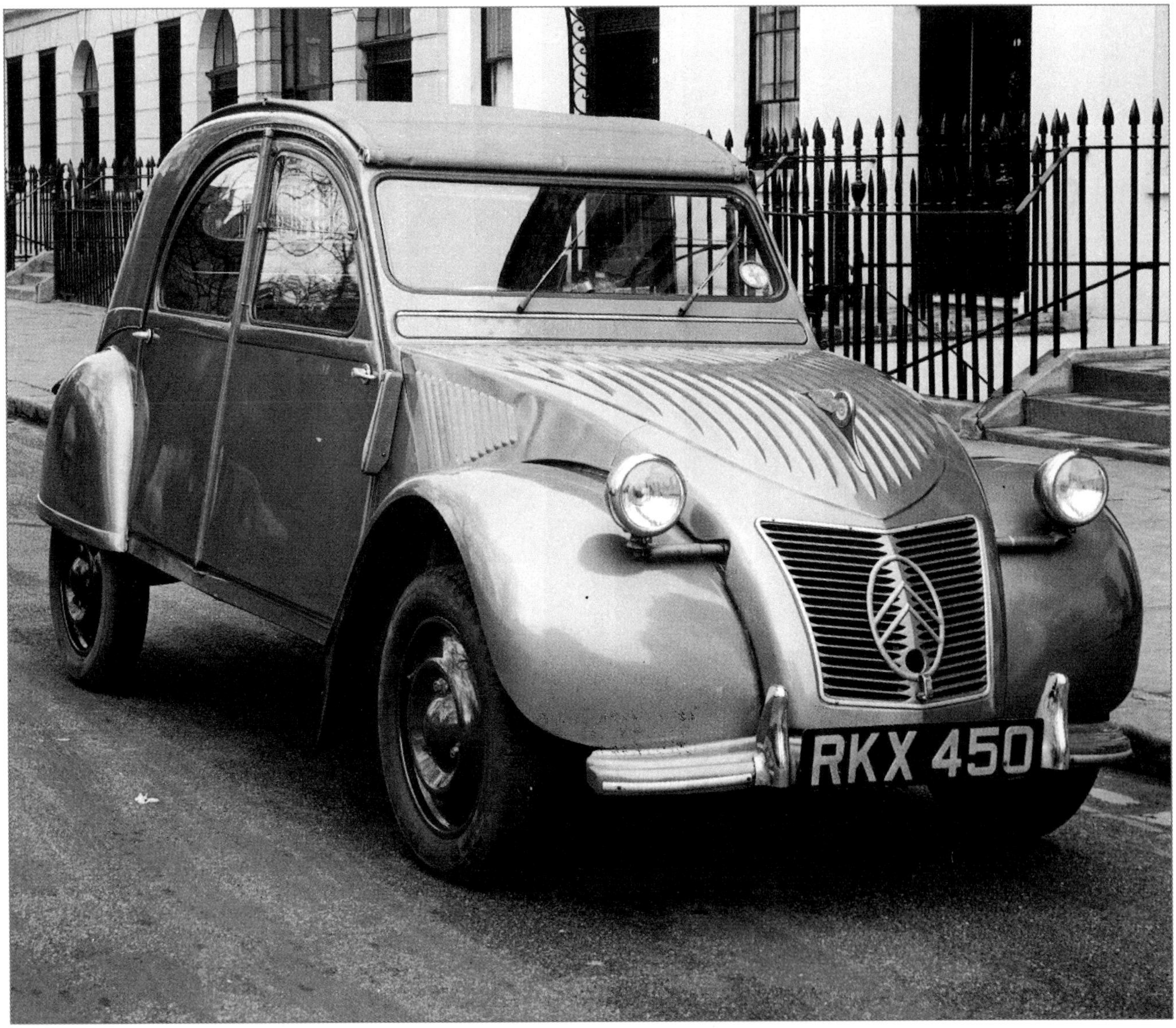
RKX 450

CHAPTER EIGHT

THE 2CV IN THE UK

The 2CV is such a quintessentially French car that even the most francophile Britons find it hard to believe that examples could ever have been sold bearing the label 'Made in England'. Yet from 1953 to 1964, a right-hand-drive version of the 2CV was built at Slough by Citroën Cars Ltd, for distribution throughout the United Kingdom and the British Commonwealth. And since well over half of the 752 Type A vehicles produced by the Slough Works were sent abroad to customers throughout the English-speaking world, the 2CV played a small but significant part in the British motor industry's post-war export drive.

Even harder to credit is the fact that Citroën's British assembly plant was once one of the largest and most important car factories in the UK. Opened by André Citroën in February 1926 as the first of his foreign subsidiaries, for exactly forty years, until February 1966, the Slough factory assembled components obtained both in France and in England into British-made Citroëns subtly modified to appeal to British tastes. Initially, Citroën's aim was simply to overcome the McKenna duties imposed on imports into the UK from France, but in 1929 exports from Slough were commenced, to take advantage of the system of preferential tariffs then governing trade in the territories of the former British Empire, and thus gain entry into the valuable Commonwealth markets denied to French-made vehicles.

To qualify for British-made status, at least 51 per cent of the total content value of an imported vehicle, including labour, material and overhead costs had to be of British origin. Citroën's British-made products were adapted and anglicised to take advantage of this loophole – in the process, providing welcome business for British suppliers and jobs for British workers.

Thus, well before the Second World War, the Slough Works ranked as Citroën's biggest foreign manufacturing subsidiary, at first producing the company's early, conventional, rear-wheel-drive cars, but then, from 1934 onwards, the highly advanced front-wheel-drive Traction Avant. By 1940, more than 28,000 right-hand-drive Citroën vehicles had been assembled there, for export to Australia, New Zealand, South Africa and other Commonwealth territories, as well as for sale in the British Isles.

The right-hand-drive version of the 2CV, built at Citroën's Slough factory, did not arrive in the UK until 1953. This press photo shows the third car to come off the production line. Most of the peculiarities of the British version are visible including the distinctive bonnet emblem and the semaphore direction indicators. These Slough-built cars were offered in a wide range of colours, with black-painted wheels. Later, chromed wheel trims were fitted.

In 1955, Citroën Cars brought out this improved AZ version of the right-hand-drive 2CV saloon, equipped with the enlarged 425 cc engine and beautified by large chromed hubcaps. Note the opening windows on the rear doors, not found on Paris-built versions.

During the war, however, the Slough factory was placed under the control of the Official Custodian of Enemy Property, and, forbidden to communicate with its Paris headquarters, its work was directed towards producing 23,480 Army lorries from knock-down kits imported from Ford and Chevrolet in Canada, building and fitting bodies to various other types of military vehicles, and numerous other war-effort duties. In 1946, car production was resumed, the necessary permit being granted to Citroën alone among the many foreign manufacturers applying to build vehicles in the UK at this time. Moreover, as the terms of this permit stipulated that the bulk of production should be exported, overseas sales had top priority. Out of the total of 2,309 cars built in 1948, only 500 were sold in the UK. By 1951, this situation had not changed – 2,905 cars were built, but only 498 remained in Britain.

With the same commercial objectives in mind, Citroën's Paris headquarters had originally planned that production of a right-hand-drive version of the 2CV should start at Slough as soon as volume manufacture got under way in France, in 1949. But this plan hit a snag when it was discovered that current British Ministry of Transport regulations prohibited vehicles equipped with inboard brakes. It was therefore not until these rules were relaxed in 1953 that the manufacture and marketing of a British-made 2CV could begin.

As with the other anglicised Citroëns before it, the Slough-built 2CV was something of a hybrid. Its chassis, suspension, engine, transmission and body panels came from France, while its seats, trim, glasswork, lighting equipment and tyres were made in England. The Slough factory itself was responsible for adapting the tubular

Despite its unrivalled economy, the 2CV saloon was regarded in the UK as overly expensive, at least when compared with the Morris Minor. Well over half the examples produced were exported, mainly to Australia and South Africa, where its rugged dependability and durability were better appreciated.

front cross-member containing the steering rack to right-hand-drive form. Assembled on its own track alongside the post-war Traction Avant (or 'Light 15', as it was always known in England), its appearance was subtly adapted to suit British customers, as were its controls, and the result was a car that differed from its Continental-built equivalent in a number of ways.

Perhaps most immediately noticeable was the choice of colour, which, unlike Paris-built examples of the period, could be black, white, cream, green or maroon as well as grey. Another unique external distinguishing feature was the circular badge bearing the words 'Citroën Front Drive' mounted on the bonnet like a figurehead, and a script-lettered Citroën badge at the rear, both of which were fitted in defiance of protestations from Paris about the excess weight penalty this would involve! Unlike their French and Belgian counterparts, British-made 2CVs were also equipped with chromed hubcaps and bumper overriders and semaphore-type direction indicators as standard, and had flap-up half-opening windows in the rear doors as well as in the front.

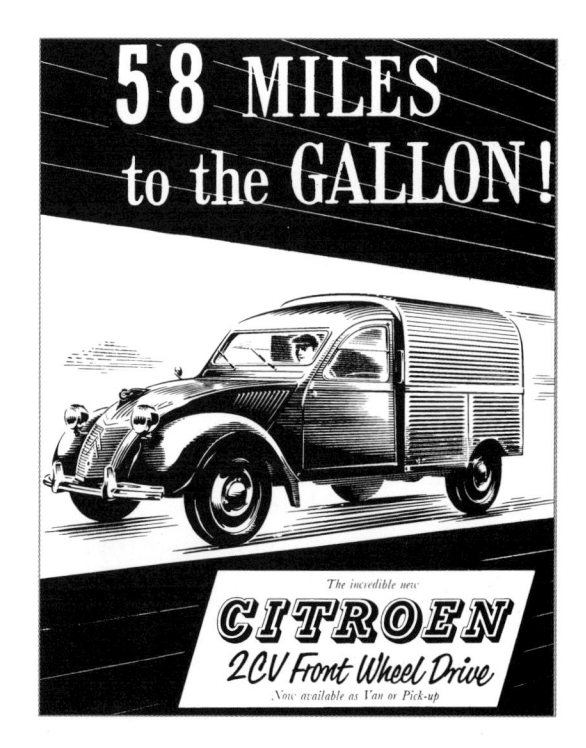

Despite its economy, the right-hand-drive van version failed to catch on among British farmers and tradesmen. Of the 231 examples built, only 84 were sold in the UK.

A view of the interior of the Slough works, c. 1960. Examples of the DS19, also built there at that time, are parked behind the 2CV saloons and vans.

A further Slough innovation present from the outset was a revised type of roof made from leathercloth and fitted with a clear PVC rear window and a metal boot lid, a departure from the norm that the French rudely christened '*la capote anglaise*' ('English cloak' – the French equivalent of 'French letter'). Inside, however, apart from the repositioning of the steering wheel, pedals and instruments from left to right, very little else was altered. The same basic 2CV saloon model was offered throughout the whole seven-year period of production from 1953 to 1960, although, naturally, a succession of progressively uprated engines were fitted as they became available from France, in step with the improvements gradually being made to French- and Belgian-built 2CVs. During that period, 673 saloons were made, of which 340 were exported. But besides these – the Type A (375 cc 9 bhp SAE from 1954 to 1955) and the Type AZ (425 cc 12 bhp SAE from 1954 to 1955 and 425 cc 13 bhp SAE from 1957 to 1960), the Slough factory also produced two commercial variants, the Type AZU van and the Type AZP pick-up, of which a grand total of 363 were made, 147 going abroad. None of the 72 pick-ups made were exported, but 65 went overseas all the same – in service with the Royal Marine Commandos on board the aircraft carriers HMS *Bulwark* and HMS *Albion*, and painted in regulation bronze-green paint. In military trim, minus doors and windows, their light weight and rugged construction made them ideal for helicopter-lifted assault operations, a role they fulfilled until helicopters capable of lifting larger, heavier vehicles came into service with the Fleet Air Arm. At the time of writing, only sixteen of these anglicised, Slough-built 2CVs are known to have survived – 9 saloons, 4 vans and 3 pick-up trucks, all civilian models.

Surprisingly, the 2CV enjoyed a very good press in the UK, being fulsomely praised by many of the motoring

164

journals which road-tested it. 'A vehicle with almost every virtue except speed, silence and good looks,' reported *Motor*, sentiments echoed by its rival *Autocar* which avowed that 'Comment other than praise is confined to criticism of the position of the rear-view mirror' – a trifling quibble considering the extraordinary contrast the car must have made with competing contemporary British and American products. Even that great doyen of British motoring journalists William Boddy, editor of *Motor Sport*, confessed to being impressed. In April 1954, after covering some 2,000 miles in eighteen days at the wheel of a 2CV, he declared that it was 'a splendid, fascinating little car. Its designer, who must be a brilliant engineer indeed, has approached fearlessly the problem of providing a modern people's car. From now on I shall look with scorn at cars of low power output which employ heavy lumps of cast iron surrounded by water for engines, and I shall refuse to regard as an economy car any vehicle which does not give a genuine 60 miles per

The RHD 2CV from Slough was exported throughout the British Commonwealth, including Kenya, where this example was photographed c. 1955.

THE BIJOU

Although it was an official enterprise undertaken with the full backing and approval of the parent company in Paris, the fibreglass-bodied Bijou coupe produced at Slough between January 1960 and August 1964 represented a complete contradiction of the ideas and principles established by the 2CV's creator, Pierre-Jules Boulanger.

When laying down his criteria for the *Toute Petite Voiture* in 1936, he specified that his minimalist car should be 'a simple Spartan form of transport for rural motorists of modest means', ultra-lightweight and devoid of all traces of luxury and beautification. Yet the Bijou followed none of these precepts. Not only was it aimed at affluent suburban motorists, and therefore elaborately styled and trimmed to appeal to middle-class British tastes, but it was also a heavy car, weighing 225 lb (102 kg) more than the standard steel-bodied 2CV saloon – equivalent to carrying an extra adult passenger.

Naturally, all this extra weight affected the Bijou's performance quite dramatically, an effect that was further magnified by its aerodynamically-efficient body shape. For although its 0–40 mph acceleration time of 31.3 seconds was 4 seconds slower than that of the standard car (with which it shared the same 12.5 hp SAE 425 cc engine), its top speed of 50.3 mph (81.00 km/h) was noticeably faster than the 47.2 mph (76 km/h) of the original all-metal version.

But one important aspect of the Bijou's performance was superior by far – its fuel economy and efficiency. Remarkably, it achieved overall fuel consumption figures that were up to 10 per cent better than the standard 2CV – 62.3 mpg (4.5 litres per 100 km) compared to 54 mpg (5.2 litres per 100 km). This was due to its extremely low drag coefficient (cd 0.37) – even better than that of the then current DS19 (cd 0.40), itself acknowledged to be one of the most aerodynamically efficient vehicles of its day. It also represented a massive 30 per cent improvement over the standard 2CV, which, although it had the same frontal area, was measured as having a cd of 0.53 in the comparative tests undertaken at the Motor Industry Research Association's establishment at Nuneaton in September 1960.

Consequently, it can be claimed that the short and truncated life-story of the Bijou was not entirely without merit, as in a number of ways it anticipated many of the future concerns of automobile engineers and designers, producing solutions that pointed the way ahead to the cars of today.

The prototype of the Bijou. Production versions had a greatly enlarged air intake at the front.

The Bijou was offered to the British public from 1960 to 1964, but only 211 were sold. None were assembled or marketed in France.

THE 2CV IN THE UK

One of the first examples of the Bijou goes on sale at a Citroën dealership at Worthing, Sussex, in the autumn of 1960.

Seen here in the delivery hall of Citroën's Slough factory, the fibreglass-bodied Bijou was assembled alongside the DS19. It shared many minor parts with the DS19, including its single spoke steering wheel.

A batch of completed Bijoux leaves the Slough Works in 1964, the year that production ceased. At the outset it had been planned to make 1,000 cars a year, but the rate of production averaged only one per week.

167

A Life on the Ocean Wave

Ironically, Citroën Car's greatest 2CV sales success was a contract negotiated with the Royal Navy to supply sixty-five pick-up truck versions for use in helicopter-lifted operations by the Royal Marine Commandos. Finished with a coat of military bronze-green paint, these vehicles saw active service in Aden, Malaya and Borneo during the counter-terrorist campaigns of the early sixties, based on the Commando carriers HMS *Albion* and HMS *Bulwark*. Apart from the Mini-Moke (which had inadequate ground clearance for military work), the 2CV was the only vehicle light enough to be carried by the Whirlwind Mk7 helicopters then in service with the Fleet Air Arm.

In 1964, however, the Whirlwinds were superseded by Wessex helicopters with a lifting capacity great enough to carry a Land Rover, so the 2CV pick-ups were eventually demobilised. Some soldiered on for a while, employed by the Navy for onshore tasks at dockyards both in the UK and the Far East, but others too worn-out for further service were unceremoniously scrapped by being pushed overboard from the decks of the aircraft carriers in the middle of the Indian Ocean. Certainly, by the end of the sixties, all had vanished.

Evidently very durable and reliable in action, these 2CV pick-ups were reported to be very popular with the troops. To save weight, the Marines removed the doors and window glass and other items, which also allowed them to open fire from within the vehicle if attacked. But unlike the French paratroop units, which used another French-made version of the 2CV pick-up, the Marines never mounted heavy machine guns and recoil-less anti-tank guns on board their pick-ups, as the SAS did with their Land Rovers. Besides acting as a patrol car, carrying a crew of four, the 2CV's main role was to provide cross-country transport for heavy radio equipment and to evacuate casualties.

The first 2CV pick-up to be tested in sea-going conditions was actually a civilian version, with the registration number 33 CPP. This is seen here suspended beneath a FAA Whirlwind helicopter during HMS *Bulwark*'s cruise to the West Indies in 1958.

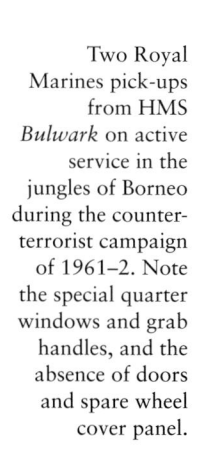

Two Royal Marines pick-ups from HMS *Bulwark* on active service in the jungles of Borneo during the counter-terrorist campaign of 1961–2. Note the special quarter windows and grab handles, and the absence of doors and spare wheel cover panel.

The 2CV in the UK

The prototype Royal Marines 2CV pick-up differed from the standard civilian version only in its bronze green military paint. Consequently, it had all the normal Slough features such as bonnet badge, wing mirrors, semaphore indicators and bumper-mounted numberplates, not fitted to the series RM vehicles.

The 2CV gets the nod from the bowler-hat brigade. A squad of Royal Marines demonstrates the portability of the pick-up to the Minister of Defence, Duncan Sandys in 1957.

gallon.' Praise indeed from this most incisive motoring critic.

Unfortunately, the great British motoring public declined to agree with the professionals. Almost in defiance of these glowing tributes by the experts of the press, the car refused to sell. Part of the reason was the price: when launched in 1953, it cost about £565, of which no less than a third was purchase tax, compared with £511 for a Ford Anglia and £529 for a Morris Minor. Yet, undoubtedly, a far greater drawback was the car's lack of perceived value among British motorists, who have never prized fundamental engineering qualities as highly as their Continental

169

counterparts. Viewed superficially, the 2CV appeared spartan and unrefined, and sounded worse – hardly the kind of neat and nippy second car that would be regarded as a desirable asset by the suburban housewives who represented perhaps its greatest potential market. After all, what was the point of investing a small fortune in a strange, eccentric-looking cross-country vehicle capable of doing 60 mpg through deserts and jungles when all you wanted was a smart little runabout to take the children to school or pop down to the shops or the hairdresser?

After five years of uphill struggle against all the odds, in 1958 Citroën Cars decided on one last desperate effort to win the 2CV a place on the roads of Britain. To make it acceptable to surburban British tastes, its engine and chassis would have to be hidden by sleek new bodywork, offering a proper boot for the shopping. And because the Slough factory had neither the facilities nor the funds for producing steel body pressings, this body would have to be made from fibreglass-reinforced polyester resin, which had the added advantage of being corrosion-free. Accordingly, the well-known designer Peter Kirwan-Taylor (who had already produced that most successful of fibreglass designs, the Lotus Elite) was engaged to style a new two-door, hard-top coupé look for the car. Completely different inside and out, this featured a modish, ultra-modern, aerodynamic body shape, resembling that of Citroën's latest wonder car, the DS19, by then also being built at Slough, and available, like the DS, in a range of

A conventional right-hand-drive 2CV leads a procession of Bijoux from the factory at Fairlie Road, Slough, c. 1960.

THE 2CV IN THE UK

> ### THE 2CV COMMANDO
>
> After its reintroduction on the UK market in 1974, sales of the 2CV took some time to get rolling, but by the end of the decade it had found its niche in Britain and was selling well among the younger generation, the Spot and Beachcomber special editions in particular. This gave the marketing department of Citroën Cars the idea of producing a limited special edition of its very own, with paintwork and trim specifically designed to appeal to British tastes.
>
> The outcome, produced in 1980, was a prototype that has remained an official secret at Citroën ever since – the unique 2CV-6 Commando. Equipped with bolt-on extras such as a jerry-can petrol tank mounted on the rear door, an entrenching tool and a combat radio complete with whiplash aerial, the Commando echoed the military look that was fashionable among young motorists at the time. But instead of being painted in olive drab camouflage paint (which was thought to be too aggressive), the Commando came in a peaceful shade of white, just like the vehicles used by United Nations peacekeeping forces.
>
> Initial market research suggested that the Commando would put up a brave fight in the never-ending battle for sales, so a request was made to France for permission to proceed with the production of a trial batch for press and publicity purposes. Alas, this recommendation was rejected by Citroën's supreme headquarters in Paris, which disapproved of such independent, unilateral marketing campaigns, especially those involving the 2CV. Thus the Commando never saw action on the streets of the UK, and the whole idea was quickly forgotten at Slough, until some photos came to light again.

striking colours. The result was the Bijou, truly one of the oddest (and rarest) cars ever made and sold in Britain. In appearance, if not performance, the Bijou was a kind of DS in miniature, for the trim incorporated many DS components, such as door handles, minor controls and the famous single-spoke steering wheel.

Although this new bodyshell was actually 50 kg heavier than the 2CV's original metal bodywork (equivalent to the burden of an extra adult passenger), the Bijou achieved up to 10 per cent better cruising fuel consumption than the standard car, due to its remarkably low drag coefficient – cd .37 – which was as good as that of the DS. The first prototype was shown at the 1959 Earls Court Motor Show, and production began the following year, with assembly of the Bijou replacing that of the conventional 2CV. The mechanical specification of the Bijou was identical to that of the 425 cc-engined standard 2CV AZ saloon which it superseded.

Alas, the unexpected arrival of the BMC Mini at the very same show put paid to Citroën Cars' hopes of success in the small car field. Now, even with this elaborate disguise, there was absolutely no chance of persuading British motorists to buy the 2CV in sufficient quantities to make the expense of continued UK assembly a worthwhile proposition, so production was discontinued four years later, in 1964. Throughout its short production life, only 211 examples of the Bijou were made, of which a mere 34 are known to

The 'Made-to-Measure' Deux Chevaux

As described in Chapter Two, not least among the requirements listed by Pierre-Jules Boulanger when setting down his famous *cahier des charges* for the design of the *toute petite voiture* had been that it should have adequate headroom to accommodate a tall man wearing a hat. A lean and lanky individual (over 1.7 m tall), who invariably wore a trilby rather than the customary Frenchman's beret, Boulanger insisted that he should be able to enter and exit the car without removing his hat, and this is undoubtedly the reason for the vehicle's unusually high roofline and domed silhouette.

When combined with the 2CV's superbly comfortable seating and flexible suspension, this virtue made the Deuche the ideal contemporary form of transport for invalids or otherwise incapacitated drivers, as was quickly recognised by the medical profession. Many doctors actually went so far as to prescribe the little car as the perfect remedy for patients suffering from backache, slipped discs, and other spinal problems, who would normally find travelling by automobile uncomfortable.

One tall customer that Boulanger could never have envisaged riding in his peasant's car, though, was the crippled British Army officer who was among the first to buy a right-hand-drive example when they went on sale in the United Kingdom towards the end of 1953, four years after production had commenced in Paris.

The notion of a bespoke vehicle, hand-crafted to suit the tastes or physical requirements of affluent drivers from the professional and officer classes as well as the aristocracy, was a tradition in the UK, of course. Numerous coach-building firms still existed to supply tailor-made bodies, constructed to their customer's exact specifications, which could then be fitted on relatively inexpensive chassis supplied by firms like Humber and Armstrong-Siddeley and not merely luxury marques such as Rolls-Royce or Bentley. But a humble 2CV, made-to-measure just like a Saville Row suit? The idea must have seemed ridiculous!

Nevertheless, strange as it may seem, early in 1954 the sales department of Citroën Cars Ltd at Slough received an unusual request from a firm specialising in the supply of cars specially converted or modified to meet the needs of invalids and disabled motorists. Would it be possible for the Slough factory to supply a custom-built version of the 2CV, adapted to suit the particular requirements of one of its customers, whose doctors had specifically recommended the soft suspension of the 2CV? The customer in question was a certain Major E.O. Wanliss of

The unique 2CV saloon custom-built at Slough for Major Wanliss in 1954.

The 2CV in the UK

Lytham St Annes in Lancashire. A regular British Army officer serving with the East Lancashire Regiment at Fulwood Barracks near Preston, the Major had contracted spinal tuberculosis while stationed in Hong Kong before the war, as a result of which he had been forced to undergo a series of operations on his backbone which had left him a semi-invalid, forced to wear a rigid surgical corset to keep his back straight at all times. As a result, the Major – who was six feet three inches tall (1.87 m) – could not bend forward to lower his head, and therefore found it very difficult indeed to get into and out of the driver's seat of a normal car, as well as to drive one. Of all the vehicles that he had tested, only the 2CV combined a comfortable, jolt-free ride with easy entry and exit.

Ever anxious to satisfy prospective customers, the Slough factory agreed to supply (for an unknown price) a custom-built car tailored to accommodate the Major's height and overcome his discomfort at the wheel. The result was, and remains, unique in the history of the Citroën 2CV.

The dimensions of Major Wanliss's car differed from a standard Deuche in a number of interesting ways. Firstly, the driver's individual seat was raised an inch (2.54 cm) off the floor, and its height increased by the fitting of an extra elastic strap to the backrest. Secondly, the

The raised roofline of Major Wanliss's car can be clearly seen in this side view. It was four inches higher than normal.

On account of its outstandingly comfortable ride – unrivalled at the time – the 2CV was specifically recommended by the medical profession for people suffering from back problems.

THE CITROËN 2CV

The Slough-built 2CV had a large full-width back window made from plastic instead of the small glass aperture of the French version. It also had a lockable metal boot lid, not introduced on Paris-built cars until much later.

The Slough-built 2CV carried a special Citroën Front Drive badge on its bonnet. In France no identification was considered necessary apart from the Double Chevron emblem.

steering column was lengthened by an inch, to allow for the increased height of the seat. Thirdly, the gear-change lever was modified and relocated slightly, to correspond with the new higher driving position that would be adopted by Major Wanliss. Fourthly the entire roofline, together with the upper edge of the windscreen, was raised in height by four inches (10.16 cm), not only to provide the necessary extra headroom but also to allow the Major to enjoy the correct field of forward and lateral vision, corresponding to the line of sight experienced by a person of normal height driving a standard, unmodified 2CV. This modification was achieved by separating the upper portion of the side panel pressings from the door frame surrounds, raising the front and centre roof cross-members, extending the door pillars upwards, and then inserting extra metal to fill the resulting gap. A new, much taller windscreen glass was also required, of course.

The car was completed and delivered in the summer of 1954, as is confirmed by its chassis number 8/530102. Few details of the car's service during Major Wanliss's ownership survive, although it is known that it was used for frequent holiday trips to France and Switzerland. On one of these runs its original 375 cc engine was exchanged for the second, 423 cc, version, with which it is equipped today.

Although severely neglected after the Major's death, his 2CV survived in the Preston area, and has recently been restored by its new owner, who acquired it in 1991 in a derelict condition. Though lengthy and extensive, the restoration was quite straightforward; the main difficulty lay in finding suitable modern materials to replace the leather-cloth used by the Slough Works for making the fabric roof and upholstering the seats.

have survived to the present day, despite its non-corroding fibreglass bodywork. Thus, by the close of play, a total of 1,245 2CVs of all types had left the Slough factory – and 493 of these had been despatched abroad.

Within another two years, the entire Slough production line was destined to close, a victim of the decline in demand which began in 1959, following the decision of first the South African government and later the Australian government to impose high rates of import duty on complete vehicles, in order to promote local production. With the establishment of Citroën assembly facilities in Australia and South Africa, supplied direct from France, the Slough factory's principal export markets were lost, leaving spare production capacity that could not be absorbed by home sales. Therefore, in 1966, Citroën Cars' French management deemed that further production was unviable, and the assembly line – by then producing the DS only – was shut down, leaving Slough with a new, reduced role as Citroën's UK sales and replacement parts base.

In 1965, a few Belgian-built right-hand-drive vehicles (originally intended for Nigeria) were imported to fill the gap – but then a further problem arose that was to halt further official 2CV sales in Britain for the next ten years. The introduction of new British seatbelt regulations requiring the fitting of three-point mountings meant that the 2CV would require a modified, stiffened door pillar on which to fit the diagonal belt, and with right-hand-drive sales so low, this was considered uneconomic.

Thus it was not until the global energy crisis of 1974 that the British market again had the chance to recognise the 2CV's outstanding economy and value for money, and demand revived enough to make importing the 2CV in its original form a commercial proposition for Citroën. In the meantime, seatbelt and safety regulations had been standardised throughout the EEC and the 2CV had duly been adapted to conform to this legislation, with front-hinged doors and stronger locks as a bonus. Moreover, its Dyane sisters had already been introduced in right-hand-drive form by Citroën Cars Ltd in 1968, and these, augmented by the ever-increasing numbers of privately imported 2CVs now appearing on British roads, ensured that the reputation of the Citroën 2CV quickly became firmly established in the

A view under the bonnet shows that there were few mechanical differences between Slough- and Paris-built cars. But British export models were always fitted with a large oil-bath aircleaner, primarily for the benefit of the Australian market.

UK among younger, trendier, more adventurous drivers.

Even so, despite the flourishing second-hand market, Jasper Carrott's jokes and Citroën's own witty self-knocking publicity campaign, increases in sales of brand new 2CVs took a long time to materialise. It was not until 1986 (when peak UK imports of 7,520 cars were recorded) that the 2CV reached the zenith of its popularity among British buyers – but by then its star was waning fast in its homeland.

When Citroën Cars Ltd started bringing 2CVs into the UK again in the autumn of 1974 in response to the sudden interest in smaller, more economical cars aroused by the energy crisis, it ignored the 435 cc versions then available and imported only the 602 cc-engined 2CV-6 model. Subsequently, the 2CV-6 Special, Club, Charleston and

LICENSED TO THRILL

After featuring in so many famous films over the years, and appearing alongside many of the cinema's greatest stars, such as Brigitte Bardot, Jeanne Moreau, Jean-Paul Belmondo, and Philippe Noiret, it was inevitable that in 1981, the 2CV should finally achieve international stardom in its own right. Audiences around the world gasped at its amazing performance in the James Bond movie *For Your Eyes Only* – but then, as any 2CV driver will tell you, the 2CV has always been licensed to thrill!

Four cars were specially prepared for the film, fitted with roll-over cages, strengthened suspension systems and 1,015 cc GS engines. With this extra get-away power beneath their bonnets, their top speed was reported to be 95 mph. Escaping from the villains, Bond and his female companion took off through the air in a death-defying leap to evade pursuit. The 2CV's agility had saved lives before, but never in quite so spectacular a way as this! To capitalise on this free publicity, Citroën produced a limited edition of 300 bright-yellow James Bond 2CV-6 007s, complete with bullet-hole decals on the bodywork, but fitted, alas, with standard engines.

The special edition 2CV-6 007, painted bright yellow and decorated with bullet hole decals. Just 300 examples were built, for the French market only.

Dolly models were all introduced to the UK in right-hand-drive form, and also the 1977 2CV Spot special edition, fitted with a 602 cc engine instead of its normal 435 cc unit. The Sahara and the Mehari versions were never sold in the UK, and as for the 2CV and Acadiane vans, no commercial variants were made available in Britain following the demise of 2CV production at Slough. The sales of imported 2CV-type cars, firstly by Citroën Cars Ltd and subsequently by Citroën UK Ltd between 1968 and 1990, finally reached a total of 68,254 2CV saloons and 39,408 Dyanes. Therefore, more than 108,000 Deux Chevaux of all types and origins were sold in Britain by Citroën during the model's lifetime, of which 752 were actually made there. At the time of writing (end of 2004) some 6,260 examples of the 2CV and Dyane remain in regular use on British roads according to the records of the Driver and Vehicle Licensing Authority.

CHAPTER NINE

EXPLORATION & ADVENTURE

Jean-Claude Baudot and Jacques Seguela cross the Atacama Desert in Peru in the course of their 10,000 km round-the-world marathon drive in 1958/9, during which they spent more than 2,247 hours at the wheel. Their travels covered over 100,000 km through fifty countries.

Thanks to its modest thirst for fuel and the nimble way it crosses rough country, the tough but frugal little 2CV has always attracted a particularly footloose and adventurous kind of driver. Right from the start, its robust reliability made it a favourite vehicle among intrepid explorers and long-distance travellers, who recognised a kindred pioneering spirit in its indefatigable energy and enthusiasm for marathon journeys – especially over difficult and dangerous terrain or in adverse climates, where, time and time again, it overcame conditions which defeated far more complicated and expensive machinery. Whether crossing soft, sun-baked desert sand, steaming swamps and jungles or mountainous slopes of rock, ice and snow, the 2CV proved capable of surviving the challenge, unbroken and unbowed. And when the going got really bad, enterprising 2CV explorers found that they could always get out of trouble by dismantling the car and carrying it around the obstacles, piece by piece!

It's true that, lacking power, the very first examples found mountain-climbing something of a problem when fully loaded, so their passengers often had to get out and push on the uphill stretches. But that did not stop Jacques Cornet and Henri Lochon breaking the world altitude record for car travel when, in 1953, they drove their tiny 375 cc vehicle straight to the top of the 17,780 ft Mount Chacaltaya in the Bolivian Andes.

At the time, Cornet and Lochon just happened to be driving from Quebec in Canada to Punte Arenas in Chile, a 52,000 km, 367-day tour of North and South America that also involved crossing the USA from coast to coast. Reaching Chile, they decided to press on to the very tip of Tierra del Fuego, the most southerly point of the continent, and in doing so they travelled over 800 miles further south than any vehicle had ever reached before. Altogether, they crossed seven deserts and sixty-five rivers, and spent 240 nights in the open air, camping in their little car, which, apart from wearing out four sets of tyres and suffering 310 punctures, did not once complain about its ordeal.

The 2CV's long, distinguished expeditionary career really began the year before, when two Parisians, Michel Bernier and Jacques Hugier, left Paris on a 13,588 km circular tour around the Mediterranean coasts of Europe, the Middle East and North Africa. Today, with the Mediterranean encircled by multi-lane highways, this does not sound like much of a trip, but in those days, communications in the countries of the Middle East and North Africa had changed little since the Middle Ages, and there were few made-up roads of any kind for the greater part of the journey.

Having caught the wanderlust in no uncertain fashion, the following year, Michel Bernier put his 2CV on board a freighter in Amsterdam and sailed for Cape Town, this time with a new companion, Jacques Duvey, as mechanic and co-driver. On 19 December 1953, the intrepid pair of globe-trotters left the Cape and headed northwards into the African bush, carrying just the minimum of spares – two spare spark plugs, two valves, two contact-breaker sets, two spare headlight bulbs, two metre-long lengths of perforated metal track and a nylon tow rope. Their destination was Algiers, via Rhodesia, the Congo, Nigeria and the Sahara, a trek they completed in twenty-five days, driving non-stop.

Arriving home in Paris on 13 January 1954, Bernier and Duvey scarcely paused for rest, and just had time to change the oil, plugs, tyres and brake shoes of their car before setting off again. This time they had entered their 2CV in the Monte Carlo Rally! Starting in Oslo two days later, they went on to

Jacques Cornet and Henri Lochon break the world altitude record for motor travel in 1953, by taking their 375 cc-engined 2CV to the top of Mount Chacaltaya (5,420 metres) in the Bolivian Andes, while driving from northern Canada to the southernmost tip of Chile.

179

While passing through London, Baudot and Seguela pause briefly outside St James's Palace.

cover the 17,500 km course in twenty-four days without serious problems, and would have come first in their class had it not been for a dynamo problem which cost them a vital forty minutes. On their next racing outing in the 1955 Mille Miglia, however, they were more successful, completing 1,597 km in twenty hours to be placed 271st out of 652 entrants, all of them in very much bigger and more powerful sports cars.

Naturally, the very first French car to be driven round the world was a 425 cc Type AZ 2CV saloon, owned by Jacques Seguela and Jean-Claude Baudot. Setting out from Paris in October 1958 and returning in November the following year, the pair passed through fifty countries and covered over 100,000 km, travelling an average of 250 km a day. En route they crossed six seas and five continents, traversed eight deserts and five mountain ranges, spent a total of 2,247 hours at the wheel, and used 5,000 litres of petrol – thus achieving an average fuel consumption of 46 mpg.

Apart from being attacked by bandits in Siam and suffering a serious collision with a runaway truck in Pakistan, there were no major mechanical disasters, except for a trifling incident in the middle of the Atacama Desert in Chile. Here, loosened by vibration caused by the rutted, corrugated road surface, the car's gearbox drainplug fell out, spilling the oil – but the car was able to continue on its way regardless, lubricated by a bunch of squashed bananas. Later, in India, Baudot and Seguela noticed that the 2CV's engine required attention. Removing it from the car unaided, the two friends carried it with their luggage to the nearest cheap hotel. Here they dismantled it and reground the valves on a bedside table.

Indeed, by the late fifties, the car's reputation for adventure was already so well established that Citroën had begun to offer travellers an annual prize for the most hazardous long-range journey undertaken in a 2CV, the Prix Citroën Tour du Monde. The generous prize of a

EXPLORATION & ADVENTURE

million old francs encouraged enthusiasts to venture even further afield, and in ever greater numbers, so that in the end the competition had to be abandoned due to its sheer popularity. In their enthusiasm, some reckless drivers were literally going too far!

To replace it, Citroën's Director of Public Relations, Jacques Wolgensinger, came up with an exciting new idea – to stage an officially organised mass 'raid' or rally from Paris to Kabul in Afghanistan and back, by the toughest, most demanding route. No fewer than 1,300 young motorists from eighteen countries took part, taking twenty-eight days to drive 494 assorted 2CV-type vehicles a total of 17,000 km during the summer of 1970. So successful was this adventure that the following July, a similar 'raid' to Persepolis in southern Iran was organised. This time, 467 crews selected from almost 4,000 applicants joined in the fun, representing Holland, Germany, Switzerland, Belgium, Luxemburg, Italy, Spain, Portugal, Norway and Sweden, as well as France. The third, final and most impressive mass 2CV rally organised – and led – by Wolgensinger was the famous Citroën-Berliet Raid Afrique of 1973, an arduous mission that combined adventure and discovery with episodes of bold and enterprising publicity. On 22 September that year, a convoy of hand-picked cars and crews set out from the Place de la Concorde in Paris, on an expedition to cross the wilderness of North West Africa, on a 50,000 mile route traversing the Hoggar Mountains and the forbidding Ténéré Desert region of the Sahara, a vast area of shifting sand almost twice the size of France and never before conquered by conventional 2×4 wheeled motor cars.

After travelling to Africa by sea from Le Havre, the sixty 2CVs and Dyanes of the expedition left Abidjan on the Ivory

Le Raid Afrique 1973. One of the convoy of sixty 2CVs crosses the North African desert, en route from Abidjan to Tunis. Some 8,000 km were covered in thirty-four days by a team of one hundred young drivers and co-pilots.

THE CITROËN 2CV

Ten years before the advent of the Paris–Dakar race, the 2CV pioneered the way! Despite the extreme conditions, not one single car retired.

The route crossed the vast Ténère wilderness, normally forbidden to conventional vehicles and never previously conquered by an ordinary road-going family saloon.

Coast on 29 October 1973, heading north to Tunis and crossing the countries of Upper Volta, Niger, Algeria and Tunisia. On board were a total of 200 participants, made up of 100 young French 2CV enthusiasts (98 males and 8 females) plus 49 mechanics, 10 assistants, 10 medics, 9 cameramen and sound recordists, 11 photographers, 7 journalists and 4 artists. Accompanying the crews were eight Berliet lorries carrying fuel, water, food supplies, radio equipment and spare parts, plus further support personnel, including representatives of Citroën's Competition and Publicity departments.

By early December, all had arrived safely back in France, having reached Tunis on 28 November, exactly on schedule. En route they had covered 8,000 km in thirty-four days of hard driving across trackless, unsignposted territory, encountering blistering temperatures by day and freezing cold by night. Not a single car suffered a major breakdown or significant structural damage. Ten years before the first Paris–Dakar all-terrain vehicle race was run across the same region, the 2CV had shown the world exactly how a car should be designed and built to survive the risks and dangers of such an expedition, beyond the very fringes of civilisation.

Another of Jacques Wolgensinger's innovations was the idea of 2CV Cross – speed trials carried out on a rough and bumpy cross-country circuit. The very first meeting took place in July 1972 in a disused quarry at Argenton-sur-Creuse, officially organised and sponsored by Citroën. Pop-Cross proved so successful that it soon caught on all over Europe, developing into a fully fledged sport rivalling stock-car racing in popularity with drivers and spectators alike. By 1976, over a thousand European drivers were regularly competing in 2CV Cross events, which attracted very large crowds. Unlike stock-car racing, however, under 2CV Cross rules, deliberate collisions and dangerous ramming were forbidden. The course was carefully constructed to prevent competitors exceeding the 45 mph speed limit, and the cars themselves were not allowed to be modified or souped up, although for maximum safety the window glass and rear doors were removed, a roll bar was fitted, a steel panel was welded into the

EXPLORATION & ADVENTURE

The sport of 2CV Cross, introduced in France in July 1972, soon proved immensely popular right across western Europe, including the UK.

roof and a maximum of a mere 5 litres of petrol was permitted at the start of a race. The drivers wore crash helmets, gloves and full safety harnesses, so although spectacular crashes sometimes occurred, these accidents were seldom disastrous, and injuries were rare. As might be expected with the 2CV, competitors claimed that Pop-Cross was much more fun – and far less expensive – than traditional motor racing and rallying.

Today, the popularity of Pop-Cross has declined somewhat – perhaps because the availability of cheap 2CV

Despite appearances, 2CV Cross was a harmless pastime. Unlike in stock-car racing, deliberate collisions and dangerous ramming were banned!

183

A poster produced by the Yacco oil company, the sponsors, celebrating the 2CV's success in establishing nine international endurance records in 1953.

A RECORD-BREAKER

Apart from achieving numerous motor industry records for production and longevity, believe it or not, the 2CV also won a notable motor sport competition.

On 27 September 1953, at the Montlhéry track near Paris, a special-bodied, modified 2CV sponsored by the French oil company Yacco and driven by Pierre Barbot and Jean Vinatier established nine new international Class Y (350 cc) speed and distance records, including twelve hours at an average speed of 56.85 mph and twenty-four hours at an average speed of 53.14 mph. For this attempt, the car's engine capacity was reduced to 348 cc and its weight to 475 kg.

bangers has also diminished. With cars becoming scarcer and more valuable, its place has been taken by Le Mans-style endurance races, such as the twenty-four-hour race held at Mondello Park near Dublin, attracting seriously enthusiastic, highly experienced semi-professional racing drivers.

CHAPTER TEN

2CV Publicity & Advertising

Many motorists, unaware of the mysterious inner workings of the motor industry, are baffled by the enormous effort and expense that goes into selling even the simplest and cheapest of cars. Why is advertising necessary when a model is already on the road in vast numbers and has become a familiar sight, openly available for inspection in any high street garage or parking lot? Why, in particular, did the creative energy expended in publicising the 2CV increase in step with its advancing years, rather than diminish? And why was this huge investment expended on advertising and marketing, rather than on improving and updating the product itself?

Initially, the 2CV sold well without the back-up of a big publicity machine, and in the seller's market of its early years, when cars were scarce and demand exceeded supply, word-of-mouth recommendation was enough to bring in potential buyers in huge numbers. Indeed, Pierre-Jules Boulanger's personal dislike of publicity was so strongly entrenched that the 2CV was launched in 1948 almost entirely without the benefit of advertising and promotion: a modest leaflet produced by Boulanger himself was all that was offered to prospective customers by way of information.

But by the late fifties, the situation had altered. Production of the 2CV had reached over 200,000 units a year, and the urgent demands of its ever-moving assembly lines, pushing out more than 500 vehicles a day, meant that Citroën was forced to actively seek out new customers and encourage a revival of interest in the car. So, in 1960, its current Managing Director, Pierre Bercot (who had taken over after Boulanger's death in 1950), at last took the step of establishing a proper marketing and advertising policy for the 2CV. To increase sales, the strategy was to widen the market by creating a completely new image for the car – one which, although stressing its simplicity and economy, would play down its utilitarian, agricultural origins, and position it upmarket as the perfect means of every-day transport for hard-up young professionals, and the ideal runabout or second car for more affluent, middle-class, urban motorists. A promise of relaxed, informal reliability and a friendly, unthreatening unconventionality was the keynote of this marketing campaign.

The Citroën 2CV

One of the earliest examples of 2CV advertising was this modest little leaflet produced by P.-J. Boulanger. When it finally went on sale, the Deuche sold well enough by word of mouth, without the need for expensive publicity.

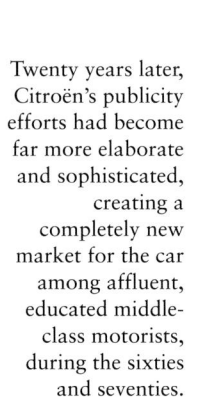

Twenty years later, Citroën's publicity efforts had become far more elaborate and sophisticated, creating a completely new market for the car among affluent, educated middle-class motorists, during the sixties and seventies.

To help establish this new, laid-back, fun-loving personality in the public's mind, Citroën engaged a team of young and talented publicity experts, who in turn employed the services of some of France's most celebrated graphic designers, illustrators and photographers. Undoubtedly, the resulting series of attractive and effective advertisements, posters, brochures and catalogues that followed throughout the next decade gave the 2CV a second lease of life.

The witty and inventive advertising was the work of Citroën's own Director of Publicity, Claude Puech (who reputedly had ten new ideas every day), while the stylish and imaginative brochures were designed by Robert Delpire, head of the Delpire Agency. In these brochures and catalogues, the copy came from the pen of Citroën's own Director of Public Relations, Jacques Wolgensinger. 'More than a car – a way of life,' was the headline in a notable example.

It can be argued that apart from Boulanger and his original team of engineers and designers, no individual made a greater contribution to the long-term success of the 2CV than Wolgensinger. It was largely through his influence that in the sixties the car gradually shed its sombre, grey paintwork and began to appear in a range of vivid primary colours – and it was he who encouraged this new, youthful image by devising the famous series of 2CV 'raids', rallies and Pop-Cross events in which he actually took part. By all accounts, it was Wolgensinger who recruited Hergé's much-loved cartoon character Tin-Tin to appear in the 2CV's sales literature, and it was he who persuaded Citroën to restore the pre-war prototype that was discovered in 1968, hidden in a barn at La Ferté-Vidame, and then put it on show around the world. No wonder that, enhanced and polished by Wolgensinger's inspired and untiring efforts, the 2CV's reputation shone ever more brightly year by year, until it achieved the status of an international cult. Soon, as 2CV ownership spread through all strata of society, not just in France but right across Europe and beyond, the car became a legend, instantly recognised in every corner of the motoring world.

Later, this same marketing strategy was repeated in the UK, with equal success. When the 2CV was reintroduced on to the British market in 1975, sales were initially disappointing, interest being still confined to a narrow band of fiercely loyal Citroën enthusiasts. But then, in the late seventies, a highly original and intelligent advertising campaign was launched, aimed principally at educated but impecunious middle-class professional customers – for example, francophile social workers, school teachers or polytechnic lecturers – and

The 2CV was always noted for a relaxed and humorous style of publicity in its native land, in complete contrast to the portentous and bombastic tone normally adopted by car advertising.

The Citroën 2CV

This informal, honest approach to advertising was also adopted with great success in the United Kingdom. An award-winning newspaper campaign running in the *Guardian* during the late seventies helped to create a revitalised, youthful image for the car, making it *de rigueur* as a mode of transport for non-conformists.

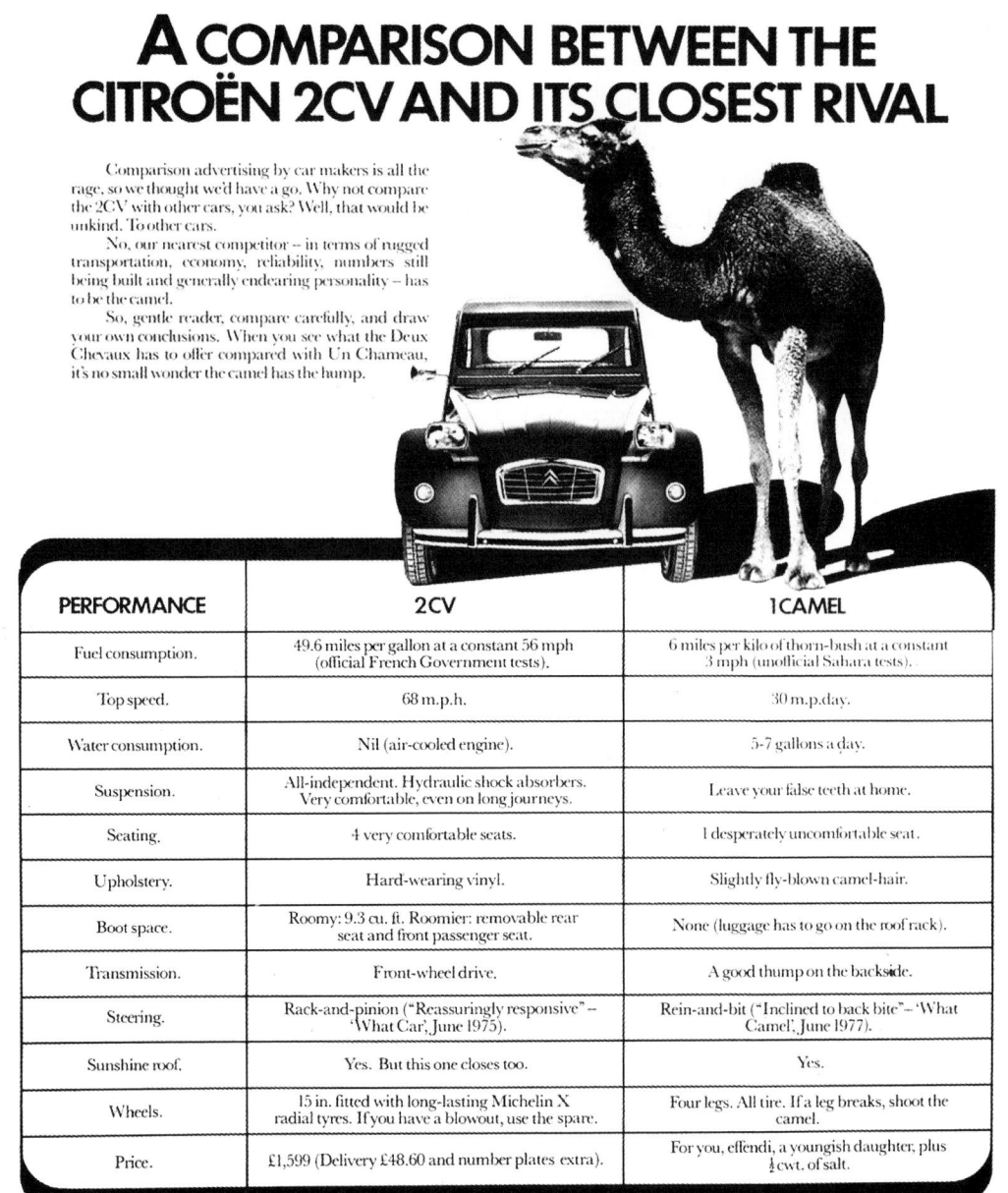

A COMPARISON BETWEEN THE CITROËN 2CV AND ITS CLOSEST RIVAL

Comparison advertising by car makers is all the rage, so we thought we'd have a go. Why not compare the 2CV with other cars, you ask? Well, that would be unkind. To other cars.

No, our nearest competitor – in terms of rugged transportation, economy, reliability, numbers still being built and generally endearing personality – has to be the camel.

So, gentle reader, compare carefully, and draw your own conclusions. When you see what the Deux Chevaux has to offer compared with Un Chameau, it's no small wonder the camel has the hump.

PERFORMANCE	2CV	1 CAMEL
Fuel consumption.	49.6 miles per gallon at a constant 56 mph (official French Government tests).	6 miles per kilo of thorn-bush at a constant 3 mph (unofficial Sahara tests).
Top speed.	68 m.p.h.	30 m.p.day.
Water consumption.	Nil (air-cooled engine).	5-7 gallons a day.
Suspension.	All-independent. Hydraulic shock absorbers. Very comfortable, even on long journeys.	Leave your false teeth at home.
Seating.	4 very comfortable seats.	1 desperately uncomfortable seat.
Upholstery.	Hard-wearing vinyl.	Slightly fly-blown camel-hair.
Boot space.	Roomy: 9.3 cu. ft. Roomier: removable rear seat and front passenger seat.	None (luggage has to go on the roof rack).
Transmission.	Front-wheel drive.	A good thump on the backside.
Steering.	Rack-and-pinion ("Reassuringly responsive" – 'What Car', June 1975).	Rein-and-bit ("Inclined to back bite" – 'What Camel', June 1977).
Sunshine roof.	Yes. But this one closes too.	Yes.
Wheels.	15 in. fitted with long-lasting Michelin X radial tyres. If you have a blowout, use the spare.	Four legs. All tire. If a leg breaks, shoot the camel.
Price.	£1,599 (Delivery £48.60 and number plates extra).	For you, effendi, a youngish daughter, plus ¼ cwt. of salt.

CITROËN 2CV

appearing exclusively in the *Guardian* newspaper; in other words, exactly the kind of motorists that were subsequently depicted as typical 2CV drivers in Posy Simmonds's *Guardian* cartoons. Low-key and soft-selling in tone, off-beat, humorous and self-knocking in content, these ads found their target with precision, widening interest and opening up a valuable new niche market for the car.

With the Citroën 2CV firmly identified as the archetypal anti-car for chic radicals – a vehicle that made a statement about the owner's scale of values, displaying scorn for conspicuous consumption or expense-account living and a rejection of the automobile's role as a status symbol – sales took a sudden upward leap, and kept on climbing. At the high point, in 1986, over 7,500 were sold in the UK.

Ironically, although they had been among the last to latch on to the 2CV's unique attractions, Citroën's British customers were among the first to protest at its impending demise. In 1987, as a mark of their disapproval at news of the imminent cessation of production at Levallois, the British enthusiasts' club, 2CV GB, organised a 'Save the 2CV' campaign, and arranged for a special 'protest car' to be presented to Citroën's management in Paris. Besides the message '*Vive la Deux Chevaux*', the body panels bore thousands of signatures collected from the members of other 2CV clubs all over Europe, acting as a mobile petition demanding that the 2CV's life should be spared.

Engineers and designers may give birth to a car, and motoring journalists may ensure that the infant vehicle gets off to a successful start in life, but ultimately it is the work of advertising and marketing people that keeps a car alive and fresh in the minds of the public, preserving its long-term popularity, and preventing its makers from sending it to an early grave. The story of the 2CV provides a case in point. Beginning its career on the road as a masterpiece of engineering and design, by the end of its life it had become as much a marvel of the art of publicity and promotion as a triumph of science and technology.

Off-beat, self-knocking humour was cleverly used to position the 'Tin Snail' as the essence of radical chic – the only real motoring alternative for the alternative society!

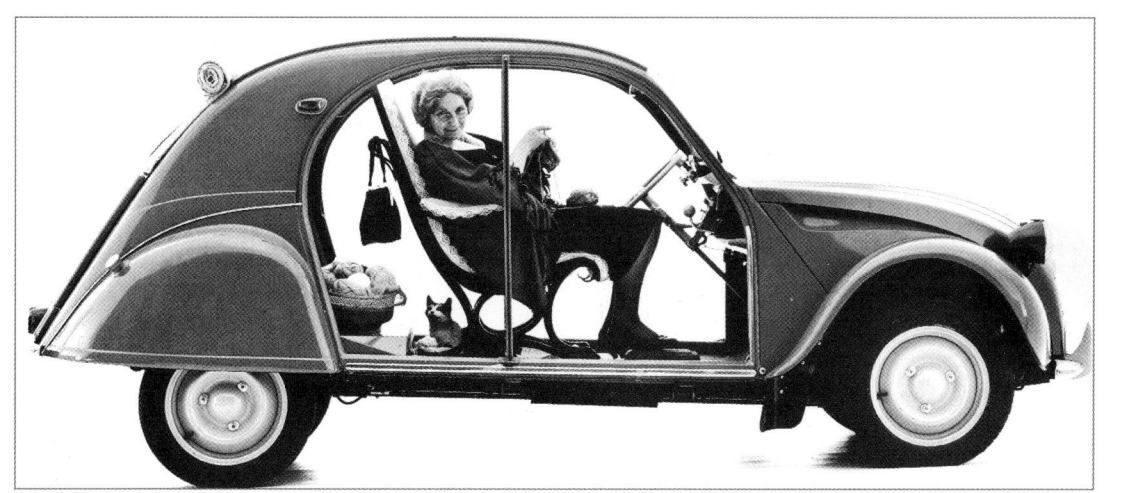

A publicity shot taken for a French brochure, published in 1963. The copy read: 'It's exactly as if I was in my armchair at home. The doctor has prescribed the 2CV for my backache, says grandmother.' *Incroyable mais vrai* – the claim was actually based on medical facts!

The Citroën 2CV

By the early eighties, the 2CV had become so popular among the francophile *bien-pensants* of London NW1 that Posy Simmonds had begun to include it in her famous *Guardian* cartoon strip, Lingua Franca. This example was published in September 1982.

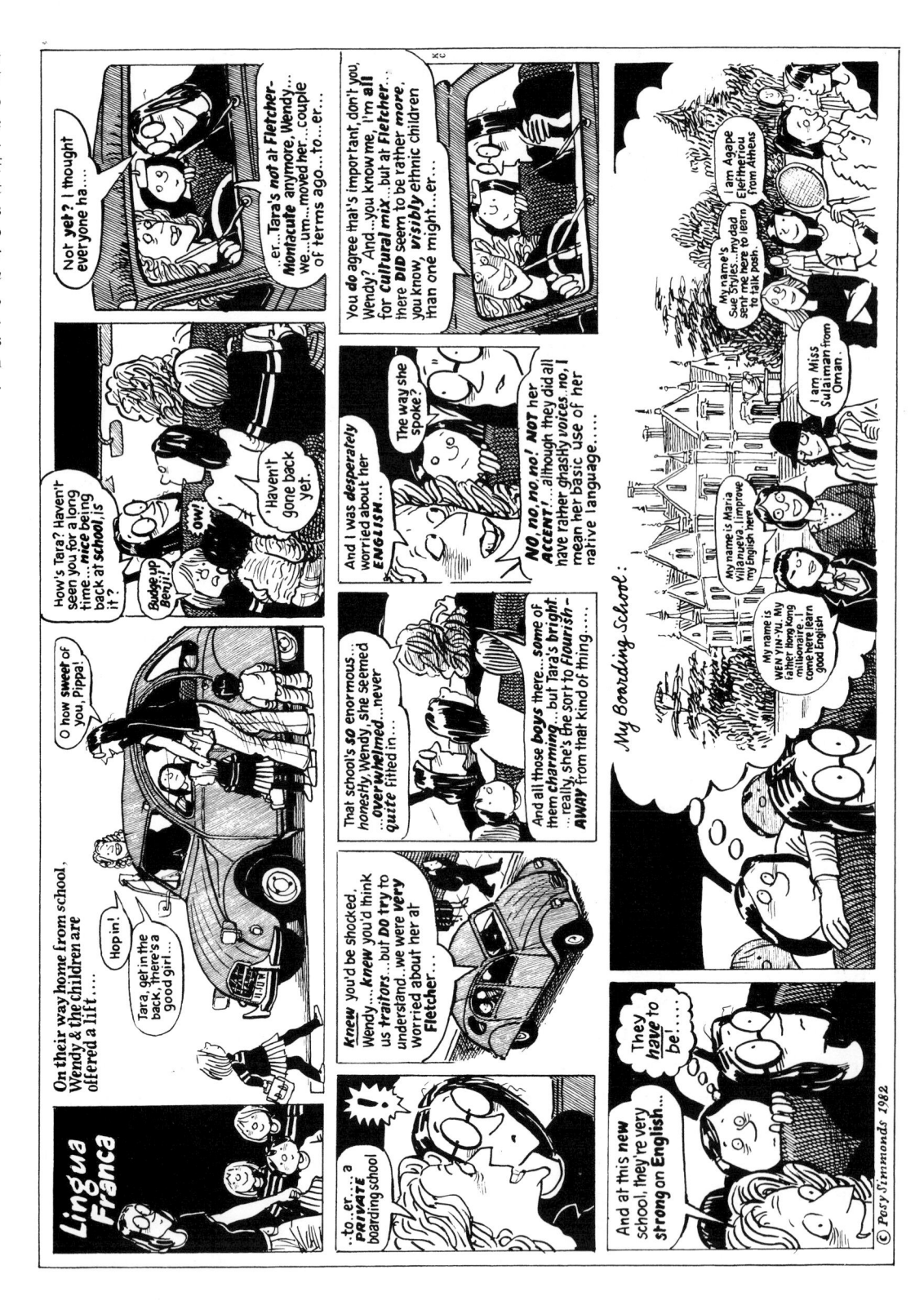

CHAPTER ELEVEN

THE 2CV'S CONTINENTAL COMPETITORS

The social and political changes that occurred on the Continent during the late thirties had a profound and lasting impact on the motor industry of France, as elsewhere in Europe. The introduction of higher wages and paid holidays that followed recovery from the Depression brought about much higher standards of living among ordinary working families, creating in turn a new and ever more lucrative source of demand for automobiles, hitherto the preserve of the middle and upper classes. Motor manufacturers and designers responded to this development with alacrity, but motivated as much by a sense of philanthropy as by opportunism. The concept of a 'people's car' that would bring mobility and independence to the masses became an industrial crusade. As we have seen, the idealism that energised the creation of the 2CV was just one expression of this enlightened objective, the realisation of which was postponed by the outbreak of war in 1939.

After this interruption, in the Europe of the late forties, at least four other important and influential cars emerged to fulfil this pent-up demand, in addition to the 2CV. Conceived, like the 2CV, well before the Second World War, but not produced or sold in great numbers until long after it was over, these vehicles were the Renault 4CV and the Panhard Dyna in France, the Fiat Topolino in Italy and, of course, the Volkswagen Beetle in Germany. The two great British contenders for the title of 'people's car', the Morris Minor of 1949 and the BMC Mini of 1959, arrived far too late to pose any competition to the 2CV, at least in its native land. But it is interesting to note that they, too, were created by a designer with a European background, Sir Alec Issigonis. Unlike some of his more insular British colleagues, Issigonis always adopted an international perspective in his work, being greatly influenced by Continental automobile engineering practice, and particularly by the ideas then emanating from Citroën.

Yet although these other rival 'people's cars' were all very different from the 2CV, they were also entirely different from the small cars of the twenties, such as the Peugeot Quadrillette, Austin 7 and André Citroën's own *Petite Citron*, the 5CV Type C2 and C3. Instead of merely being miniaturised versions of the big cars of their era, these minicars (as they were called in the motoring press even

The Citroën 2CV

The first European people's car was the Fiat 500 or Topolino. Although designed in Italy, it actually made its first appearance before the public in France in April 1936, three months before it arrived in Italy.

then) were fully fledged automobiles intended for all-round transport duties, not just runabouts. The design philosophy behind them all was entirely uncompromising: although minimal in dimensions, their size resulted merely from the need to reduce manufacturing and running costs to the minimum, rather than any urge to eliminate all traces of engineering complexity and sophistication. They represented, in effect, a return to the concept of the Model T Ford, a car of universal capabilities and appeal, designed to be produced and sold in vast numbers at the cheapest possible price, but to offer a very high standard of all-round performance and value for money.

In fact, the first of these five important 'people's cars' to appear on the market in Europe, and therefore in France, did so well before the war. This was the Fiat 500, designed by Dante Giacosa in Italy. Launched in 1936, it rapidly earned the affectionate nickname 'Topolino' ('Mickey Mouse'). Powered by a 596 cc side-valve engine driving the rear wheels through a propshaft and differential located in the conventional way, it was capable of carrying two people plus 110 lb of luggage to the dizzy top speed of 53 mph. Unfortunately, the confined interior layout imposed by fitting a conventional engine and transmission within a short 2 m wheelbase meant that seating space was severely restricted – when carrying extra adults (one) or children (two), the passengers had to ride on cushions placed in the boot! Nevertheless, by virtue of the excellent ride and road-holding conferred by its independent front suspension and hydraulic brakes, the Topolino exerted a powerful influence and incentive on automobile designers and manufacturers in France, spurring them on to compete in the popular-car market, but using rather different technical solutions. As the Simca Cinq, the Topolino was marketed in France under licence by Simca from 1936 until 1940, and again from 1946 until 1949.

Of even greater long-term technical significance, at least in France, was the highly advanced, front-wheel-drive Panhard Dyna X, which first appeared at the 1946 Paris Motor Show. Entering production in 1948, it continued in assembly until 1953, powered, like the 2CV, by an extremely sophisticated and compact air-cooled flat-twin engine. Noted for its lively performance and high cruising speed – around 80 mph – the four-door, four-seater Dyna X was fitted with an ultra-lightweight, aerodynamic bodyshell weighing only 98.5 kg, which helped reduce its kerb weight to less than 400 kg.

In fact, this car was a revamped version of a much older 'people's car' design, the so-called Aluminium-Français-Grégoire (AFG) prototype, which had evolved from pre-war studies. The brainchild of Jean-Albert Grégoire (the leading French exponent of front-wheel drive, who earlier had been closely involved in the design of the Citroën Traction Avant, the Amilcar Compound and the creation of his own Tracta marque in the thirties), the AFG was another concept car developed in secret before and during the Occupation. First produced in prototype form in 1942, its principal *raison d'être* was to demonstrate the virtues of aluminium alloys in automobile construction. Powered by a 594 cc flat-twin air-cooled engine also designed by Grégoire, it featured all-independent suspension, rack and pinion steering, and a chassis formed from Alpax light-alloy castings bolted together, on which was mounted a bodyshell comprising a frame and panels also made from light-weight aluminium. The engine was mounted ahead of the front transaxle, so that the car's mass was concentrated in the nose, as on the 2CV. Tipping the scales at only 396 kg (69 per cent less than the Fiat Topolino, of identical wheelbase and track dimensions), the AFG had a top speed of over 60 mph and an average fuel consumption of 71 mpg at a constant 30 mph.

As we have seen from the story of the 2CV, light-alloy panels and castings were viewed as the wonder materials of the future by the French motor industry in the early forties, and not just by serving to overcome the problems caused by a general shortage of steel. It was also hoped that by allowing substantial savings in the weight of vehicles, all-aluminium construction would produce dramatic improvements in performance and fuel economy, to the national advantage, France then being somewhat less than self-sufficient as an energy producer. In fact, later experience

During the Second World War the task of producing an inexpensive popular car for the post-war years was investigated by designers other than those working on the 2CV at Citroën! Another notably advanced design developed in secret during the Occupation was the light-weight, all-alloy prototype designed by Jean-Albert Grégoire for the Aluminium Français company. Like the 2CV, this also featured an air-cooled flat-twin engine driving the front wheels.

After the war, a scheme to build a right-hand-drive version of the AFG prototype in England was proposed by Grantham Productions Ltd, a company run by Denis Kendall, the Member of Parliament for Grantham, who had previously been the head of production at Citroën's Quai de Javel factory. Called the Kendall 6HP and priced at only £200 plus tax, its publicity described it as 'The minor car with major performance' – 60 mph and 60 mpg were claimed. But the venture collapsed in 1947, before a single vehicle had been built or sold.

showed that such materials were not just expensive and difficult to use in mass-production practice, but they also consumed more energy overall. Indeed, it soon became apparent that in the field of motor transport at least, any energy savings achieved by lowering fuel consumption through a reduction of the weight of vehicles were soon cancelled out by the very high energy consumption involved in the smelting of aluminium alloys and the manufacture of such light-alloy components.

Four further AFG prototypes were funded immediately after the war by the Aluminium Français company and loaned to the four big French manufacturers, Citroën, Renault, Peugeot and Simca, for testing purposes, in the hope of persuading one of them to acquire the manufacturing rights. But there were no takers, for by then each of these companies had its own secret 'people's car' project well under way.

So, under the provisions of the state-sponsored Plan Pons, the AFG design eventually passed to the Panhard firm, which made it the foundation of its post-war revival, though using an alternative flat-twin air-cooled engine designed by Louis Delagarde, having a capacity of 610 cc and a power output of 22 bhp, later increased to 850 cc and 42 bhp. Capable of running for over 100,000 km without overhaul – unusual reliability for that era – this engine boasted such refinements as roller-type main bearings and torsion bar valve springs. Mounted on a conventional steel chassis frame, the distinctive, redesigned four-seater bodies (four-door, as opposed to the two-door configuration of the AFG, and also having a different front end treatment) were made by Facel-Metallon, a specialist in light-alloy construction, which later achieved distinction in its own right as the creator of the prestigious Facel-Véga marque.

Successively revised and improved, the Dyna design concept, based on the AFG, remained in production until 1967 in the shape of the Panhard 24CT Tigre, although, stage by stage, the aluminium used in its construction was entirely replaced by steel, except in the case of the engine. Ultimately, the swept volume of this tiny power plant was expanded to 848 cc, producing 60 bhp, so that the Panhard Tigre could cruise effortlessly at 100 mph while returning 35 mpg overall.

There were plans to build a right-hand-drive version of the AFG in the UK at that time. Late in 1945, the buccaneering entrepreneur and MP for Grantham, Denis Kendall, announced an ambitious scheme to manufacture a British 'people's car' capable of 60 mph and 60 mpg. Billed as 'the minor car with major performance' and priced at only £250, including £50 purchase tax, the vehicle was to be yet another version

Grégoire's AFG design was finally taken up by Panhard in France, which built it in modified four-door form as the 3CV Dyna X. First exhibited at the Paris Motor Show in October 1946, it entered production in 1948 and remained on sale in its original form until 1953.

of Grégoire's design, powered by the 6 hp 594 cc engine, and built under licence in large numbers at a factory in Kendall's Grantham constituency. An automobile engineer by profession, Denis Kendall had gained experience with General Motors and the Budd Corporation in America before working in France during the thirties as head of production at André Citroën's Quai de Javel factory in Paris, so he knew most of the leading figures of the French auto industry, including Grégoire, as friends and colleagues. But the ambitious Grantham Productions project failed within a few months, in 1947, before so much as a single production car had been built and sold. After the liquidation of the Kendall company, the tooling and prototypes of the right-hand-drive AFG car were disposed of by the receiver to the Australian firm Hartnett of Melbourne, which managed to build about 120 examples before it also went to the wall, in the early fifties.

Naturally, the newly nationalised Renault firm was also one of the very first potential manufacturers to carry out an appraisal of the AFG, but here the little front-wheel-drive car met with scant interest. Throughout his lifetime, the company's founder, Louis Renault, had always opposed the notion of front-wheel-drive, and after his demise, his successors continued to uphold his prejudices. Another of their reasons for rejecting the AFG was that they already had a 'people's car' of their own almost ready for production. The existence of this vehicle, the Renault 4CV, was revealed to the world at large at the Paris Motor Show in October 1946, though its manufacture and marketing did not begin until the autumn of the following year. Apart from sharing a similar type of road wheel with spoked cast alloy centres which, lined with cast-iron cylinders, also served as brake drums (a bright idea that Renault had borrowed from Grégoire), the car itself was the complete technical antithesis of the AFG, having a rear-wheel-drive layout, similar to that of the VW Beetle.

The Renault 4CV was yet another French car that had been designed and developed in secret during the war, like the 2CV, in defiance of the German decree forbidding such activities. Inspired and influenced by the thinking of Ferdinand Porsche, its creators had begun their studies virtually at the outset of the Occupation in 1940, constructing their first clandestine prototype as early as 1942, so by the time of the Liberation, its final design was fully resolved. Consequently, in 1945, when the French government reached its brave decision to rebuild the war-ravaged Renault factories and to recommence production of private cars on a grand scale, it fell to the Renault 4CV to be the vehicle that, above all others, put the French motorist back on the road. In fact, it was the first high-volume production European 'people's car', for its rate of assembly at the Ile de Séguin factory in Paris during those early post-war years far outstripped that of the VW Beetle at Wolfsburg.

Initially painted in an odd pale creamy-yellow shade, reputedly using stocks of paint once used on the vehicles of the German Afrika Korps, it rapidly acquired the nickname 'the little pat of butter'. Given top political priority and state backing using funds provided by the USA under the Marshall Aid Plan (an advantage not enjoyed by Citroën), by 1948 production of the Renault 4CV was running at 300 vehicles a day, and by 1950 it was 400, or roughly 120,000 per year, a vastly higher rate of production than that experienced by the 2CV at that point in its career. It was not until the mid-fifties that the sales success of the 4CV was overtaken by that of the VW Beetle. By 1960, over a million examples of the 4CV had been built, making the 'butterpat' the first French car ever to achieve this distinction.

Capable of a top speed of 68 mph and of returning an average fuel consumption of 49.5 mpg, the four-door, four-seater Renault 4CV saloon was powered by a 17 bhp four-cylinder water-cooled engine mounted at the rear and located aft of the rear axle, overhanging the wheelbase. When coupled, as it was, with Porsche's unfortunate swing-axle rear suspension arrangements, similar to those seen on the Beetle, this adverse distribution of weight gave the car decidedly skittish and slippery handling characteristics, so much so that the 'butterpat' allusion may well have been an ironic pun coined by contemporary French motorists! In 1961, after fourteen years of continuous production, the 4CV was abandoned in favour of an entirely new replacement called, simply, the Renault 4, total production having reached 1,105,547 examples.

Disapproval of the Renault 4CV was not confined to its poor road-holding,

The first European people's car to sell in large numbers was the rear-engined Renault 4CV, first exhibited at the Paris Motor Show in October 1946, but developed in secret during the Occupation. Its technical debt to the Volkswagen Beetle can clearly be seen from this prototype, built in 1942.

however. Its lack of passenger and luggage space also prompted criticism, for thanks to its rear-wheel-drive layout, its interior seemed cramped and confined, even when compared to that of the 2CV. Consequently, in designing its replacement, Renault's engineers abandoned tradition and took a leaf out of Citroën's book, producing a car that followed exactly the space-efficient principles laid down by André Lefebvre some twenty years earlier: a pontoon-type chassis platform bearing a body built up from unstressed panels; a soft, compliant suspension system having adequate wheel travel and with the wheels positioned at all four corners so that the passengers rode well within the wheelbase, and of course, front-wheel-drive transmission. Unlike the 2CV, though, its original 747 cc 24 bhp engine remained a four-cylinder in-line water-cooled unit, mounted aft of the front transaxle, with the gearbox positioned ahead of it, in a layout resembling that of Citroën's old Traction Avant. Moreover, just like the Traction Avant, the Renault 4 had rack and pinion steering with torsion bar suspension both front and rear, rather than the coil springs previously favoured by the Renault firm.

Introduced in 1961, the new Renault 4 was not a slavish copy of its Citroën rival, however, as it featured many important innovations of its own, including a sealed engine cooling system designed to overcome the maintenance problems that had bedevilled such arrangements in the past by providing a degree of reliability at extremes of temperatures which rivalled that of air-cooled units. But it was really its spacious bodywork that showed the way ahead. Although no less utilitarian and practical than that of the 2CV, it was decidedly stronger and more durable. It also followed a true estate car configuration, with a large opening hatchback rear door plus rear seats that could quickly be folded forward to turn it from a saloon into a van.

Following the launch of the R4, Renault never again designed a rear-wheel-drive car, for this car soon proved the company's greatest ever success. A significant vehicle which helped, like the 2CV, to define the future technical direction of the European motor industry, it remained in production for over thirty years, constantly modified and improved. Between 1961 and 1992 (when the final example left the last remaining production line in Yugoslavia), 8,162,044 units were built, almost as many as the total output of all Citroën's 2CV-type vehicles combined.

Production of the Renault 4CV commenced in 1947. By the end of 1948, output was running at over 300 units a day. Ultimately over a million examples were built. This right-hand-drive example was assembled at Renault's UK factory at Acton. Note the unusual design of the wheels and hubs which were derived directly from the AFG.

THE VOLKSWAGEN BEETLE

Because they were so different in conception, the VW Beetle and the Citroën 2CV were never direct commercial competitors in their native lands, although the 2CV enjoyed a certain vogue in Germany during the seventies, as the chosen motor transport of the Greens. Where the two rival 'people's cars' competed was not so much on the streets or in the showrooms as in the hearts and minds of automobile designers.

In every respect – mechanical, aesthetic, commercial, social and political – the two cars present the most striking and significant contrast in the history of the mass-produced automobile. Conceived and developed almost simultaneously before the war and then launched on to the market at more or less the same time after it, these two unorthodox cars were both designed to bring motoring within the reach of the masses, but in ways that, in engineering terms at least, were diametrically opposed. Each succeeded beyond their creators' wildest dreams, so much so that both went on to achieve cult status. Initially, each in their own way offered the public a simple, economical and reliable means of family mobility. Then later on, when other cars grew ever more extravagant and expensive, both came to represent symbols of reason and restraint in an age of unrestricted travel and unbridled consumerism.

Although often credited as being the first such 'people's car' by a very wide margin of time, the Beetle did not enter large-scale civilian production until 1950, only a year or so ahead of the 2CV. And although its development history can be traced back to June 1934,

Although the Volkswagen people's car project was commissioned as early as 1934, a definitive prototype did not appear until 1938.

The 2CV's Continental Competitors

German motorists did not get an opportunity to buy their people's car until civilian production got into its stride at Wolfsburg in the late forties, at about the same time that the 2CV began to appear in small numbers in France. This is the version that competed against the Deux Chevaux at that time, the classic 1200 cc Beetle of 1949/50 – roughly 46,000 units were built that year, in contrast to about 6,000 2CVs. Note the split rear window, phased out in 1953.

when Adolf Hitler awarded its designer, Ferdinand Porsche, a contract to produce Nazi Germany's '*Kraft durch Freude*' ('Strength through Joy') car, no prototypes appeared on the test track until late in 1936, much less a fixed pre-production design. This stage was not achieved until late in 1938, by which date the 2CV had also reached the same point in its evolution. As is well known, before the war, all production from the new Wolfsburg factory (the foundation stone of which was laid by Hitler in May 1938) went to the German *Wehrmacht*, and the Beetle failed to reach a single civilian paying customer under the Nazi regime. Indeed, no proper sales and service network existed to serve such a market. And when production was resumed after the war, in 1945, for the first few years output was again reserved for military use by the British and American Occupation Forces. So, in reality, the story of the Beetle's illustrious sales career did not begin until it was roughly twenty years old, just as was the case with the 2CV!

Eventually, the Beetle became the best-selling automobile ever built. Still in production in Mexico after well over fifty years of service, it enjoyed an international export success completely denied to the 2CV: at one time it was sold simultaneously in over 150 countries throughout the world. So far, over 22 million examples have been constructed – thus, in both volume and longevity, it ranks as the most popular and successful motor vehicle of all time, easily surpassing the record set by its nearest rival, the Model T Ford.

With a mere third of that total to its credit, the 2CV appears to be a much less successful product at first sight. But whereas, despite its early imitators, the rear-wheel-drive Beetle was destined to remain a technical blind alley in the development of the automobile, it was the inventive, innovative front-wheel-drive layout of the 2CV that inspired the

199

The Citroën 2CV

In 1961 Renault took a leaf out of Citroën's book, and introduced a replacement for the 4CV that borrowed many of the ideas pioneered by the 2CV. The Renault 4 eventually proved to be the most successful car in the company's history. Over eight million examples were constructed by 1992, when production finally ceased.

imaginations of future generations of designers, thus setting the technical pattern for the small family cars of today. So it could well be argued that by spawning countless millions of other similarly engineered vehicles, it is the Citroën rather than the Volkswagen which has the strongest claim to fame – through its seminal influence on other manufacturers, if not its outright sales.

So which has the stronger claim to immortality in the Valhalla of motoring's most illustrious makes and models – the world's most successful small car, or the world's most successful small car *design*? To resolve the question, it is interesting to compare a couple of representative examples of the last versions of the two designs ever produced: a Paris-built 1986 2CV Special, and a Mexican-built 1,200 cc Beetle dating from 1979.

On paper, the specifications of the two rivals would suggest that there's no contest, at least in performance terms. The Beetle, with its 1,192 cc (34 bhp DIN) engine, weighs in at 760 kg compared with the 585 kg kerb weight of the 2CV, powered by a 602 cc (29 bhp DIN) engine. Yet, surprisingly, despite having an engine half the size of the Beetle's, the 2CV's lighter construction and superior power-to-weight ratio means that this great disparity is far less noticeable on the move. Contemporary data credited the Beetle with a top speed of 80 mph, compared with the 2CV's 71.5 mph, but the extremely economical 2CV scored higher on fuel consumption, with an average 52.3 mpg, compared with the Beetle's 38.5 mpg. Moreover, the Beetle was always the heavier of the two on price, as well as on running costs: in 1978, the Beetle sold for £2,626 on the British market, while the 2CV was over 20 per cent cheaper at £2,071, including VAT.

The body-language of the rivals speaks volumes too. Viewed at a standstill, the complex double curves and smooth, rounded shape of the Beetle look subtle and sophisticated compared with the simple, flat-sided panels and glasswork of the 2CV. Clearly, here are two vehicles that were originally designed to be produced by completely different production methods and machinery, the Beetle requiring complicated and expensive press-tools, the 2CV merely the very simplest metal-forming and assembly techniques. When opening and closing the driver's door, this contrast in build quality and production methods is instantly evident to both eye and ear – the Beetle's, with its high-quality handles and latches, operates with a soft and satisfying click; the 2CV's door bangs shut with all the finesse of a dustbin lid.

Once at the wheel, however, the fundamental virtues of the Citroën are immediately apparent to the driver. Here, thanks to the clear, unobstructed floor, the driving position feels superbly comfortable and the seating arrangements are relaxing and unrestricting. The controls – though rudimentary – are thoughtfully positioned, with the pendant pedals particularly well located so that the movement of the driver's foot from accelerator to brake in an emergency is swiftly and surely accomplished.

In the Beetle, however, an awkward, angled footwell and offset pedals force the driver to sit askew, with the upright steering wheel placed uncomfortably close to the chest, as if at the helm of a sailing ship. Although light to operate, the Beetle's steering gear is slow in response and imprecise in action, as are its brakes, which, thanks to a badly located brake pedal with over-generous free travel, give a spongy, unreassuring feel.

On start-up, however, the one common feature of the two designs is loudly evident – their air-cooled engines. That of the Beetle seems smoother and quieter despite its greater size and power, although its rear-mounted position may well account for this. At tick-over speeds, it rumbles gently like a monster coffee grinder; working harder at cruising pace, it hums along, sounding more like a busy bumble bee than a bug. Put your foot down and the torque comes in at low revs, which makes for a surprising degree of flexibility in town traffic. But try accelerating on the open road or motorway and the car soon runs out of steam, unless you quickly change down from top gear. Yet even though the Beetle's four-speed box has to be used constantly to keep up momentum, doing so is never a chore – its crisp action and well-engineered linkages make it a pleasure to handle.

The 2CV's front-mounted motor, on the other hand, sounds crude and coarse, completely belying the quality of its construction, and to get the most from its limited torque, heavy use of the right foot is demanded at all times to keep up the revs – and this produces that unmistakable shrieking, rasping sound that devotees say is part and parcel of the 2CV's personality and charm! Again, the Citroën's unique fascia-mounted gear lever has to be kept constantly in use, but its logical push-pull-twist action makes for easy shifting between second and third when crawling in town traffic. Clutch operation is pleasantly light and sensitive on both cars.

On the open road, the basic difference in the character of these two venerable machines becomes even more apparent. The Beetle's firm suspension (the 1979

Sometimes the bitter rivalry between the 2CV and the 4CV for domination of the streets of France during the fifties and sixties reached the level of outright confrontation. But despite the evidence presented here (or perhaps because of this), it was the Renault that eventually came off worst. By the seventies, when sales of the 2CV revived to hit a new peak, the 4CV was just a memory for French motorists.

example has transverse torsion bars front and rear, with a semi-trailing rear axle) gives a smooth, stable ride on the straight and far more trustworthy handling on cambered bends than was the case with the notoriously unpredictable swing axle layout fitted on earlier types. But although effortless to turn, the Beetle's worm and roller steering seems vague and imprecise in feel, making it difficult to position the car with any accuracy. In contrast, the supple, interlinked coil-sprung suspension of the Citroën provides a superlatively comfortable ride across all surfaces. Riding inside, that famous body roll feels far less alarming than it looks to startled spectators – and, driven with determination, the 2CV can be hustled through bends with surprising agility. Moreover, the 2CV's rack and pinion steering is direct and precise, providing plenty of feedback from the road, so that its driver always knows where the wheels are pointed when going through corners.

Under motorway conditions, the biggest contrast in the character of the two cars is soon made crystal clear. As is well known, the Beetle was specifically designed by Professor Porsche to cruise at high speed for long distances on the *Autobahn* network then being planned in Germany – hence its semi-streamlined shape. The Citroën, on the other hand, was built for rural – indeed agricultural – use, and therefore, although it is capable of cruising fast on open country roads, it does not feel at home on congested autoroutes. Chancing one's luck among the juggernauts in the slow lane during a rainstorm calls for courage on the part of a 2CV driver, especially when overtaking manoeuvres cannot be avoided or postponed! By contrast, the comparative strength and solidity of the Beetle's bodyshell gives its driver and passengers a sense of confidence and security which is perhaps over-optimistic. Earlier swing-axle Beetles certainly had a disconcerting habit of hopping from lane to lane in crosswinds on the motorway, due to their poor weight distribution and consequent directional instability at high speeds.

In short, the 2CV with its frail body epitomises the concept of *active* safety – the avoidance of accidents through its superior braking, handling and road-holding qualities. The Beetle represents the virtues of *passive* safety – cocooned in its strong steel shell, some drivers and passengers experience a sense of well-being and invulnerability that others, accustomed to the 2CV's open-air ambience, might well find claustrophobic.

But apart from the arcane subtleties of handling and road-holding, what about the practicalities of daily use? From the point of view of versatility, there's no doubt that the four-door 2CV wins hands down. It's a true four-seater that is suited to virtually every kind of purpose, from the shortest shopping trips to the longest holiday hauls. Rear legroom is ample, so there's space for almost everyone and everything on board, no matter how large or awkwardly shaped. And if there isn't, the owner merely has to remove the rear seats and open up the roof to make more room. All that the 2CV lacks is a proper cover for the well in the rear (housing the spare wheel) to give it a long, flat load area and convert it into an estate car when the occasion arises.

When tasked as a load- and people-carrier, however, the two-door Beetle is just not up to the job. Inside, the rear cabin space is cramped and uncomfortable, so it ranks more as a two-plus-two than a family car. Outside, under the sloping, streamlined bonnet, the petrol tank has pride of place and there's scarcely space for a suitcase, so as a shopping or leisure car, it's less than *wunderbar*. Clearly, despite its designer's intention to make it the streamlined showpiece of Nazi Germany's new long-distance superhighways, the Beetle was really only a commuting car. Yet, thanks to its unburstable, ever-ready, air-cooled engine and its super-efficient heater, against all expectations, it came to provide an unfailing means of getting German (and American) workers to their factories and offices on time, thus providing a major motive force behind Germany's miraculous post-war economic recovery.

The conclusion must be that, like certain other notable products of the German automobile industry, the Beetle is best described as a triumph of development over design. Constantly revised, modified and improved in detail throughout its lifetime to incorporate the latest new ideas in automomotive technology, production engineering and quality control, the Beetle underwent a process of continual evolution. Despite appearances to the contrary, the last versions produced at Wolfsburg were entirely different vehicles from the first. In fact, only one component remained unchanged from the beginning of production to the end – a minor metal part holding a rubber sealing strip to the rim of the engine and luggage compartment covers.

The 2CV's life story was also woven together by a thread of permanence and continuity, but one of unchangeability rather than of seamless improvement and progress. The fact is that following the revisions introduced in the early eighties, no further significant investment was made in enhancing the 2CV's specification or in modernising its method of production. As we have already seen, apart from certain superficial, cosmetic details, the cars of the final batch from Levallois were more or less identical to those made there twenty years earlier. At the end, the car was still equipped with the same antiquated steering column lighting switch design that first made an appearance in 1938, on Citroën's Traction Avant.

The global struggle for leadership in the motor-industry is like a never-ending marathon race in which the front-runner may never slacken pace or pause for breath. And so it must be concluded that, just as with the story of the tortoise and the hare, in the contest between the Beetle and the Tin Snail it happened that the livelier, more interesting and inventive concept was inevitably overtaken in world-wide production, sales and popularity by a duller, altogether less imaginative and innovative design.

PART FIVE
CONCLUSION

THE CITROËN 2CV

CHAPTER TWELVE

THE END OF THE ROAD?

As the 2CV is now well past its 56th birthday (and the 70th anniversary of its conception), the time has come to assess its impact on the motoring world and attempt an explanation of its demise. However, although – officially at least – the *Deuche* has now been declared deceased for over a decade, it is much too soon to be taken as an obituary!

Although the 2CV and its sisters have now been officially dead for over seven years, it is much to soon to write the valediction of this much-maligned and misunderstood little car, still very much alive and running. With so many examples remaining on roads around the world today, and with facilities for restoring these surviving cars already highly developed, it seems inevitable that, like it or loathe it, the 2CV will continue to be a familiar sight on the streets of Europe well into the twenty-first century, attracting as much controversy as ever.

Despite the fact that its place in automobile history is assured, motoring historians will doubtless wrangle over the reasons for the 2CV's demise for many years to come, conducting endless inquests and post-mortems. So much secrecy surrounded the official execution of the 2CV that the affair is already regarded as one of the most intriguing motoring murder mysteries of modern times – indeed, for some fervent enthusiasts, a crime so ghastly that it demands nothing less than an investigation by Inspector Maigret himself.

So, whodunnit? Was the 2CV assassinated by ruthless cost-accountants whose calculations decreed that further production would be both unprofitable and undesirable? Was it killed off by the plotting of faceless bureaucrats and legislators, imposing unreasonable modern safety and emission-control standards on a venerable but obsolescent design? Did it fall victim to a rival sibling in the Citroën stable, whose growth starved it of the development investment that was essential to revive and refit it for future service? Or did it merely die from neglect on the part of its erstwhile customers, no longer desired by the French motoring masses who once had been its most ardent and devoted admirers?

Certainly, the evidence shows that although they continued to profess their undying affection, the French had actually been falling out of love with the 2CV for a long time – and not without reason: the France of today is a very

Plus ça change ... This photograph depicts a scene so permanent and enduring that even an expert would find it hard to say exactly when it was taken! In fact, it was shot at Chablis in Burgundy, as recently as 1992. The car was built in 1958.

THE CITROËN 2CV

The 2CV was in essence a hand-built car, entirely dependent on labour-intensive manual assembly methods and therefore costly to produce despite its simplicity.

Another view of the 2CV production line at Levallois during the late fifties. Here, whole bodyshells hang from the roof like sides of beef at an abattoir.

different country from the France of Pierre-Jules Boulanger's time. Geographically, its road network is now as smooth and level as anywhere else in Western Europe, so the need for French cars to have suspension systems with superb rough-road capabilities is long gone. Moreover, the arrival of France's new autoroute system called for cars that can cruise safely and comfortably in heavy traffic at speeds exceeding 70 mph, if only to keep clear of the giant juggernauts – a task for which the 2CV was never intended.

Socially, too, the nation has changed. Once predominantly rural and agrarian, with its population of peasant farmers governed by a classically educated intelligentsia, France is is now an urbanised, industrialised society administered by a meritocracy of technocrats, just like other European countries. The distinction between the rural and the urban car market has disappeared, and a single type of standardised vehicle, the conventional family saloon or estate car, now satisfies both town- and country-dwellers alike. Moreover, French motorists no longer view the automobile as merely a utilitarian machine in which to travel from place to place, but now expect it to serve as a vehicle of social mobility also, by carrying them ever onwards and upwards to a higher position or prestige and greater material success. Just like other twentieth-century consumers elsewhere, the car-buyers of modern France now demand upwardly mobile, status-conscious consumer products that convey their aspirations and express their lifestyles – which explains why, of the 43,000 2CVs produced in 1987, only about 7,500 went to French customers, compared with 12,500 German and 7,200 British buyers. In the eyes of sophisticated, unsentimental Parisians at least, the 2CV's cultural heritage was insufficient reason to keep it alive, just as age-old British customs and traditions were not enough to preserve the Morris Minor.

If the tastes of French motorists had altered noticeably during the 2CV's lifetime, becoming ever less insular and idiomatic, then the nature of the double chevron marque had also been drastically modified by the relentless pressure of world economic forces. In 1974, with Citroën's financial health gravely weakened by soaring costs and slumping sales resulting from the energy crisis, Michelin relinquished control and the company was taken over by its erstwhile rival, Peugeot, a firm with a very different design and engineering philosophy; one that represented quite another face of French motor manufacturing practice: cautious, conservative and, above all, money-conscious.

In theory, Citroën was to maintain an independent, autonomous marque identity in the vast, new PSA multinational conglomerate created by the merger, competing with Peugeot as intensely as before. But in practice, the decision to pool research efforts and to share manufacturing facilities led to a fundamental shift in management attitudes at Citroën, away from the elitist, idealist, rationalist philosophy inherited from the Boulanger era to a new, more pragmatic outlook dominated by the prosaic disciplines of production engineering, cost-accountancy and marketing. No longer would Citroën's new model policy be distinguished by a characteristic pattern of bold,

The finishing line, *c.* 1959. The cars queuing up to leave the factory have a long list of customers waiting for them – at that time the quoted delivery period for orders was years rather than weeks or months!

Twenty years later, *c.* 1975, nothing much had changed at Levallois, except that the 2CV had been joined on the production line by the Dyane. But thanks to the energy crisis, once again the 2CV was in huge demand!

adventurous leaps in design followed by long recuperative production runs to recover its vast investment in research and development. No longer would it be allowed to depend on a hard-core market of fiercely loyal fanatics and devotees for its business, and no longer would its designers be encouraged to work in splendid isolation, forbidden to examine other manufacturers' cars lest the originality of their ideas be weakened or compromised. In short, its entire corporate culture had changed.

During the forty years from 1948 to 1988, the whole technology of car construction had also altered immeasurably. Despite superficial appearances to the contrary, the 2CV was a relatively complicated, expensive and labour-intensive car to produce, wholly unsuited to assembly by modern, automated techniques. No robot could be made to fit together its body sections, fastened by bolts not welds; no computerised automaton could replace human hands in the delicate task of building up its engine. In truth, the 2CV was now just too different from other cars, and from other, newer Citroëns, to be a viable proposition. It did not accord with the prevailing methods and mentality of the motor industry, and while it may once have been a highly profitable product in the past, when labour was cheap, it was now extremely uncompetitive. What the company's management wanted next was a conventional small car that could be easily integrated into the PSA group manufacturing system and which fitted in comfortably with its new marketing strategy. As it stood, this survivor from a bygone age was not just an awkward anomaly but a downright embarrassment.

Moreover, despite its reputation among the Greens, the 2CV was no longer the paragon of environment-friendliness that it had been at the start of its career. Long before there was any legal requirement to do so, Becchia had designed its engine to recycle crankcase fumes and burn off any oil vapour, exhaust gases and unburnt fuel that would otherwise have been vented to the atmosphere as was the general practice in the motor industry at the time. In the forty years that had passed since then, public concern about exhaust emissions had caught up with and overtaken the little car, and although with further modification its air-cooled engine could certainly have been made to continue to comply with the ever-increasing severity of EC anti-pollution legislation, the expense would have been prohibitive. The cost of modifying the 2CV's chassis and body structure to withstand collision tests and meet impending EC safety regulations and construction specifications would also have been unacceptably high, pricing the vehicle out of the market altogether. As events turned out, before the end of 1989, Citroën was forced to withdraw the 2CV from its showrooms in Austria, Switzerland, Spain, Holland, Italy and Scandinavia for these very reasons, while sales chugged on in France, Belgium, Germany and the UK at an ever-decelerating pace.

Therefore, when the subject of a replacement for the 2CV came up for discussion some time in the early eighties, there was no talk at Citroën of producing another radical and revolutionary vehicle bristling with original, innovative and individualistic ideas that would shake the motoring world to its foundations as the 2CV had done. Some motor industry experts had suggested that the only way to produce a worthy successor would be to take Boulanger's original design brief and start all over again, using the benefits of modern methods and materials, but the new custodians of the double chevron marque had other ideas. The world had changed, the goalposts had been moved, and Citroën now had very different objectives from those that had exercised Boulanger in 1936. He had conceived the car as a frugal, spartan means of basic transport, but in the modern age, austerity and self-denial were no longer in fashion. So when it appeared in 1986, Citroën's new baby car, the AX, turned out to be a conventional but very light-weight two-box supermini, incorporating components from the PSA parts bin, closely modelled on Peugeot's own commercially successful efforts in that market sector – a commuting or shopping car for affluent, urban, European consumers, rather than a minimalist, low-cost, go-anywhere, do-anything workhorse suitable for Third World use, like its predecessor.

In truth, the 2CV's greatest defect was that it was much too successful at its job for its own good. Unequalled as a reliable and economical runabout for so many years, it was kept alive for far too long. Preserved from the normal process of ageing and decline not by nostalgia or sentimentality, but by the inherent, eternal qualities of its design, it survived well beyond its intended lifespan to find itself in a world very different from that for which it had been conceived.

Condemned by the ignorant and ill-informed as unsafe and dangerous, it was, in some ways, one of the safest and easiest cars to drive ever offered to the motoring public, so much so that, at its wheel, even the most clumsy driver was able to survive the kind of mistakes that spell instant disaster in less forgiving cars. On the other hand, its fragile body, built for lightness and simplicity of construction, eventually proved to be vulnerable when

At 1500 hours on 27 July 1990, the very last Deux Chevaux, a 2CV-6 Charleston, rolls off the production line at Mangualde in Portugal. Production had ceased at Levallois in Paris over two years earlier, in February 1988.

exposed to modern dangers. Intended merely to shield its occupants from the wind and rain, not against the onslaught of 40-ton lorries, it was designed in an age well before the advent of motorways, when traffic densities were so light that it was a rare occurrence for two cars to meet and pass each other on a country road in rural France. Consequently, when involved in the kind of accidents and collisions that are almost inevitable in today's traffic conditions, the 2CV's driver and passengers were left woefully unprotected from the mistakes of others, and exposed to serious injury in even the slightest impact.

Suffice it to say that when its epitaph is finally written, history will have shown that the 2CV's lifespan encompassed almost exactly the golden age of European motoring – that happy time before the automobile became a victim of its own success. At the outset of this great new era of motorised mobility, optimists like André Citroën foretold that the car would set people free, but all too soon it was evident that they had merely become enslaved by the motor car itself. That's why, although for some motorists the 2CV remains a symbol of the bad old days of poverty, austerity and lack of opportunity, from which they are thankful to have escaped, for others it survives as a reminder of a gentler, simpler and less hurried world, to which they would gladly return.

For all its faults, Citroën's ugly duckling was always a willing servant, faithful, friendly, unassuming and eager to please, and never an aggressive, extortionate, temperamental tyrant like some other grander, more expensive cars. Long may it continue to quack and clatter on in its inimitable way!

PART SIX

APPENDICES

PRODUCTION DATA 1: Cumulative A Series production dates and specifications

Model Range	Official Code	Production Dates	Sales Description	Engine Code
2CV	A	7/49–7/59	2CV	A – 2 ch
	AZ	10/54–10/55	2CV	AZ
	AZ	10/55–10/58	2CV	AZ
	AZ	10/58–10/61	2CV	AZ
	AZ	10/61–4/62	2CV	AZ
	AZ	4/62–2/63	2CV	AZ
	AZ (séries A et AM)	3/63–12/63	2CV AZL & 2CV AZAM	AZ
	AZ (séries A et AM)	12/63–2/70	2CV AZL & 2CV AZAM	AZ
	AZ (séries A 2)	2/70–9/75	2CV 4	AYA 2
	AZ (série KB)	9/75–9/78	2CV 4	AYA 2
	AZ (série KB)	9/78–7/79	2CV Spécial	AYA 2
	AZ (série KA)	2/70–9/75	2CV 6	AK 2
	AZ (série KA)	9/75–9/78	2CV 6	AK 2*
	AZ (série KA)	9/78–7/79	2CV 6	A 06/635
	AZ (série KA)	7/79–7/81	2CV 6 Spécial, Club	A 06/635
	AZ (série KA)	7/81–7/90	2CV Spécial, Club, Spécial E or Charleston	A 06/635
DYANE	AYA (série A et AM)	8/67–3/68	Dyane	AYA
	AYA2 (série A et AM)	3/68–2/70	Dyane 4	AYA 2
	AYA3 (séries A et AM)	1/68–10/68	Dyane 6	AYA 3
	AYB (séries A et AM)	10/68–2/70	Dyane 6	AK 2
	AYA2 (séries A et AM)	2/70–9/75	Dyane	AYA 2
	AY (série CB)	2/70–7/80	Dyane 6	AM 2
	AY (série CB)	7/80–7/84	Dyane 6	AM 2*
MEHARI	AY (série CA)	10/68–9/75	Mehari	AK 2
	AY (série CA)	9/75–7/78	Mehari	AK 2*
	AY (série CA)	7/78–7/87	Mehari	A 06/635
	AY (série CE)	9/79–7/83	Mehari 4 x 4	A 06/635
2 CV 4×4	AW	3/58–3/63	2CV 4 x 4 "SAHARA"	2 x AZ
	AW/AT	3/63–7/66	2CV 4 x 4 "SAHARA"	2 x AZ
2CV Fourgonnette	AU	3/51–10/54	2CV – AU	A – 2 ch
	AZU	10/54–12/55	2CV – AZU	AZU
	AZU	12/55–10/58	2CV – AZU	AZU
	AZU	10/58–11/61	2CV – AZU	AZU
	AZU	11/61–2/62	2CV – AZU	AZ
	AZU	2/62–3/63	2CV – AZU	AZ
	AZU (série A)	3/63–8/67	2CV – AZU (série A)	AZ
		8/67–8/72	2CV – AZU (série A)	AYA
	AZU (série B)	8/72–9/75	Citroën 250	AYA 2
	AK série AP (AZU)	9/75–2/78	Citroën 250	AYA 2
3 CV Fourgonnette	AK	4/63–5/68	AK 350	AK
	AK (série B)	5/68–8/70	AK 350	AK 2
	AK (série AK)	8/70–9/75	Citroën 400	AK 2
	AK (série AK)	9/75–2/78	Citroën 400	AK 2*
	AK (série CD)	2/78–9/80	Acadiane	AM 2 A
	AK (série CD)	9/80–7/87	Acadiane	AM 2 A*
	AK (série CD modifie)	8/80–7/87	Acadiane G.P.L (L.P.G.)	AM 2 A G.P.L
3 CV Berline & Break	AM	5/61–11/61	AMI 6	AM
	AM	11/61–9/63	AMI 6	AM
	AM	9/63–9/67	AMI 6	AM
	AMB	9/64–9/67	AMI 6 Break	AM
	AM	9/67–5/68	AMI 6	AYA 3
	AMB	9/67–5/68	AMI 6 Break	AYA 3
	AM 2	5/68–3/69	AMI 6	AM 2
	AMB 2	5/68–7/69	AMI 6 Break	AM 2
	AM 3	3/69–7/69	AMI 8	AM 2
	AM (série JA)	7/69–9/78	AMI 8	AM 2
	AM (série JB)	7/69–9/78	AMI 8 Break & Commerce	AM 2
	AM (série JC)	7/69–9/79	AMI 8 Break Service	AM 2
AMI Super	AM Série JF	1/73–7/76	AMI Super Berline	
	AM Série JG	1/73–7/76	AMI Super Break	G10/613
	AM Série JH	1/73–7/75	AMI Super Service	

*Power reduced

Cubic Capacity	POWER SAE	POWER DIN	bhp rpm	TORQUE SAE	TORQUE DIN	mkg rpm	COMPR. RATIO :1	CARBURETTOR Solex except Zn:Zenith, Wb:Weber
375 cm³	9		3500	2.0		2000	6.2	22ZACI
425 cm³	12		3500	2.2		2000	6.2	26BCI ext. dashpot
425 cm³	12.5		4200	2.4		2500	7.0	26BCI ext. dashpot
425 cm³	12.5		4200	2.4		2500	7.0	26CBI int. dashpot
425 cm³	13.5		4000	2.7		2500	7.5	26IBC or CBI
425 cm³	15		4500	2.75		2500	7.5	26IBC or CBI
425 cm³	18	16.5	5000	2.85	2.75	2500	7.5	28IBC or CBI
425 cm³	18	16.5	5000	2.85	2.75	2500	7.5	Zn28IN or IN4 alternatives to Solex
435 cm³ }								
435 cm³	26	24	6750	3.1	2.9	4000/4500	8.5	34 PICS or 34 PCIS
435 cm³ }								
602 cm³	32.8	29	6750	4.3	4.0	4500	8.5	34 PICS 4 or 34 PCIS 4
602 cm³	30	26	5500	4.3	4.0	3500	8.5	34 PICS 6 or 34 PCIS 6
602 cm³						3500		
602 cm³ }	33	29	5750	4.3	4.0	3500	8.5	26 x 35 CSIC or 26 x 35 SCIC
602 cm³								
425 cm³	21	18.5	5450	3.0		3500	7.75	32 PICS or 32 PCIS
435 cm³	26	24	6750	3.1	2.9	4000/4500	8.5	34 PICS or 34 PCIS
602 cm³	28	25.5	5400/4750	4.4		3500	7.75	40 PICS/PCIS
602 cm³	32.8	29	6750	4.3	4.0	4500	8.5	34 PICS/PCIS
435 cm³	26	24	6750	3.1	2.9	4000/4500	8.5	34 PICS or 34 PCIS
602 cm³	35	32	5750	4.7	4.2	4750/4000	9	26 x 35 CSIC or 26 x 35 SCIC
602 cm³	33.5	30	5750	4.5	4.2	4000	9	26 x 35 CSIC or 26 x 35 SCIC
602 cm³	32.8	29	6750	4.3	4.0	4500	8.5	34 PICS 4 or 34 PCIS 4
602 cm³	30	26	5500	4.3	4.0	3500	8.5	34 PICS 6 or 34 PCIS 6
602 cm³	33	29	5750	4.3	4.0	3500	8.5	26 x 35 CSIC
602 cm³	33	29	5750	4.3	4.0	3500	8.5	26 x 35 CSIC
2 x 425 cm³	2 x 13.5		4500	2 x 2.7		2500	7.5	2 x 26 CBIN
2 x 425 cm³	2 x 18	2 x 16.5	5000	2 x 2.85	2 x 2.75	2500	7.5	2 x 28 CBIN
375 cm³	9		3500	2.0		2000	6.2	22 ZACI
425 cm³	12		3500	2.2		2000	6.2	26 BCI
425 cm³	12.5		4200	2.4		2500	7.0	26 BCI
425 cm³	12.5		4200	2.4		2500	7.0	26 IBC
425 cm³	13.5		4000	2.7		2500	7.5	26 IBC
425 cm³	15		4500	2.75		2500	7.5	26 IBC
425 cm³	18	16.5	5000	2.85	2.75	2500	7.5	28 IBC or Zn. 28 IN
425 cm³	21	18.5	5450	3.0		3500	7.75	32 PICS
435 cm³	26	24	6750	3.1	2.9	4000/4500	8.5	34 PICS
435 cm³	26	24	6750	3.1	2.9	4000/4500	8.5	34 PICS
602 cm³	22.68		4500	4.3		3000	7.75	30 PICS
602 cm³	32.8	29	6750	4.3	4.0	4500	8.5	34 PICS 4 or 34 PCIS 4
602 cm³	32.8	29	6750	4.3	4.0	4500	8.5	34 PICS 4 or 34 PCIS 4
602 cm³	30	26	5500	4.3	4.0	3500	8.5	34 PICS 6 or 34 PCIS 6
602 cm³	33.8	31	5750	4.5	4.2	3500	8.5	26 x 35 CSIC
602 cm³	33.0	29	5750	4.3	4.0	3500	8.5	26 x 35 CSIC
602 cm³	27.5	25	5000	3.9	3.7	2500	8.5	LPG
602 cm³	22		4500	4.0		2500	7.25	30 PBI
602 cm³	22		4500	4.0		2500	7.25	30 PBI
602 cm³	22.5	24	4750	4.1		3000	7.75	40 PICS/PCIS
602 cm³	22.5	24	4750	4.1		3000	7.75	40 PICS/PCIS
602 cm³	28	25.5	5400/4750	4.4		3500	7.75	40 PICS/PCIS
602 cm³	28	25.5	5400/4750	4.4		3500	7.75	40 PICS/PCIS
602 cm³	35	32	5750	4.7	4.2	4750/4000	9	26 x 35 CSIC or 26 x 35 SCIC
1015 cm³	61	53.5	6500	7.5	6.9	3500	9	Wb 30 DGS1

PRODUCTION DATA 2: Annual output of A Series models (2CV and derivatives) 1949–1990

Year	2CV Saloon	2CV Van	2CV 4×4	Dyane Saloon	Acadiane	Mehari	FAF & Baby-B	Total
1949	876							876
1950	6,196							6,196
1951	14,592	1,696						16,288
1952	21,124	7,711						28,385
1953	35,361	13,121						48,482
1954	52,791	19,197						71,988
1955	81,170	23,904						105,110
1956	95,864	23,859						119,723
1957	107,250	31,431						138,681
1958	126,332	37,631						163,963
1959	145,973	50,058						196,031
1960	152,801	57,724	20					210,545
1961	158,659	56,639	274					215,572
1962	144,759	54,191	112					199,062
1963	158,035	55,775	87					213,897
1964	167,419	64,994	138					232,551
1965	154,023	59,211	35					213,269
1966	168,357	55,817	27					224,201
1967	98,683	55,281		47,712				201,676
1968	57,473	51,545		98,769		837	495	209,119
1969	72,044	53,259		95,434		12,624	300	233,661
1970	121,096	46,485		96,456		11,246	660	276,033
1971	121,264	62,074	1	97,091		10,175	2,430	293,035
1972	133,530	64,592		111,462		11,742	2,025	323,351
1973	123,819	68,357		95,535		12,567	1,125	301,403
1974	163,143	64,325		126,854		13,910	2,280	370,512
1975	122,542	44,821		117,913		8,920	4,050	298,246
1976	134,396	54,533		118,871		9,569	1,290	318,659
1977	132,458	52,721		113,474	141	9,645	2,010	310,449
1978	108,825	12,647		102,958	37,787	8,467	3,390	274,074
1979	101,222	2,535		77,605	49,679	8,995	5,070	245,106
1980	89,994	135		61,745	45,438	8,351	3,510	209,623
1981	89,472	30		39,176	30,881	4,833	2,295	166,687
1982	86,060			27,960	36,054	4,137	1,590	155,801
1983	59,673			13,908	20,377	3,349	600	97,907
1984	54,923			570	12,756	2,654		70,903
1985	54,067				8,429	1,882	30	64,408
1986	56,663				7,915	669		65,247
1987	43,255				3,936	381	30	47,602
1988	22,717							22,717
1989	19,077							19,077
1990	9,954							9,954
Totals	3,867,932	1,246,335	694	1,443,583	253,393	144,953	35,650	6,990,520

Total 2CV: 5,114,961
Total Dyane: 1,696,976

Grand Total: 6,990,520

PRODUCTION DATA 3: Total world-wide production of 2CV and derivatives 1949–1990

2CV		
2CV Saloon/Berline	3,867,932	
2CV Van/Fourgonnette	1,246,335	
2CV Total		5,114,267
Dyane		
Dyane Saloon/Berline	1,443,583	
Acadiane Van	253,393	
Dyane Total		1,696,976
Other 2CV types		
Mehari	144,953	
2CV 4×4 Sahara	694	
Baby Brousse	31,335	
FAF	2,295	
Total Misc.		79,277
Grand Total 2CV		6,990,520
Ami		
Ami 6*	1,039,384	
Ami 8*	755,955	
Ami Super*	44,820	1,840,159
Grand total		8,830,679

* Berline, Break & Service Van

(Source: Automobiles Citroën, Paris)

BIBLIOGRAPHY

In English

Clarke, R.M., *Citroën 2CV 1948–1982*, Brooklands Books, 1983

Jacobs, David, *The Citroën 2CV*, Osprey Automotive, 1989

MacQueen, Bob and McNamara, Julian, *The Life and Times of the 2CV*, Great Ouse Press, 1982

Sparrow, David and Kessel, Adrienne, *The Citroën 2CV*, Bison Books, 1992

——, *The Citroën 2CV: A Family Album*, Veloce Publishing, 1993

Taylor, James, *The Citroën 2CV and Derivatives*, Motor Racing Publications, 1983

Van Altena, Ernst, *Citroën 2CV: The Ugly Duckling* (translation of Dutch text first published 1983), Haynes/Foulis, 1986

Zeichner, Walter, *Citroën 2CV 1948–86* (translation of German text first published by Schräder Motor Chronik, 1988), Schiffer Publishing, USA, 1989

In French

Baudot, Jean-Claude and Seguela, Jacques, *La Terre en Ronde*, Flammarion, 1960 (account of round-the-world drive)

Borge, Jacques and Viasnoff, Nicholas, *La 2CV: L'amie de Toujours*, Balland, 1977

De Serres, Olivier, *Le Grand Livre Citroën: Tous les Modèles*, Editions EPA, 1988

Sabatès, Fabien, *La 2CV: 40 Ans de Amour*, Editions Massin, 1990

——, *L'Album de la 2CV*, Editions EPA, 1992

Wolgensinger, Jacques, *Raid Afrique*, Flammarion, 1974

——, *La 2CV: Nous Nous Sommes Tant Aimés*, Gallimard, 1995

Photographic Credits

The illustrations for this book were provided by the following organisations and individuals:

Automobiles Citroën: 7, 13, 16, 18, 20, 23, 26, 27, 28, 29, 34/35, 45, 46, 47, 55, 56, 57, 58, 60, 61, 65b, 65c, 66a, 66b, 66c, 67b, 68a, 68b, 68c, 69a, 69b, 70a, 70b, 70c, 71a, 71b, 72a, 72b, 74, 75, 76, 78, 79, 81, 82, 83, 84, 85, 86, 87b, 87c, 87d, 88, 89, 91, 92, 93, 96a, 97a, 97b, 99, 102, 103, 104, 105, 106, 107a, 107b, 108a, 109a, 109b, 112, 113a, 113b, 114, 115, 116a, 117, 118, 119, 120a, 120b, 124, 126a, 126b, 128, 129b, 131, 132, 138/139, 140a, 140b, 141a, 141b, 141c, 144a, 144b, 146, 151, 154, 159, 177, 178, 179, 181, 182a, 182b, 183, 184a, 184b, 186a, 186b, 187, 189b, 205, 208a, 208b, 209, 210, 211, 212

Citroën UK/Ken Smith: 19, 67a, 94, 95, 98, 116b, 129a, 162a, 162b, 164, 165, 166/167, 169a, 169b, 170, 171, 188, 189a

Neill Bruce/Peter Roberts Collection: 2, 25, 43, 77, 80, 90, 121, 122, 123a, 123b, 127, 158, 192, 195, 198, 199

Automobiles Renault: 196, 197, 200, 201

Michael Pointer Collection: 193, 194

Ludvigsen Library: 160, 162

Jean-Luc Benard: 8, 206

LAT/Haymarket archives: 41, 51, 53, 54

Michelin & Cie: 62, 63, 135

John Reynolds: 65a, 87a, 142/143

George Burton/2CV GB: 172, 173a, 173b, 174a, 174b

Giles Chapman: 96b

Zoe Harrison: 176

Wouter Jansen: 100, 108b

Bob McQueen: 180

Greg Long: 137a, 137b

Posie Simmonds: 190

Gilles Blanchet: 148

Anthony Heal: 149

Leonardo Bertoni: 155

Filmography

These are films in which the 2CV stars or plays a key role, rather than merely making a passing appearance. They are listed in chronological order:

Les Diaboliques, France, 1954, directed by Georges Clouzot, starring Simone Signoret, Vera Clouzot and Paul Meurisse

Les Amants, France, 1958, directed by Louis Malle, starring Jeanne Moreau and Jean-Marc Bory

La Belle Américaine, France, 1961, directed by Robert Dhéry, starring Robert Dhéry and Colette Brosset

Constance aux Enfers, France, 1963, directed by François Villiers, starring Michelle Morgan, Dany Saval and Claude Rich

Le Corniaud, France, 1964, directed by Gérard Oury, starring Bourvil and Louis de Funes

Le Gendarme de Saint-Tropez, France, 1964, directed by Jean Girault, starring Louis de Funes

Les Félins, France, 1964, directed by René Clément, starring Jane Fonda, Lola Albright and Alain Delon

La Vieille Dame Indignée, France, 1965, directed by René Allio, starring Sylvie, Malka Ribowska and Victor Lanoux

Le Grand Bidule, France, 1966, directed by Raoul André, starring Francis Blanche, Poiret and Serrault, and Micheline Dax

Alexandre le Bienheureux, France, 1967, directed by Yves Robert, starring Philippe Noiret and Françoise Brion

L'Ours et la Poupée, France, 1969, directed by Michel Deville, starring Brigitte Bardot and Jean-Pierre Cassel

Le Boucher, France, 1970, directed by Claude Chabrol, starring Stéphane Audran and Jean Yanne

Traffic, France, 1970, directed by, and starring, Jacques Tati

American Graffiti, USA, 1973, directed by George Lucas, starring Richard Dreyfuss

La Dentellière, Switzerland, 1976, directed by Claude Goretta, starring Isabelle Huppert and Yves Beneyton

For Your Eyes Only, UK, 1981, directed by John Glen, starring Roger Moore and Carole Bouquet

Indecent Proposal, USA, 1992, directed by Adrian Lyne, starring Demi Moore and Robert Redford

La Cérémonie, France, 1995, directed by Claude Chabrol, starring Sandrine Bonnaire and Isabelle Huppert

INDEX

advertising and publicity 26, 34, 36, 45–46, 60, 64–66, 69, 75, 78–79, 98, 107, 113, 171, 175, 177, 183, 185–190
AFG (Aluminium Française Gregoire) 193–195
air-cooling 42, 50, 56, 59, 114, 125, 143, 158, 193–194, 202, 211
Amilcar Compound 193
Antiques Roadshow TV programme 7
Atacama Desert 178, 180
Auriol, Vincent 73
Austin 7 25, 37, 191
Autocar magazine 51, 165

Barbier, Aristide 134
Barbier & Daubrée 134
Barbot, Pierre 183
Bardot, Brigitte 77, 177
Baudot, Jean-Claude 178, 180
Becchia, Walter 50–51, 56, 59, 62, 149, 156–158, 210
Belmondo, Jean-Paul 77, 177
Bercot, Pierre 57, 145, 185
Berliet 49, 181–182
Bernier, Michel 179
Bertarione, Vincenzo 149, 156–157
Bertone 152–153
Bertoni, Flaminio 56, 59, 114–115, 143, 151–156
Bertoni, Serge 155
Bionier, Louis 125
Bleriot, Louis 147
BMC
  Mini 22, 171, 191
  Mini-Moke 168
BMW 500 cc engine 46
Boddy, William 165
Borgé, Jacques 150
Boulanger, Pierre-Jules 11–12, 32–39, 41–44, 46, 48, 52, 56–57, 59–62, 64, 73, 77–78, 132–136, 145, 147–148, 153–154, 157, 166, 172, 185–187, 208, 211
Broglie, Maurice 38, 43
Brueder, Antoine 145

Budd Corporatin195
Bugatti 157
Bugatti, Ettore 156

Cadiou, Jean 46, 56
Cahiers Politiques journal 63
Camus, Albert 77
Car of the Century Award 15
Carrott, Jasper 175
Chataigner, M 37–38, 133
Chevrolet 162
Chinon, Marcel 41, 46, 59
Citroën facilties
  Brussels-Forest factory, Belgium 75, 81
  Bureau d'Études 32, 38–39, 41–42, 46–47, 49, 56, 59–60, 62, 115, 125, 145, 148–149, 151–155, 158
  Conservatoire, Aulnay-sous-Bois 34
  La Ferté-Vidame test track 12, 34–35, 41, 47, 52, 55, 60, 73, 187
  Levallois factory 47, 49, 52, 68, 77, 95, 98, 189–190, 204, 208, 212
  Mangualde factory, Portugal 15, 98, 212
  Quai de Javel factory 24–25, 28, 30, 33, 49, 59, 145, 148, 151, 155, 194–195
  Rennes-le-Janais factory 111, 117, 122
  Slough factory, UK 13–14, 51, 66, 110, 122, 141, 161–176
  Vigo factory, Spain 130
Citroën Cars Ltd 110, 122, 161, 166, 170, 172, 175–176
Citroën engines
  7CV 27
  375 cc 13, 42–43, 51, 59, 78, 105–106, 164, 174
  423 cc 174
  425 cc 13–14, 80, 82, 85, 101, 110, 125, 162, 164, 166, 171, 180
  435 cc 14, 68, 85, 89, 93, 110, 125, 175–176
  602 cc 14, 85, 89, 93–94, 97–98, 104–105, 114, 116, 121, 125, 127–128, 130, 138, 143, 175–176
  652 cc 105

221

856 cc 25
1,015 cc GS 15, 121–122, 124, 177
1,452 cc 25
Citroën models
  Acadiane Fourgonnette 15, 94, 98, 106, 110, 129–130, 140, 176
  agricultural tractor 27
  Ami Super 111, 122, 124
  Ami-6 85, 88, 105, 110–124, 143–144, 152–153
  Ami-6 Berline 122
  Ami-6 Break (Type AMB) 117–119, 122
  Ami-6 Break Club 118–119
  Ami-6 Club 118
  Ami-6 Commerciale 117
  Ami-6 Enterprise Service Van 118–119
  Ami-8 111–124
  Ami-8 Break 121–122
  Ami-8 Club 122
  Ami-8 Confort (Luxe) 122
  Ami-8 Enterprise 121–122, 124
  Ami-8 Super Berline 121–122
  AX project 36, 56, 153
  AX (1986) 211
  Bijou 14, 141–142, 166–167, 170–171
  C15 light van 130
  CX 151
  DS/DS19 (ID19) 15, 60, 111, 114–115, 141, 145–146, 148, 150, 152–153, 156, 158, 164, 166–167, 170, 175
  Dyane (Type AYA) 14, 54, 85, 89, 92–93, 98, 125–130, 138–139, 176, 181, 210
  Dyane Confort 127
  Dyane Luxe 127
  Dyane-4 15, 88, 94, 125–127, 139
  Dyane-6 15, 88, 93–94, 104, 125–127, 139–140
  Dyane-6 Caban 93, 128
  Dyane-6 Capra 93, 128
  Dyane-6 Côte d'Azur 93, 18
  Dyane-6 Confort 128
  Dyane-6 Weekend 128
  FAF 92, 94
  GS 121–122, 145, 151, 158
  GSA 158
  Maserati SM 145
  Mehari 14–15, 94, 98, 103–105, 138, 176
  Mehari Azur 95
  SM 151
  TPV 11–13, 34–38, 41, 44–45, 47–48, 52, 55, 57, 59–60, 98, 166, 172
  TPV Mark II 56
  Traction Avant (Light 15) 15, 20, 27–31, 36, 38–39, 43, 46, 49, 56, 64, 125, 145, 147–148, 152–154, 158, 161, 163, 193, 197, 204
    11CV 64
    15CV (15-Six) 29, 64
  TUB 36, 61

Type B2 25
Type B10 25
Type B12 25, 37
Type H van 61
VGD36
Visa 105, 121, 128
Visa 3CV Special 128
5CV Type C2 25, 27, 37, 191
5CV Type C3 Cloverleaf ('Petit Citron') 11, 25, 28, 191
10CV Rosalie 23
Citroën 2CV
  Type (Series)
  A saloon 13, 24–25, 27, 45, 78, 80–81, 94, 111, 125, 161, 164
  AK Fourgonnette 70, 106, 108–110
  AKS 2CV-6 Fourgonnette 70, 94, 105–106, 109–110, 130, 140
  AU Fourgonnette 13, 70, 80, 94, 100, 105–107
  AZ 65, 81, 162, 164, 171, 180
  AZA 84
  AZAM 82, 84, 137
  AZC Mixte (Combi) 84
  AZL 65, 79–81, 84, 86
  AZLP 81, 96
  AZP pick-up 164, 168–169
  AZU Fourgonette (van) 70, 106, 110, 163–164
  AZU Weekend 110
  Baby-Brousse 14, 94
  Sahara 4x4 13, 82–83, 101–103, 105, 176
  Special 68, 200
  2CV-4 90, 110
  2CV-4 AZL 89
  2CV-4 Special 85
  2CV-4 Spot 15, 89
  2CV-6 14, 67, 90, 105, 110, 126–127, 175
  2CV-6 AZL 89
  2CV-6 Charleston 15, 68, 71–72, 86, 90, 92, 98, 176, 212
  2CV-6 Club 68, 86, 88, 92, 94, 97–98, 176
  2CV-6 Commando 171
  2CV-6 Cocorico 92
  2CV-6 Dolly 91–92, 176
  2CV-6 France 3 Beachcomber 92, 95, 171
  2CV-6 Special 68, 86, 92–93, 97–98, 176
  2CV-6 Special E 93
  2CV-6 Special Bamboo 92
  2CV-6 Special Dolly 92
  2CV-6 Spot 91, 171, 176
  2CV-6 007 James Bond 91, 177
Citroën UK Ltd 176
Citroen, André 11–12, 20, 22, 24, 26–30, 32–33, 37, 43, 134–136, 148, 152–153, 161, 191, 195, 212
CKD assembly 94–95
Clément bicycle company 98
Coatalen, Louis 156

Index

Confederation of French Mechanical Engineering and Electrical Industries 63
Cornet, Jacques 178–179

Daubrée, Edouard 134
de Beauvoir, Simone 77
de Gaulle, General Charles 49
Delagarde, Louis 194
Delahaye 157
Delpire advertising agency 7, 187
Delpire, Robert 113, 187
Doisneau, Robert 151
drag coefficient 166, 171
Driver and Vehicle Licensing Authority 176
Duclos, Jacques 38–39, 46
Dunlop, John 134
Dupin, M 158
Duvey, Jacques 179

Earle, Harley 152
Earls Court motor show 1959 171
EC/EEC regulations 84, 211
Eiffel Tower 18, 26
ENAC 95, 105
energy crisis (1970s) 15, 91, 175

Facel-Véga 194
Farina 152
Fiat 149
    500 Topolino 37, 191–193
Fiat Racing Dept. 156
Ford 162
    Anglia 116–117, 169
    Lincoln Capri 117
    Model T 192, 199
four-wheel drive (4x4) 82, 94–95, 101, 104–105, 138
Four Your Eyes Only James Bond film 15, 91, 177
French Grand Prix
    1923 147–148, 156
    1937 157–158
French Resistance 49, 57
front-wheel drive 27, 29, 40, 44, 89, 118, 147, 161, 163, 174, 193, 195, 197, 199
fuel consumption 38, 180, 200

General Motors 195
Geneva motor show 1969 119
German Occupation 49, 55, 57, 74–75, 145, 155, 193, 196
Ghia 152
Giacosa, Dante 192
Girard, Lucien 56, 157–158
Grantham Productions Ltd 194–195
Grégoire, Jean-Albert 193, 195
Guardian newspaper 188, 190

Hartnett, Lawrence 195

Hergé 187
Hitler, Adolf 198
Hotchkiss 157

Issigonis, Sir Alec 191

Jaguar XK120 50
Junkers, Dr Hugo 46

Kendall, Denis 194–195
Kirwan-Taylor, Peter 170

l'Auto Journal 125
La Presse newspaper 73
Lago, Antonio 157
Lancia, Vincenzo 156
Land Rover 168
Laoste, Robert 57
le Corbusier 57, 147
Lefebvre, André 12, 29, 43–44, 46–47, 54, 60, 78, 111, 145–151, 155, 157, 197
Liberation of France 49, 57, 59, 63, 75, 196
Lingua Franca cartoon strip 190
Lochon, Henri 178–179
Loewy, Raymond 152
Lotus Elite 170
Louys, Pierre 25

Macintosh, Charles 134
Marchand, César 147
market research 39, 46, 171
Marshall Aid Plan 196
Maserati, Alfieri 156
McKenna duties 161
Michelin family 20, 31–32, 37–38, 41, 136, 148
Michelin tyre company 12, 29–31, 33–38, 47, 49, 63, 135, 150–151, 209
    Clermont-Ferrand headquarters 34–35, 37–39, 55, 62, 133–136, 148, 151
    cross-ply tyres 151
    Pilote tyre 31, 63, 84
    X steel-braced radial tyres 14, 31, 63, 84, 151
Michelin, André 134
Michelin, Edouard 32–33, 134–136
Michelin, François 37
Michelin, Marcel 134–136
Michelin, Pierre 12, 32, 37–38, 135–136
Michelotti 152
Millar, Max 51
Mille Miglia 180
Miller, Arthur 76
MIRA (Motor Industry Research Association 166
Modern Houses Ltd 135
Modern Movement 57, 147
Mondello Park 24hr race 183

monocoque bodyshells 27, 148
Montlhéry 147, 157–158, 183
Monty Carlo Rally 179
Moreau, Jeanne 77, 177
Morris Minor 116, 163, 169, 191, 209
Mors factory 56, 155
Motor magazine 52, 165
Motor Sport magazine 165
Mount Chacaltaya 178–19
Muratet, Jean 59, 154
Musée Henri Malarre 34–35

Noiret, Philippe 177

Opron, Robert 115

Panhard 103, 125, 194–195
   Dyna 191, 194
   Dyna X 3CV 193, 195
   24CT Tigre 194
Paris–Dakar race 182
Paris Salon motor show 64, 86
   1934 29
   1939 12, 34, 48–49
   1946 62, 193, 195–196
   1948 13, 22, 40, 55, 64, 73
   1949 31, 74
   1965 84
Peugeot 64, 194, 209, 211
   Quadrillette 37, 191
Pinay, Antoine 57
Plan Pons 63–64, 74, 194
Plan Voisin 147
Pons, Paul-Marie 63
Pop-Cross events 14, 182–183, 187
Porsche 196
Porsche, Dr Ferdinand 40, 52, 196, 198, 202
Prix Citroën Tour du Monde 180
Production figures 14–15, 22, 25–26, 30, 34, 59, 64, 70, 73–78, 80, 83, 89–91, 94–95, 98, 105, 111, 117, 121–122, 130, 141, 161–162, 164, 166–167, 171, 175–176, 185, 209, 216–217
   limited editions 71, 89, 92, 102–103, 171, 177
PSA group 209–211
Puech, Claude 187
Pugh-Barker Elizabeth 134
Puiseux, Robert 136, 185

RAC horsepower system 32
Radioën radio 81
'raids' (rallies) 14, 187
   Afrique 4, 181
   Paris to Kabul 14, 181
   Paris to Persepolis 14, 181
   records (altitude, distance, endurance, speed) 178–179, 183
Renault 32, 43, 47, 49, 62, 64, 147, 194–198

Acton factory, UK 197
Billancourt factory 28
Ile de Séguin factory 196
Renault models
   4 22, 40, 196–198
   4CV 32, 40, 55, 63, 74, 191, 195–199
Renault, Léon 60
Renault, Louis 147–148, 195
Revue Automobile Suisse magazine 73
Rootes brothers 157
Rosengart 37
round-the-world marathon 178, 180
Royal Marine Commandos 164, 168–169

Sainturat, Maurice 46, 59, 158
Sallot, Georges 150
Salomon, Jules 24
Sartre, Jean-Paul 77
SEAB 103
seatbelts 175
Segrave, Henry 149, 156–157
Seguela, Jacques 178, 180
Service des Mines 12
Seznec, Hubert 150
Simca 37, 193
   Cinq 37, 193
Simmonds, Posy 188, 190
Somerset-Leeke, Nigel 166
Steck, Maurice 59
Sunbeam 149, 156
Sunbeam-Talbot-Darracq 149, 156–157

Talbot 157
   T120 engine 157
Talbot-Lago 56
   T150SS sports car 157–158
Tierra del Fuego 178
Tin-Tin 187
Toubain, Georges 39
Tours 147–148, 156

Vinatier, Jean
Voisin 147, 149–150, 157
Voisin, Gabriel 43–44, 147
Voisin racing team 147–148
Volkswagen 42, 52
   Beetle 22, 40, 63, 191, 195–204

Wall Street crash 43
Wanliss, Major E. O. 172–174
Wolgensinger, Jacques 11, 181–182, 187, 189–190

Yacco Oil Co. 147, 183

Zenith-Stromberg 157

2CV Cross speed trials 182, 184
2CV GB 189